In Praise of *Circles, Lines, and Squiggles*

Cleverly using qualities of his own Sun sign of Gemini as a narrative tool, W. Nikola-Lisa presents complex astrological materials in a fun, engaging format. I highly recommend *Circles, Lines, and Squiggles* to anyone interested in the primary concepts that have animated the art of astrology since the dawn of civilization. *Brian Allemana, Astrologer, Soulrise Astrology,* www.soulriseastrology.com

W. Nikola-Lisa has managed the impossible: finding a fun and engaging way to root the fundamentals of astrology into an interesting narrative. Understanding the underpinnings of the astrological system is challenging, but the author's metaphors create clear images of astrology in motion that anyone can understand. *Sarah Pickett, Sarandipity the Chicago Astrologer,* www.facebook.com/sarandipitythechicagoastrologer

In *Circles, Lines, and Squiggles* the author gives us a way to begin a dialogue on the esoteric, literary, philosophical, and related scientific background of astrology, especially the underpinnings of its theories. *Bonnie Hartenstein, Artist, Teacher, Natural Healer,* www.bonniehartenstein.com

Circles, Lines, and Squiggles

Selected Works by W. Nikola-Lisa

Bein' With You This Way

Dear Frank: Babe Ruth, the Red Sox,
and the Great War

Dog Eared: A Year's Romp Through
the Self-Publishing World

Dragonfly: A Childhood Memoir

Folk Stories

From Lectern to Laboratory: How Science and Technology
Changed the Face of America's Colleges

Hey, Aren't You the Janitor?

How We Are Smart

The Men Who Made the Yankees: The Odyssey of the World's
Greatest Baseball Team from Baltimore to the Bronx

Please Don't Say an X Word

Shark Man: A Middle Grade Novel

Summer Sun Risin'

Tangletalk

Circles, Lines, and Squiggles

ASTROLOGY FOR THE CURIOUS-MINDED

W. Nikola-Lisa

Gyroscope Books
Chicago

For orders by US trade bookstores, retail outlets, and public libraries, contact the Ingram Content Group: Tel: Retail (800) 937-8000; Libraries (800) 937-5300; or visit www.ingramcontent.com

Vector Illustration of Gemini Twins: Foolchico, Shutterstock.com
Introductory quotation: Steven Forrest, *The Night Speaks: How Astrology Works*,
     Part I, The Boundless Symbol, Chpt. 1, "Night"
Natal Chart Reproduction: Four Elements Chart Forms, 1984
Design Consultant: Deb Tremper, Six Penny Graphics

Summary: With the discovery of an old natal chart in his files, the author sets out to understand the principles of astrology and what his chart says about his life as a writer.

Publisher's Cataloging-In-Publication Data
(Prepared by The Donohue Group, Inc.)

Names: Nikola-Lisa, W., author.
Title: Circles, lines, and squiggles : astrology for the curious-minded /
     W. Nikola-Lisa.
Description: Chicago : Gyroscope Books, [2021] | Includes bibliographical
     references.
Identifiers: ISBN 9781734192360 (paperback) | ISBN 9781734192377 (ebook)
Subjects: LCSH: Astrology. | Nikola-Lisa, W. | Astrology and vocational
     guidance.
Classification: LCC BF1708.1 .N55 2021 (print) | LCC BF1708.1 (ebook) | DDC
     133.5--dc23

To Robin and Michael—

a binary star of immense magnitude

To Doug and Frank—

feet on the ground, head in the stars

And to B.C.—

a universe unto herself

Contents

1. A Picture of the Heavens 3

2. As Above, So Below 13

3. Great and Not-So-Great Circles 30

4. Actors and Experiencers 47

5. The Great Pattern-Matching Game 67

6. A Battlefield in France 91

7. A Turn of the Kaleidoscope 114

8. Suspended in Air 128

9. Fields of View 152

10. N/1, N/2, N/3, N/4, N/5 173

11. Finger of God 193

12. In All Line of Order 219

13. Healers and Seers 239

14. Universal Scheme of Things 257

    Reader's Guide 280

    Bibliography 291

    Acknowledgments 297

    About the Author 300

Author's Natal Chart, 1984

We're born, and from that moment we carry
inside ourselves a little hologram of the sky.
As long as we live, it resonates with the rhythms
of planets and tides, stars and seasons.
That hologram is our life. Its breath is the
breathing of an intelligent, conscious universe.
Studying that hologram is the delicate,
ever-changing art we call astrology.

Steven Forrest
The Night Speaks: How Astrology Works

Circles, Lines, and Squiggles

A Picture of the Heavens

For the people of the ancient world things we define today as belief and superstition were inseparable from their everyday lives and experience. Everything had meaning and power; everything had a spiritual cause. The world was a complex matrix in which the hidden was greater than the seen.[1]
Karni Zor, *Stories of Ancient Astrology*

This book starts not with the stars, but in my office. I know it's here somewhere amidst the rubble of books and papers— my astrological chart, that is. I had it cast quite a few years ago. After considering it, I stashed it in a file where it has stayed ever since. But now, several moves later, where is it? While I look for it, let me tell you about some of the things the astrologer told me. First of all, the astrologer was no crystal-gazing, turban-wearing fortune teller: he was a computer analyst at the local university. I went to see him with my girlfriend after my wife and I got a divorce. Yes, I needed help and I thought the stars just might provide the key to my turbulent past and uncertain future.

We huddled around a small table in the university cafeteria (not your usual clandestine meeting place with a soothsayer). As we settled into our chairs the computer-analyst-qua-astrologer produced a piece of faux parchment upon which several concentric circles were inscribed attended by a number of mysterious symbols. I don't recall the physical arrangement of the entire chart, but I do remember a few of the things he said to me that day. The first thing he said was that in my lifetime I would have more than one child, which made me laugh because I already had two by my first wife. The next thing he said was that the relationship between my girlfriend and me was karmic. Apparently, in the past—a past lifetime, that is—I had come to my girlfriend's aid when she needed it, and now, in a kind of grand karmic payback scheme, she had come to mine when I needed it. What he said next really caught my attention: "If you don't work on your relationship it will disappear overnight as soon as your karmic debt has been repaid." Well, we must not have worked hard enough because our relationship evaporated before year's end. There's one more thing I remember the astrologer telling me during our meeting: "You have all of the Writers Destiny Marks except one: contact with publishers." Ouch. Talk about the kiss of death. It was a particularly damning prognostication because at the time I was starting to get serious about my writing, which I had been doing on the sly for several years (probably one of the many tensions that led to my divorce). However, since I was at the beginning of my writing career, I considered this juicy little tidbit, then dismissed it out of hand.

Back to my astrological chart, the physical one, the one the computer-analyst-qua-astrologer cast for me. Where is it? I spent the last hour searching various bookshelves and file cabinets in my office, but to no avail. Then I remembered where I put it—in the lockbox under my desk. I used to keep important papers in a safety deposit box at the bank, but after losing the key a couple of times (and paying a sizable fine to replace it), I decided to buy a small fireproof lockbox and stash important papers in it under my desk. After retrieving the box, I opened it and shuffled through various papers, namely my passport, car title, list of computer passwords, international drivers license (expired, of course), various editions of my last will and testament, TSA pre-approval affidavit, and a household inventory form that I never got around to filling out. Then I found it. Yes, here it is, the original copy of my astrological chart. And what an exquisite piece of artwork it is with all of its circles, lines, and squiggles—and all hand drawn (after all, this was the mid 1980s before astrologers began using computer software to pump out natal charts).[2]

As beautiful as it is, even with several smudge marks, what does it mean? I'd like to tell you, but I can't, at least not yet since I'm not a trained astrologer. In order to make sense of this, I'm going to have to do a bit of research. Before I do, however, I have to make a confession: I write this book based on the assumption that astrology works, works in the sense that it's a useful tool in helping ordinary people like me find out more about themselves (just one of a number of approaches addressing the idea of personality types). I'm not interested in proving or disproving the "scientific" principles that underlie this more than five-thousand-year-old endeavor (I'll let those more versed in the matter do that). What I'm interested in, along with its long and varied history, is its usefulness in aiding the individual along the path of psychological individuation. But where to start? I suppose with the natal or birth chart itself.

The main device in any astrologer's toolbox is the birth chart. Like ancient philosophers grappling with a way to capture the enormity of the universe, astrologers use a variety of metaphors to capture the essence of the chart cast at the moment of birth. Steven Forrest calls it a "developmental path" with many stages.[3] Yasmin Boland sees it as a "map" to help you face life's obstacles.[4] Amy Herring describes the birth chart as a "freeze-frame snapshot," a photograph of the heavens taken at the moment of your birth.[5] April Elliott Kent uses multiple images to describe the birth chart: for this astrologer, it is "the tiny hand- and footprints on your hospital birth certificate, a photo taken moments after your earthly debut, or a newspaper clipping from the day of your birth..."[6] In his exhaustive study of the history of astrology, especially its predictive capacity, Benson Bobrick refers to the birth chart as a "clock of heaven" that gives an overall picture of the person, his life, and fate.[7]

Dane Rudhyar, founder of person-centered astrology, an approach to astrology based on the tenets of humanistic psychology, sees the birth chart as nothing less than a seed-pattern containing the genetic code of an individual's total being. In *Person Centered Astrology*, his most complete writing on the subject, Rudhyar writes, "The fundamental concept on which astrology is based is that everything that is 'born' (i.e., that begins to operate as an individual factor in a specific environment) at a particular time and point of space is organized according to a particular seed-pattern or archetype symbolized by its birth chart. This seed-pattern defines what that organism (or organized field of activity) SHOULD be if it fulfills its function in the universal scheme of things...."[8]

Universal scheme of things? That's what William Lilly, a well-known astrologer in seventeenth-century England, concluded about the birth chart: it's a "scheme of heaven" (although he didn't mean "scheme" as in a ploy or ruse; rather he meant it as in an intricate pattern or diagram of the heavens above). The most poetic description of the nature and design of the birth chart, however, comes from Alexander Boxer, a data scientist with an insatiable curiosity about all things astrological, who, borrowing a term from biology, says that the birth chart is "like the 'pluripotent cells' of storytelling, capable of producing many, but still not quite every possible outcome."[9] Boxer follows this up by marveling at the birth chart's particular genius, the fact that it can "encode all of the complex astronomical data needed for its operations so perfectly within a single, abstract image."[10] Writing some half century before Boxer (well before the discovery of pluripotent cells), Rudhyar echoes this sentiment: "Astrology's supreme contribution to human thinking and human search for order and simplicity is its ability to reduce all functional activities (physiological, vital-emotional, mental, behavioral) to a few essential categories, each of which is symbolized by a planet. The picturing of an individual human being in a circular birth chart, including the cruciform lines of horizon and meridian and ten 'planets' and related factors, is a triumph of simplicity and synthesis. It is a highly potent hieroglyph, a 'magical formula,' a mandala.

Every potentiality or vital, emotional, mental, socio-cultural and metamorphic development is there, condensed and reduced to its essential outline and potency. But what is essential is the organization of these potentialities; it is their interrelatedness, their interaction and interdependence. It is the 'form' of the whole."[11]

The form of the whole. That's something occult philosopher Rudolph Steiner, founder of the Anthroposophical Society in the early twentieth century, also wrote about. In one of his most insightful writings about the relationship between the individual and the cosmos, Steiner asks us to think about the contours of the newborn's brain, which he likens to a spherical mirror, and the positions of the stars and planets in the celestial sphere at the time of birth: "If we could take a picture of the entire brain with all of its details visible, we would get a different picture for each person. If we photographed a person's brain at the moment of birth and took a picture of the sky directly above his or her birthplace, the two pictures would be alike. The stars in the photograph of the sky would be arranged in the same way as certain parts of the brain in the other picture. Thus our brain is really a picture of the heavens, and we each have a different picture depending on where and when we were born. This indicates that we are born out of the entire universe."[12]

What this means is that each of us carries within us, depending upon the time, date, and place of our birth, a picture of the cosmos that is unique to us and to us only. It is a picture, a map, a blueprint, a snapshot, a seed-pattern, a scheme of heaven that affects and influences us throughout

our lives. But how do we take the immensity of this idea—
the cosmos imprinted in us at the moment of birth—and
represent it graphically? Since the seventeenth century,
astrologers in the West have adopted a fairly uniform circular
format, or "architecture" as astrologer Alison Gunn calls it.[13]
This was not always the case.

When I say chart, especially in reference to my birth
chart, I'm really talking about three related components:
the circular chart showing the placement of signs, planets,
and houses; a rectangular "aspect" grid showing various
angular relationships between planets; and several pages of
handwritten notes interpreting the above in an attempt to
make it more palpable to the uninitiated. Before we dig into
the minutiae of these details, let me introduce you to a couple
of astrology students of mine: Messrs. Castor and Pollux,
otherwise known as the Gemini Twins.

Author: Greetings, I'm glad you could join us.

Castor: Our pleasure.

Pollux: Yes, *our* pleasure, though I don't like it when Castor
speaks for me.

Author: I've invited you here to help me make sense of my
birth chart.

Castor: Terrific. I love learning about new things.

Pollux: Yes, but don't go overboard with it.

Castor: *Overboard?*

Pollux: You know what I mean.

Author: Now, boys, settle down, and let me continue.
I'd like to begin with a phrase I found in Madeline Berwick-
Brodeur and Lisa Lenard's book. The authors open their book

with this mathematically elegant formula: *Planets* + *Signs* + *Houses* = *You*.[14] I'd say that pretty much sums it up, but it's not as simple as it appears: each of these domains is laden with meaning that could take an initiate years to master. Here's what Howard Sasportas, co-founder of London's Centre for Psychological Astrology, has to say about them: "Planets represent particular psychological drives, urges and motivations. Like verbs, they depict a certain action which is going on—for example, Mars asserts, Venus harmonizes, Jupiter expands, Saturn restricts, etc. The signs represent twelve qualities of being or attitudes towards life. The drive of a planet is expressed through the sign in which the planet is placed. Mars can assert in an Arien way or Taurean way; Venus can harmonize in a Geminian or Canceran fashion, and so on. Houses, however, show the specific areas of everyday life or fields of experience in which all this is occurring. Mars in Taurus will assert itself in a slow and steady manner, but its placement by house determines the exact area of life in which this slow and steady action can most obviously be observed— whether it is in the person's career that he or she acts that way, or in his or her relationships, or at school, etc. Put very simply, the planets show what is happening, the signs how it is happening, and the houses where it is happening."[15] Using Sasportas's description above, we can flesh out Gerwick- Brodeur and Lenard's formula a bit more: Planets (the *what*) + Signs (the *how*) + Houses (the *where*) = All You Need to Know About Yourself (astrologically speaking, that is). Although this is the underlying dynamism of any birth chart, we're not going to follow the discreet elements of the formula in precisely that order. Rather, taking my natal chart as the example, we'll follow it ring by ring (as best we can), starting with the first and outer ring.

Castor: Ooh, I like that—*ring by ring*. Very mysterious.

Pollux: Enough, Castor.

Notes

1.   Zor, Karni. *Stories of Ancient Astrology*, Chpt. 8, "Gods and Planets of the Olympus."

2.   The natal chart that appears in the front matter of this book is the original natal chart cast in the mid 1980s (I did clean it up a bit, removing ink smudges, etc.). The blank form was created by Four Elements Chart Forms of Grafton, California (© 1984). I've tried to locate the proprietors of this form, but to no avail. Although the chart uses the Koch house division system, most of the online chart generators I've consulted for this book use Placidus. The major difference is in the placement of house cusps and not sign/planet relationships, aspects, or aspect patterns. If there is a difference between the latter factors, it is more a function of the astrologer I consulted in the mid 1980s than the house division system he used.

3.   Forrest, Steven. *The Night Speaks: How Astrology Works*, Chpt. 10, "In Practice."

4.   Boland, Yasmin. *Astrology*, Chpt. 1, "What Is Astrology?"

5.   Herring, Amy. *Essential Astrology*, Chpt. 3, "The Natal Chart Map."

6.   Kent, April Elliott. *The Essential Guide to Practical Astrology*, Chpt. 2, "Reading Your Chart."

7.   Bobrick, Benson. *The Fated Sky*, Chpt. 6.

8.   Rudhyar, Dane. *Person Centered Astrology*, Chpt. 8, "Astrology as a Discipline of Mind."

9.   Boxer, Alexander. *A Scheme of Heaven*, Introduction.

10. *Ibid.*
11. Rudhyar, Chpt. 11, "What Is Form?"
12. Steiner, Rudolph. *Astronomy and Astrology,* Chpt. 3, "Cosmic Influences on the Individual and Humanity."
13. Gunn, Alison. "Astrological Architecture: Does Form Follow Function," *Beyond the Stars Astrology:* http://beyondthestarsastrology.com/2011/07/06/astrological-architecture/
14. Gerwick-Brodeur, Madeline and Lisa Lenard. *The Complete Idiot's Guide to Astrology,* Chpt. 1, "Astrology Is More Than Your Horoscope."
15. Sasportas, Howard. *The Twelve Houses,* Chpt. 1, "Basic Premises."

2

As Above, So Below

As we approach the interpretation of a birth chart we should never lose sight of the fact that the chart is a two-dimensional projection of the whole universe in relation to a particular "organism" which began its individual existence at a particular time and on a particular locality on the Earth.[1]

Dane Rudhyar, *Person Centered Astrology*

Every seed contains within it the potential for new life. Plant the seed, nurture it, and watch it grow. Everything it exhibits, from the titillatingly velvet feel of its flowers to the hard-nut crunchiness of its seedpods, is pre-programmed, woven into the plant's genetic code. In many ways, an individual's birth chart is like a plant's genetic code, shaping an individual's personality traits and behavioral tendencies. And like a plant, an individual is sensitive to environmental conditions as much as he or she is to familial and social forces that either promote growth or inhibit it. Nothing can be taken for granted, life is not predetermined: external forces combine with internal pressures to contribute to the full maturation of each individual. The natal chart represents nothing more than the potential that each individual can achieve in this lifetime. Understand the birth chart and you will have a road

map to help you through life's travails. Like any map, the
birth chart points toward reality, but it is not reality. And it
points toward it using a language of symbols, symbols that are
universal enabling anyone to "read" a chart no matter what
their vernacular language happens to be. A French-speaking
citizen can read my birth chart just as easily as a German-
speaking citizen, because the language of astrology is unique
unto itself (this is not to say that all astrological symbols—or
even astrological systems—are the same, just that there is a
close overlap among most contemporary approaches). As
a language, we can break astrology's symbolic system into
three components: its alphabet, its vocabulary, and its syntax
or grammar, all of which combine to tell a story, the story
of an individual's path toward individuation. We start with
astrology's alphabet.

Castor: A, B, C, D, E, F,...

Pollux: Not that alphabet, Castor.

Author: No, not that alphabet, but it's not a bad place to
start. Like any alphabet, individual letters are made up of
smaller units. For instance, in English, the letter "A" is made
up of three lines (two inclined verticals joined by a horizontal
bar). On the other hand, the letter "B" is composed of two
half-circles fixed to a vertical line. Depending upon your point
of view, the letter "C" is either a circle with a wedge cut out of
it or a somewhat overgrown semicircle. The late nineteenth-
century British astrologer Alan Leo argues that the symbolism
of astrology is built from three basic symbols: the circle,
the semicircle, and the cross. Each one of these symbols
carries with it a set of meanings inherent to it. Regarding the

circle, Leo writes, "Spirit, life, consciousness, energy, all are symbolized as springing from the point in the centre of the circle; the circumference signifying the boundary line of space within the Solar universe." The semicircle, on the other hand, that can represent the space above or below the horizon (the "light" or the "dark"), represents the soul of man, "that which is neither wholly spiritual nor wholly material, but partakes of the nature of both and is the connecting link between the spirit and the physical body." Finally, the equal-armed cross symbolizes the manifest universe in all its varied forms, i.e., "it is an ever-changing symbol out of which all possible geometrical figures may be formed."[2]

For Leo, the cross represents the creative power of life; it is where the macrocosm and the microcosm meet, where spirit (the vertical bar) and matter (the horizontal bar) commingle. Taken together, the circle, semicircle, and cross symbolize three important life forces—*will* (Sun), *wisdom* (Moon), and *activity* (Earth). Although his perspective is built upon his esoteric Christian beliefs, Leo can help us understand how the graphic symbols or "glyphs" for these celestial bodies are constructed: the Sun by a circle with a dot in its center, the Moon by two similar-facing semicircles connected at their points, and the Earth by a cross inscribed within a circle. Indeed, every celestial body, zodiacal sign, and planetary aspect crucial to an understanding of Western astrology is represented by some combination of circle, semicircle, and cross. Here is Leo describing the first three planets and their glyphs: "Mercury, semicircle over circle over cross, represents the complete union of the three symbols in one, denoting perfectibility. Venus is the symbol of Spirit triumphant over matter, circle over cross. It represents beauty, grace, refinement and all that expresses the human state. Mars, really the cross over the circle, is the symbol of spirit constrained by matter. It represents strength, force, physical energy and the animal in man—the animal-man state."[3]

Castor: So it's not as easy as 1, 2, 3... A, B, C.

Author: That's right, Castor, astrology is like an onion, peel away one layer and you are faced with another, and another, and another, each one with subtle differences of meaning.

Pollux: Why use symbols in the first place?

Author: Reducing astrological content to graphic symbols, each one with its unique and often hidden meanings, enables more information to be encoded in the birth chart. Sometimes astrologers go a bit too far, however. John Dee, the brilliant, but somewhat eccentric, astrologer and physician to Queen Elizabeth I, saw hidden meanings in almost everything. Dee went so far as to divide the planets into a lunar and solar group depending upon the presence or absence of the semicircle in their symbols.[4] Nonetheless, if you extend the reductiveness of symbol-making to all celestial bodies, zodiacal signs, natal chart houses, and planetary aspects, you have a considerably large and diverse vocabulary, the building blocks to form larger units of meaning.

Pollux: As in words.

Castor: That combine to make sentences.

Author: Now you're catching on. The symbols of astrology make it possible to "read" a birth chart. Take my chart, for instance. Since I'm a Gemini rising (or a "double Gemini," which I'll explain later), I know that Gemini is in the first house and that the Sun is somewhere in that house, too. It's not until I look closer that I see the following:⊙23° Ⅱ 26', which indicates that my Sun (⊙) is 23 degrees and 26 minutes into the sign of Gemini the Twins.

Castor: Hey, that's us!

Author: Yes, it is. Now, regarding the location of my Sun, it's a lot easier to write⊙23° Ⅱ 26' than it is to say that my Sun is 23 degrees and 26 minutes into the sign of Gemini the Twins. In fact, I can go around my chart and locate any number of celestial entities. For instance, the North Lunar Node (☊) is 14 degrees and 1 minute in Pisces (♓) in the tenth house, which, in symbolic shorthand, reads ☊ 14° ♓ 1' 10th.

Castor: Cool.

Author: The ability to reduce the narrative components (reduce the form, but not the meaning) to a simpler equation allows us to fold more and more information into the birth chart, which after all is the name of the game. Another set of data that is quite important to the birth chart is the set of planetary angles or aspects. These are presented in one of two ways: either directly on the birth chart's circular clock face as a set of lines indicating the angles between two or more celestial objects (which today's computer generated charts do as a rule), or in a separate aspect grid containing the same information but with more clarity, especially as it often involves the use of aspect glyphs.

Pollux: Aspect glyphs?

Author: Yes, I know it's confusing, but these are the graphic symbols related to the angles that various heavenly

bodies hold in relationship to each other. In other words, it's
not enough to know where celestial bodies are at the moment
of your birth, but also what relationship they hold to each
other. This is the dynamic aspect of a birth chart. Looking at
my planetary aspect grid, I see that Mars is trine (approx. 120°
away from) Neptune, a very positive relationship, which is
written ♂ △ ♆. A less sanguine relationship is Jupiter square
(90°) Saturn, written ♃ □ ♄. All of the above combines to tell
a story, the story of the native whose natal chart is in question.

Castor: Native? You don't mean...

Author: No, I don't. I mean *native* as in "the one
whose chart is being read," and *natus*, another term I'll use
occasionally, meaning "the one born."

Pollux: There's really a lot to think about here.

Author: Yes, I know it's a lot to take in—and we've only
just begun. In order to get a complete picture of the native,
you'd have to continue through all of the signs, houses,
planets, planetary aspects, and global chart patterns until a
fully revealed individual stands before you in all of his or her
astrological radiance. (See appendix titled *Reader's Guide*)
However, the symbols or glyphs populating a natal chart are
not the only entities that carry meaning and symbolic power;
the very design or architecture of the chart itself speaks
volumes about an astrologer's belief system. Let's take the first
circle in my chart, the one that contains the "ouroboros," the
serpent devouring its tail.

Castor: Now we're talking.

Author: As you've probably figured out, I cut my
existential teeth during the turbulent days of the late 1960s.

It was a heady time. A time of sex, drugs, and alcohol—
and political unrest. We protested against everything:
our preoccupied parents, our disinterested teachers, our
untrustworthy politicians, and, of course, "The War."
We marched, waved signs, raised our voices against "The
Machine," and we sang songs, protest songs by Bob Dylan,
Pete Seeger, Phil Ochs, and Joan Baez. One of my favorite
songs was "Will the Circle Be Unbroken?" I sang it with
friends at impromptu potluck dinners. I sang it with yoga
devotees at Sunday morning kirtan. I sang it alone just to
ease the existential pain that every young adult experiences.
It's a comforting song, a soulful song, written originally as
a Christian hymn in the early 1900s by Ada Habershon, but
recorded during the counterculture revolution of the 60s and
70s as one of many anthems signifying the times. The song
I remember—more funeral dirge than church hymn—was a
modified version by the Carter family released in 1935 and
later reworked by the Nitty Gritty Dirt Band in the early 1970s.

Thinking about it some forty years later, I'm reminded
of an aphorism from the ancient Egyptian-Greek text
The Emerald Tablet attributed to Hermes Trismegistus,
the legendary deity of Hellenic origin thought to be a
combination of the Greek god Hermes and the ancient
Egyptian god Thoth. The aphorism goes like this: "As above,
so below, as within, so without, as the universe, so the soul."[5]
Buried within this enigmatic saying lies not only what we
were searching for during the turbulent counterculture days,
but also the very definition of astrology itself, at least as it's
understood and practiced in the West. It's a recognition of the

relationship between the macrocosm (what is above) and the microcosm (what is below). Embedded in any definition of astrology is this central concept, the relationship—or, to put it in a Jungian context, the "meaningful coincidence"—between celestial events and human experience.[6]

Pollux: Jungian context?

Author: That's Swiss analytical psychologist Carl Gustave Jung, who was quite interested in astrology. In the introduction to *Jung on Astrology*, Keiron Le Grice and Safron Rossi paraphrase Jung's definition of astrology: "Simply stated, astrology is the practice of interpreting the meaning of observed correlations between human experience and the positions, interrelationships, and cycles of the planets (including the Sun and the Moon) in the solar system. The movements and positions of the planets are plotted against the zodiac, a symbolic frame of reference based on the ecliptic, the line formed by the apparent movement of sun around the Earth over the course of a year."[7]

There's more to Le Grice and Rossi's statement, but as it is there's a lot to unpack. And it is my aim to do so, just not all at once. The focus of this discourse is derived from the first line quoted above: "astrology is the practice of interpreting the meaning of observed correlations between human experience and the positions, interrelationships, and cycles of the planets...." This is not an unusual beginning for any definition of astrology. Yasmin Boland writes that astrology is "an investigation into how the positions and movements of the Sun, Moon, planets and fixed stars correlate with what's happening on Earth, and in our lives."[8] This is echoed in the opening paragraphs of April Elliott Kent's *The Essential Guide to Astrology* when she writes that astrology is "the study of the connection between celestial activity phenomena and earthly events."[9]

Castor: *As above, so below.*

Pollux: *As within, so without.*

Author: *As the universe,...*

Castor and Pollux: *...so the soul.*

Author: Now you're catching on. This is not just a casual observation built up over time either, but reflects a philosophical view that astrologers have been wrestling with from the earliest days of man's existence: that humankind is a miniature version of the cosmos. This view became popular well before the Christian era as ancient Greek philosophers grappled with the idea. According to the "human-as-microcosm" concept, "everything in nature has a parallel in human beings, and thus humankind and the universe are linked together in a system of correlations."[10] The idea implies that man is a microcosm of something greater, a microcosm of the universe. It also implies, at its most radical level, that the two—microcosm and macrocosm—form an inextricably related whole. The concept is bound up in the term *Unus Mundus*, a Latin phrase for "One World," which is founded on the assumption that the multiplicity of the empirical world rests on an underlying unity, a reality where everything is interconnected, where everything forms an organic whole.

Castor: When do we get to the tail-devouring serpent?

Author: Patience, Castor, we're almost there. Writing in *Psyche and Matter*, Marie Louise von Franz connects this idea to Jung's concept of synchronicity, "When he created the concept of synchronicity, Jung laid a foundation which might lead us to see the complementary realms of psyche and matter as one reality."[11] Jung says as much early in his career when he wrote: "Since psyche and matter are contained in one and the same world, and moreover are in continuous contact with one another and ultimately rest on irrepresentable, transcendental factors, it is not only possible but fairly probable, even, that psyche and matter are two different aspects of one and the same thing."[12]

The idea of a correspondence between the great world (the macrocosm) and the small world (the microcosm) can be found in a variety of mythological, religious, and philosophical works. One of the clearest statements of the doctrine of correspondences can be found in an esoteric text titled *Holy Guide*, published by the English Rosicrucian John Heydon in 1667: "That which is inferior or below is as that which is superior or above, there being one universal matter and form of all things, differenced only by accidents and particularly by that great mystery of rarefaction and condensation, the inferior and superior, to work and accomplish the miracle of one thing, and to show the great variety and diversity of operations wrought by that spirit that works all things, in all things."[13]

Symbolically, the doctrine of correspondences is represented by the circle, and nowhere so majestically described as in the following statement, "God is an infinite sphere, the center of which is everywhere, the circumference nowhere," found in the *Liber XXIV Philosophorum* (*Book of the 24 Philosophers*), a Latin text consisting of twenty-four definitions of God ascribed to the fourteenth-century grammarian and philosopher Marius Victortinus.[14] The doctrine has echoed throughout the ages in one version or another by many distinguished scholars, from twelfth-century French theologian and poet Alain of Lille to twentieth-century comparative mythologist Joseph Campbell. The most detailed explanation of this idea, however, comes from fifteenth-century Italian scholar, Catholic priest, and astrologer Marsilio Ficino, one of the most influential humanistic theologians of the early Italian Renaissance: "Thus God is the center of all, because He is so in all things that He is more internal to each thing than it is to itself. He is also the world's circumference because, in existing outside all things, He so transcends all things that His dignity immeasurably excels the highest summit of each thing. Again, He is greatest of all in power to the extent He is least of all in quantity, if this is permissible way of putting it. As He is the center, He is in all, but as the circumference, He is outside all; in all, but not included because He is also the circumference; outside all too but not excluded because He is also the center. So what is God? One might call Him a spiritual circle whose center is everywhere, whose circumference is nowhere."[15]

Castor: But when do we get to the ouroboros?

Author: Now, Castor, now. No matter how the Infinite, the All-Knowing, the Supreme Logos is described, the central image of this one continuous reality—of God—is the circle, symbolically represented at the dawn of history by the ouroboros, a symbol depicting a serpent (or worm, or snake, or dragon) swallowing its tail.

Castor: Ooh.

Author: Pollux, you seem to know your Latin. Do you know what the word ouroboros means?

Pollux: Let's see, *oura* is the Latin translation of the Greek word for "tail," and, if I'm not mistaken, *boros* is the Latin translation of the Greek word for "devour".

Castor: *Sweet*. Ouroboros, the Tail-Devourer.

Author: Yes, and like the mythological Phoenix, it represents the eternal cycle of birth, death, and rebirth. This is the endless process of cyclical regeneration, evoking the concept of the eternal return, where the beginning is the end, the end the beginning. It's a reminder that the vitality of energy cannot be destroyed, only transformed. In addition to being associated with repetition, regeneration, and immortality, the circular form of the ouroboros also suggests wholeness and completion, especially when the tail-devourer appears as a double circle or loop (or, in some cases, as two serpents entwined around each other). In any case, the ouroboros suggests the constant flow of creation from chaos to order, and back again. Specific allusions to the tail-devouring serpent date back some four thousand years, to an inscription inside of the pyramid of Unas, the ninth and final king of ancient Egypt's Fifth Dynasty, which describes two serpents entwined around each other, an allusion both to the union of opposites and to the fecundity of nature. Several centuries later, the ouroboros appears in *The Egyptian Book of the Dead*, a collection of spells and magic formulas which enable the soul of the deceased to navigate the afterlife. In the collection, the Sun god Atum is said to have ascended from the depths of the primal waters with a snake that renewed itself every morning. Another reference to the ouroboros appears in the *Dama Heroub Papyrus*, created between the eleventh and tenth centuries BCE. In this more complex depiction, Horos the Child sits within the solar disk that rests upon the Akhet Lions, which in turn are surrounded by a tail-devouring serpent.

Castor: Lions, and tigers, and...*serpents?*

Pollux: Quit interrupting, Castor.

Author: As cultural symbols did so many times in the Mediterranean, the ouroboros migrated, in this case from Egypt to ancient Greece. By the seventh century BCE, we find a reference to the mythic serpent in the Orphic religion, a mystery religion based on the teachings and songs of the legendary Greek musician Orpheus. In the oldest Greek creation myth, the *Pelasgian*, the Goddess Eurynome creates the first living creature from air, the giant serpent Ophion, mates with it, and gives birth to the "World Egg." To protect the egg from outside destructive forces, Ophion curls around the egg three times until the egg hatches, bringing forth the heavens, the earth, and the underworld.

The image of an encircling serpent appears throughout Greek culture. Ancient Greek philosophers identified *Chronos* (time) with *Oceanos* (the Earth-encircling river) that also encircled the universe in the form of a serpent with the constellations of the zodiac on its back. Followers of Gnosticism, a religion that flourished in Greece and

Hellenistic Egypt between 200 BCE and 400 CE, believed that the ouroboros marked the boundary between heaven and earth. Some sects even equated the ouroboros with the Biblical snake in the Garden of Eden, seeing it as a hero—rather than a villain—that helped Adam and Eve obtain the first "gnosis" (knowledge) by eating the forbidden fruit from the Tree of Knowledge. Later, the heroic serpent in the Garden of Eden came to represent the guardian of the Tree of Life and therefore the gatekeeper to immortality. One of the most distinctive images of the ouroboros from Hellenistic Egypt is found in an alchemical text title *The Chrysopoeia of Cleopatra* that dates to the second century CE. Attributed to Cleopatra of Alexandria...

Castor: We learned about her in history class.

Pollux: Wasn't she friends with Marc Anthony?

Author: Yes, but that Cleopatra is Cleopatra VII Philopator, who came before the Cleopatra I'm speaking about. The title, *The Chrysopoeia of Cleopatra*, refers to "gold-making" and, as such, indicates the author's knowledge of natural science and alchemy. Although the text originated in Egypt, it was written in Greek, so the image is sometimes referred to as the Greco-Egyptian or Alexandrian ouroboros. Two things distinguish the image: first, its half-dark, half-light body that suggests the Gnostic idea of the duality of existence, and, secondly, the inscription contained within the tail-devourer's body, which translates "All is one" or, more enigmatically, "One is the All."[16]

Carl Jung saw the ouroboros as having archetypal significance for the human psyche, noting how the tail-devourer made its way into man's consciousness through the alchemical tradition. Acknowledging that medieval alchemists knew more about the nature of the individuation process than most modern psychologists, Jung writes: "In the age-old image of the ouroboros lies the thought of devouring oneself and turning oneself into a circulatory process, for it was clear to the more astute alchemists that the prima materia of the art was man himself. The ouroboros is a dramatic symbol for the integration and assimilation of the opposite, i.e., of the shadow. This 'feed-back' process is at the same time a symbol of immortality, since it is said of the ouroboros that he slays himself and brings himself to life, fertilizes himself and gives birth to himself."[17]

The image of the ouroboros is not limited to the alchemical tradition, nor to the mystical religions of ancient Egypt and Greece. It appears in one form or another in many cultures, from the Yin-Yang symbol of ancient China to the tail-eating serpent-god Quetzalcoatl in Mesoamerica. In late medieval Europe, the tail-devouring serpent surfaces in a variety of settings: on watermarks, tarot cards, the frontispiece of alchemical texts, and even on the seals of secret societies. In Victorian England, where esoteric traditions experienced a renaissance, the ouroboros became a visible emblem among Rosicrucians, Freemasons, Theosophists, and members of the somewhat obscure neo-Hermetic Order of the Golden Dawn.

Castor: Wow, everyone used it.

Author: Yes, and given the interconnectedness of alchemy, tarot, and other occult traditions, it's no wonder that the image of the ouroboros found its way into astrology. Could it be the inspiration for the graphic symbol of Cancer the Crab, the fourth sign of the zodiac? Cancer's glyph is created by two swirl-like commas, one hovering above the other, in an apparent attempt to catch—or devour—each other's tail. The astrological symbolism suggested by some astrologers lies in the commas' "heads," which might refer to the Sun and the Moon respectively, two heavenly "lights" that often oppose each other. Of course, the tail-devourer's association with astrology could also be to the mysterious and often overlooked thirteenth sign of the zodiac, Ophiuchus, the Serpent-Bearer.

Castor: Gee, there sure are a lot of serpents in your stories.

Author: Yes, but that's mythology for you. To wrap this discourse up, let me end by saying that this leads to the fact that the outer circle or wheel of my natal chart is not merely decorative, but reveals a deeper meaning about the fundamental nature of the universe: that it is predicated on wholeness and unity, born of the creative-destructive process that marks every process, natural and spiritual. But the birth chart is more than just a symbolic signpost; it is a practical tool designed to help the astrologer locate the natus within the cosmos at the moment of his or her birth, and in doing so connects the natus (the microcosm) with the universe (the macrocosm) in a meaningful and poignant union.

Pollux: This sure is a lot to think about.

Castor: I'll say.

Notes

1. Rudhyar, Dane. *Person Centered Astrology*, Chpt. 15, "The 'Signature' of the Whole Person."

2. Leo, Alan. *Symbolism and Astrology*, Chpt. 5, "Planetary Symbols."

3. *Ibid.*

4. Burns, William E. "Dee, John (1527-1609)," in William E. Burns (ed), *Astrology through History*.

5. Boland, Yasmin. *Astrology*, Chpt 1, "What is Astrology?"

6. Rossi, Safron and Keiron Le Grice. *Jung on Astrology*, Part I, "Contexts and Opinions."

7. *Ibid.*, Introduction.

8. Boland, Chpt 1, "What is Astrology?"

9. Kent, April Elliott. *The Essential Guide to Astrology*, Chpt. 1, "The Language of the Stars."

10. Woolfolk, Joanna Martine. *The Only Astrology Book You'll Ever Need*, Chpt. 1, "Sun Signs."

11. Von Franz, Marie Louise. *Psyche and Matter*, "Symbols of the Unus Mundus."

12. Wehr, Gerhard. *Jung & Steiner: The Birth of a New Psychology*, Chpt. 2, "A Biographical Comparison."

13. Phelps, Ruth. *The Universe of Numbers*, Chpt. 2, "Other Aspects of Number Symbolism."

14. Grant, Edward (ed.). *A Source Book in Medieval Science*, Entry 72, "On a God-Filled Extramundane Infinite Void Space."

15. *Marsilio Ficino: Platonic Theology*, Vol. 6, Books XVII-XVIII, Chpt. 3, "Animae Creature Quotidie."

16. BBC Culture [Dec. 4, 2017], https://www.bbc.com/culture/article/20171204-the-ancient-symbol-that-spanned-millennia/.

17. Schwartz-Salant, Nathan (ed.). *Jung on Alchemy*, Chpt. 1, "The Prima Materia."

3

Great and
Not-So-Great Circles

As we look into the heavens, although we are
looking into an endless depth of time and space,
with stars and galaxies at different distances, we can
visualize instead that we are looking at the inside
surface of a very large sphere—the "celestial sphere."[1]
Nick Anthony Fiorenza, *The Lunar Planner*

I'm sitting outside at a coffeehouse on a side street in
Chicago, part of my morning routine. It's a scorcher of a
day, well over 90° with only a slight breeze to bring some
relief. The Republican National Convention is in its third
day and the coasts of Texas and Louisiana are bracing for
the onslaught of Hurricane Laura. Those events are in my
mind, just not front and center. What's front and center is my
birth chart: I have the hand-drawn chart up on my computer
so I can study it. The circle after the outer ouroboros is
divided into 360°, though the degree marks are not equally
emphasized (the line marking every fifth degree around the
circle is enhanced, dividing the 360° into 72 units of 5° each).
Again, like the ouroboros in the first circle, are these marks

practical or merely decorative? To answer this question, imagine our living, breathing solar system like an egg cooked sunny-side up.

Castor: I don't like eggs.

Pollux: It's just a simile.

Castor: Good.

Author: If you can hold off on your opinion of eggs, sunny-side up or otherwise, I'll continue. In my egg analogy, the yolk represents the Sun in the middle of the solar system and the egg white the planetary paths around it. Unlike the Aristotelian-Ptolemaic conception, the egg white does not form a series of perfect circles around the yolk, but is filled with slightly misshapen circles, more elliptical than circular. The point is to suggest that the solar system is more or less flat with a handful of major planets—and a whole lot of minor stuff— orbiting around a central star, our Sun, in less-than-perfect circular orbits. But that's not what we see from planet Earth.

From our Earth-bound or geocentric perspective, we see the Sun and the planets orbiting around us. The Earth, not the Sun, is central, but central only because we—the observer—are bound to it. This begs the question: What's the best point of reference to use when we talk about the nature and structure of the solar system? Astronomers, of course, use the Sun as the reference point; astrologers, on the other hand, use the Earth (one of the major reasons astronomy and astrology parted company after the Scientific Revolution).

In either case, planetary objects circle around a central point. Even though today we know that celestial objects don't orbit in perfect circular pathways, the circle nonetheless is at the heart of astrology and can be lumped into two types: "great circles" and "not-so-great circles," the former being the most important. However, the list of great circles varies, according to which astrologers you read. Benson Bobrick cites three great circles fundamental to the art and science of astrology—the ecliptic, the horizon, and the celestial equator.[2] Judy Hall names four great circles—the ecliptic, the terrestrial equator, the celestial equator, and the zodiac.[3] Meanwhile, Amy Herring points to three great circles worth noting—the ecliptic, the horizon, and the native's birth or local meridian.[4] I could cite other astrologers, each one with a slightly different list of circles, both great and not-so-great, but the circles cited above should keep us preoccupied for awhile. Of course the first question that comes to mind is, Just what is a "great circle?"

Castor: I suppose it's a really big circle.

Pollux: A circle that has a special meaning?

Author: You're both correct: it's really big and it has a special meaning. Look up "great circle" in any basic astronomy textbook and you'll find that a great circle is any circle on the surface of a sphere whose center is at the center of the sphere. The most common example offered is the Earth's equator, which we learned in elementary school is the imaginary line drawn around the Earth midway between the North and South Poles, effectively dividing the globe into two hemispheres. Curiously, the Earth's equator is the only great circle of latitude; any other circle of latitude (i.e., a line that runs parallel to the equator) doesn't have the Earth's center as its center. That doesn't mean that there aren't other important circles of latitude, there are. Before considering them, let's return to the Earth's other great circles, the most important being the prime meridian that circles the Earth at 0° longitude as it slices through the grounds of the Royal Observatory in Greenwich, England.

Castor: Why Greenwich, England?

Author: Why not? After all, when the prime meridian was created, England ruled the world.

Castor: Oh.

Author: The prime meridian is important because the community of world astronomers use it as the starting point for the current system of international time zones. Unlike longitude, all meridians are great circles because they circle the globe through the two poles with the Earth's center as their center. In fact, theoretically, you could have thousands of meridians—each one a great circle—if you counted every second of every minute of every degree of longitude.

Pollux: That's a lot of counting.

Castor: And a lot of meridians.

Author: Quite so. However, rather than think about circles that circumscribe the terrestrial sphere, astrologers prefer to think about great circles extended to the celestial sphere, not that the two are completely different. For instance, the celestial equator is nothing more than the Earth's equator—the terrestrial equator—extended to the background of fixed stars. If this great circle formed a solid, two-dimensional surface, it would create a plane that extended from the center of the Earth through the Earth's equator all the way to the distant stars. Likewise, the terrestrial prime meridian extended to the background stars becomes the celestial prime meridian. The same is true for the horizon that can also be extended to the celestial sphere, and, by the way, is different for each person depending upon his or her location on Earth. There is another great circle that we need to consider, perhaps the most important in all of astrology. Unlike the aforementioned circles that extend from the Earth to the celestial sphere and are somewhat easy to find, this circle is more illusive.

Castor: Do you mean invisible?

Pollux: Probably just hard to understand.

Author: Well, kind of both. The great circle I'm talking about is the "ecliptic," the circle that marks the Sun's apparent journey around the Earth each year (apparent only because it's the Earth's annual revolution around the Sun that determines this circle). We know from the study of astronomy that the Sun appears to orbit the Earth. That's why the earliest astronomers put the Earth at the center of the universe ("universe" as our ancestors knew it: what was visible to the naked eye). From their perspective, the Sun orbited the Earth following an imaginary line that marked the solar body's annual pilgrimage around the Earth. Although it refers to the apparent motion of the Sun around the Earth, the term ecliptic is only marginally derived from these two heavenly bodies, having more to do with the nature and position of the Moon than anything else.

Castor: Why the Moon?

Author: The term "ecliptic" is derived from the fact that all lunar and solar eclipses occur only at the intersection of the ecliptic and the Moon's orbit. The question is, How is the ecliptic represented on a terrestrial globe? To understand this, we need to look at some of the not-so-great circles that parallel the Earth's equator. Two of them are germane to this discussion: the Tropic of Cancer in the northern hemisphere and the Tropic of Capricorn in the southern hemisphere. Let's visit the website HyperPhysics, a site developed for high school physics teachers by the faculty of Georgia State University's Department of Physics and Astronomy, to help us here. In a diagram titled "Celestial Sphere," the Earth is shown standing on end with its axis, often called its "spin axis," running through the middle of the Earth's core, North Pole at the top, South Pole at the bottom, both of which extend to the celestial sphere marking the North Celestial Pole (zenith) and the South Celestial Pole (nadir) respectively.[5]

Castor: I think I'm getting a headache.

Author: It's really not that difficult. Try to follow me if you can. Midway between the poles, and perpendicular to the Earth's axis, is the terrestrial equator, which, as mentioned earlier, when extended to the backdrop of fixed stars, becomes the celestial equator. In the diagram the ecliptic slices through the Earth's core and extends to the celestial sphere at an angle of approximately 23.5° relative to the celestial equator. If we had a fully articulated globe in front of us, we could see that the number of degrees from the equator to either of the tropics is 23.5°, the same amount of degrees as the Earth's axial tilt. In other words, it's the axial tilt of the Earth relative to the equator that determines the two not-so-great circles we call the Tropic of Cancer and the Tropic of Capricorn.

Castor: Maybe a picture would help.

Author: Fortunately, there are a number of visual aides available, most of them on the internet in the form of informational charts or video demonstrations. However, I prefer to go right to the source: Staines & Son Orrery Makers.[6]

Castor: What kind of makers?

Pollux: Orrery makers, aren't you listening?

Castor: I thought he said ornery.

Author: The English father-and-son team specialize in the construction of handcrafted brass orreries, which are small working models of the solar system. Toolmakers by trade, father Derek and son Timothy offer three types of orreries to the public under the trademark names "Tellurion Orrery," "Inner Planet Orrery," and "Genesis Orrery," which correspond roughly to the three basic types of "planetaria,"which is the generic name for any working model of the solar system, the earliest recorded mechanism dating back to Archimedes in the third century BCE. Staines & Son's most basic model, the Tellurion Orrery, depicts the Earth and its satellite, the Moon, orbiting the Sun. The Inner Planet Orrery adds Mercury, Venus, and Mars and their respective satellites to the lineup. Finally, the Genesis Orrery, the largest and most complex model, includes nine orbiting planets and their respective satellites (eight major planets along with the minor or "dwarf" planet Pluto).

Castor: I didn't know Pluto was a dwarf.

Pollux: It's not, at least not in that sense. As of 2006, Pluto was demoted from major to minor or "dwarf" status for several reasons, one being its more acute orbital inclination—a little over 17°—in relation to the solar plane.

Castor: Show-off.

Author: As you might have noticed the three models offered in the Staines & Son catalog are surnamed "orreries." An unusual name whose origin goes back to the early eighteenth century when Charles Boyle, the 4th Earl of Orrery, commissioned instrument-maker John Rowley to build a "modern" planetarium based on the revolutionary Copernican or heliocentric model of the solar system from the design of clockmakers George Graham and Thomas Tompion. Rowley named the device an "orrery" in honor of his patron.

Pollux: Kind of like the word "sandwich," which is named after the 4th Earl of Sandwich.

Castor: Speaking of sandwiches, I'm hungry.

Author: We'll take a lunch break soon, but first back to orreries. Over time, the name "orrery" supplanted the more generic term "planetaria," with the "tellurion" (from the Latin *tellus* meaning "of or pertaining to the Earth") the most basic form of the mechanical device. Basic or not, a tellurion (also spelled tellurium) is quite useful for demonstrating the Earth's axial rotation and revolution around the Sun (in addition to the Moon's movements relative to the Earth).

Staines & Son's Tellurion Orrery is a simply geared device built around a central stand of hardwood, upon which a representation of the Sun—in the form of a solid brass ball—sits atop a tall metal column. From the central stand, a two-tiered metal arm containing a variety of gears extends horizontally to another vertical column to which the Earth and its satellite are attached, each duly geared to perform its necessary rotations and revolutions. When a metal crank protruding from the base of the tellurion is turned, four movements are initiated: the Earth begins to revolve around the Sun while rotating on its axis and the Moon begins to revolve around the Earth while rotating on its axis (which, coincidentally, is at the same speed of the Earth's rotation so that the same side of the Moon always faces Earth).

The combined movements of the Earth and the Moon illustrate for the viewer the causes of the seasons, the frequency of eclipses, the phases of the Moon, and the duration of day and night at different times of the year. When it was first created, the tellurion was quite an exquisite piece of engineering, though a century later John Herschel, son of the great German-born English astronomer William Herschel, would call them "very childish toys."[7] Toy or not, it's a perfect tool—still used in schools today—to demonstrate the motions of the Earth and its satellite relative to the position of the Sun.

Pollux: We have one in our science cabinet at school.

Author: One reason why a tellurion is so demonstrative is that the ball representing the Earth appears not as a solid, uniformly painted sphere, but as a fully articulated globe with all of its meridians clearly delineated. In fact, since globe-making has been with us over two thousand years, with the oldest surviving globe dating to 150 BCE, most tellaria from the eighteenth century on sport a fully articulated globe for the Earth. Another reason why a tellurion is so demonstrative, especially the Staines & Son model, is that the Earth's north-south axis is tilted 23.5° with respect to the celestial equator. It's the axial tilt of the Earth relative to the terrestrial equator that gives us the four seasons. But it's not just the axial tilt that causes the seasons, it's the fact that the Earth's axis remains "fixed" (at least during our lifetime and our children's) in its orientation as it revolves around the Sun. Let's return to our sunny-side-up egg analogy.

Castor: Remember, I don't like eggs.

Author: Fine, but I'm thinking about the salt and pepper shakers on the table, not what you're eating. Take the pepper shaker and place it in the middle of the table. Then hold the salt shaker about a foot away from the pepper shaker. Tilt the salt shaker (the Earth) approximately 23.5° and begin moving it around the pepper shaker (the Sun), but without changing the orientation or direction of the salt shaker's tilt. What you'll notice as you complete one revolution around the Sun, I mean the pepper shaker, is that you go through four distinct phases from the perspective of someone living in the northern hemisphere. When the top of the salt shaker points toward the pepper shaker, you have the summer solstice. When the salt shaker is tilted but points neither toward or away from the pepper shaker, you have the fall or autumnal equinox. When the top of the salt shaker points away from the pepper shaker, you have the winter solstice. And, again, when the salt shaker is tilted but points neither toward or away from the pepper shaker, you have the spring or vernal equinox.

Castor: *Achoo!* I'm allergic to pepper.

Pollux: *Castor.*

Author: Moving right along. If we were to transfer these four phases or points of seasonal change to the Earth's surface, they would appear as the summer solstice (Tropic of Cancer), the fall or autumnal equinox (equator), the winter solstice (Tropic of Capricorn), and the spring or vernal equinox (equator), which means that the two tropics—Cancer and Capricorn—are nothing more than the upper limit of the Earth's axial tilt, the farthest degree of latitude where the Sun hits the Earth directly, that is at a 90° angle. Any location more than 23.5° above or below the Earth's equator will only receive indirect sunlight.

Pollux: Why are the tropics called Cancer and Capricorn?

Author: In order to answer that question, we're going to have to talk about the four major chart angles and the signs of the zodiac, which I'm planning to do—just not yet, so please hold that thought for now. As I was saying, the tropics also signify the point at which the Sun—in its apparent revolution around the Earth—pivots or turns (which is what the Latin word "tropic" means) at the top of its northern journey and the bottom of its southern journey. If we were to cut out the zone between the two tropics (known as the "tropic" or "torrid" zone) and lay it flat on the table, we would see that the Sun's path over the course of a year follows a sine wave, undulating back and forth between the Tropic of Cancer and the Tropic of Capricorn. This "wave" is the ecliptic made visible on the Earth's globe, the result of the Earth's axial tilt of 23.5°.

Castor: I think I get it.

Pollux: It's about time.

Author: But this is not what we see from Earth.

Pollux: What do you mean?

Author: From Earth, we see the ecliptic as the solar pathway, the Sun's apparent pilgrimage around the Earth—and it's not hard to find, especially at night. All you have to do is take a giant magic marker and draw a line from one planet to the next, making a kind of necklace of planets; in doing so, you have illuminated the pathway of the Sun—the ecliptic. Well, sort of. Actually, there are three layers or bands with their own separate meanings and associations. Think of it as a highway, a celestial highway, with the ecliptic, the Sun's apparent pathway, as the center line with the planets orbiting, or "wandering," as the original Greek meaning of the word denotes, on either side of the center line anywhere from 0.77° (Uranus) to 7.01° (Mercury), though the minor planets and asteroids vary a bit more widely. But this is just the center line (the ecliptic) and the roadway (the planetary orbits); there's one more band to consider—the zodiac.

Before we consider it, because it's a fairly large topic, let's circle back to the original question, What does the second wheel on my natal chart represent and why is it 360°? As you might have guessed by now, the circle represents the ecliptic from which we ascertain the location of the signs, planets, and houses of the birth chart. Every object in a birth chart is understood from its precise location along the ecliptic. But if the ecliptic represents the Sun's apparent orbit around the Earth, then why is the ecliptic divided into 360 degrees, why not 365 degrees, which is a tad closer to the number of days in a solar year?

Castor: I think you lost me.

Pollux: Ditto.

Author: At the heart of the question is the ongoing tussle between astrology and astronomy. In a perfect world (of course we know there is no such thing), all things would fit neatly together. That's certainly what the ancient Greek

philosopher Aristotle thought. It's simple: the Earth is at
the center of the universe and every major object that orbits
around it—the seven "classical" planets, that is—does so in its
own imperturbably perfect celestial sphere (or, when reduced
to two dimensions, a circle of 360°). In this conception of the
universe, it's not a difficult leap from 360 degrees in a circle
to 360 days in a year except for the fact that the solar year is
not 360 days. For our most distant ancestors this wasn't really
a problem: they preferred to use the Moon as their calendar
guide (after all, that's what we're talking about—calendars).
The lunar calendar served them well as long as they weren't
interested in discerning the finer details of the celestial
objects circling above them.

Take the Babylonians, for instance. According to Mark
Ronan, Honorary Professor of Mathematics at University
College, London, the ancient Babylonians did quite well with
a lunar calendar, which was based on a nineteen-year cycle of
235 lunar months (called the Saros Cycle), until their need to
record the precise movements of the Sun, the Moon, and the
five visible planets forced them to set it aside and adopt a solar
calendar of 12 months of 30 days each. The 360-day calendar
wasn't actually new, however: it was an old administrative
calendar that had worked nicely for mundane accounting
procedures, but was less-than-perfect for recording celestial
events. What did they do? They took their cues from the
Egyptians who also divided the year into twelve 30-day
months that equalled 360 days, adding five days at the end
of every fourth year to adjust for the 365 days of the year.
Instead of tacking on days at the end of every fourth year, the

Babylonians added an occasional "intercalary" month every five or six years to make up the difference.[8]

In other words, no matter how anyone sliced it—Sumerians, Akkadians, Babylonians, Chaldeans, Persians, Greeks, or Romans—forcing the 365-day solar year into the 360-degree circle was no easy task. Which brings us back to the earlier question, Why is there 360° in a circle in the first place? Several theories abound. Caught between the 355-day lunar calendar and the 365-day solar calendar, perhaps our ancestors decided to split the baby in half, settling on a 360-day solar year, which they extended to the number of degrees in a circle. Others, more mathematically minded, noted that six equilateral triangles, each having an angle of 60° at the center, fit snugly into a circle, thus dividing the circle into six equal sections of 60° that resulted in a total of 360°. Still others, more interested in the properties of numbers than how they fit reality, chose 360 given its highly composite nature, that is, its divisibility by almost two dozen whole numbers. Actually, 360 is not just a highly composite number: technically, it's a "superior composite number" with 22 divisors. Not counting 1 and 360, it's divisible by 2, 3, 4, 5, 6, 8, 9, 10, 12, 15, 18, 20, 24, 30, 36, 40, 45, 60, 72, 90, 120, and 180, which come in handy in a number of ways.

Castor: Could you repeat that?

Author: No, but I will add this: the extraordinarily composite 360 is divisible by 2 equinoxes, 2 solstices, 4 seasons, 12 months, and 24 time zones, not to mention 24 hours, 60 minutes, and 60 seconds. In other words, who in their right mind would create a circle or a calendar—or a bucket for that matter—with anything but 360 degrees. No one, that's who, which is why through the ages we've periodically added intercalary days or months to the calendar in order to bring it back into alignment with "reality," and we still do, think: leap year.

Castor: Leap year? I've heard of that.

Pollux: Everyone has heard of that. Every four years a day is added to the end of February to account for the addition of a day every four years—or something like that.

Author: Yes, something like that. Let me suggest that we end this discussion with a podcast?

Castor: I've always wanted to make a podcast.

Pollux: I think he wants us to listen to a podcast, not make one.

Author: The podcast I have in mind is on the 360-day solar year co-hosted by Bob Enyart and Fred Williams of *Real Science Radio*. The podcast is essentially about the origin of calendars, namely the Sumerian calendar, the Babylonian calendar, the Egyptian calendar, the Greek calendar, even the Armenian calendar (who'd even heard of an Armenian calendar). What caught my attention was the last section of the podcast titled "Physical Mechanism" that explores the "hydroplate theory."[9]

Castor: *Hydroplane?*

Pollux: Hydroplate! Aren't you listening?

Author: According to the theory's originator, Prof. Walter Brown, the 46,000-mile globe-encircling crack known as the mid-oceanic ridge is somehow responsible for—or, at least, a visible remnant of—a massive tectonic plate shift that destabilized the Earth over a billion years ago, causing the Earth's rotation to speed up and as it did it changed the solar year from a perfect 360 days to our current 365.25 days. According to Prof. Brown, at the same time that the Earth's perfect 360-day orbit around the Sun sped up causing the solar year to approach 365.25 days, the Moon's perfect 30-day orbit around the Earth was upended as well, leaving it with today's 29.53-day lunar month. In other words, once upon a time, many Moons ago—or should I say, Suns—the mathematics of the universe was quite simple, not to mention more amenable to a human's ability to multiply and divide.

Pollux: Well, maybe for a few of us.

Castor: Are you insinuating that I...

Author: Now, boys.

Notes

1. Fiorenza, Nick Anthony. "An Introduction to the Great Circles & Personal Points in Your Personalized Star Chart (or in an Astrology Chart)." *The Lunar Planner*, [URL] https//www.lunarplanner.com/ ArgoNavisPublications/StarChartPersonal/STInstruction.html.
2. Bobrick, Benson. *The Fated Sky*, Chpt. 2.
3. Hall, Judy. *The Astrology Bible*, Introduction.
4. Herring, Amy. *Essential Astrology*, Chpt. 3, "The Natal Chart Map."
5. "Celestial Sphere," Georgia State University's HyperPhysics website, [URL] https//hyperphysics.phy-astr.gsu.edu/hbase/eclip. html.
6. Staines & Son Orrery Makers, [URL] https//www.orrerydesign.com.
7. *World Wide Words: Investigating the English Language Across the Globe, Orrery*, [URL] https//www.worldwidewords.org/weirdwords/ ww-orr1.htm.

8. Ronan, Mark. "Full Circle: The Long and Complicated History of Why There Are 360 Degrees in a Circle," *History Matters*, April 1, 2020, [URL] https//www.yahoo.com/entertainment/why-360-degrees-circle-heres-174537726.html/. See also: Ronan, Mark. "A Light Shining from Babylon," *Standpoint*, April 24, 2012, [URL] https//standpointmag.co.uk/cosmos-may-12-a-light-shining-from-babylon-mark-ronan-lunar-solar-eclipses-mesopotamia/.

9. Enyart, Bob and Fred Williams. "Physical Mechanism," *Real Science Radio*, Nov. 13, 2020, [URL] https://kgov.com/real-science-radio/.

4

Actors and Experiencers

The plus sign or cross that the Line of the Horizon and the
Line of the Meridian make as they bisect the natal chart not
only produces two hemispheres each (and four sections,
or "quadrants," when taken together), they also form four
points or "angles," one at the end of each intersecting line.[1]
April Elliott Kent, *The Essential Guide to Practical Astrology*

Although my birth chart is constructed from a set of
concentric circles containing the signs, planets, and houses,
it's not as simple as that. The basic architecture is circular, yes,
but it also contains within it a cruciform.[2]

Castor: A what?

Author: A cruciform. Which is just a fancy way of saying
a cross, but in this case a special type of cross: an equal-armed
cross created by the intersection of two lines on the birth
chart—the native's horizon line and birth meridian.

Pollux: *Horizon. Meridian. Circle. Cross.* This reminds me of
an earlier discussion about the symbols of astrology.

Author: Yes, something we'll never quite get away from in
any discussion of astrology. Do you remember the three major
symbols?

Castor: Ox, goat, horse?

Author: Not exactly.

Pollux: Circle, semicircle, and cross.

Author: That's better. Let me defer to British astrologer Alan Leo. Many years ago he wrote that the horoscope—the birth chart—was built upon the cross and the circle, or, as he explained, "the revolving earth turning upon its axis within a circumscribed area."[3]

Castor: That's heavy.

Author: It is heavy because it involves the weight of the Earth (the cross) and the immensity of the Celestial Sphere (the circle). Together, when flattened into a two-dimensional birth chart, these symbols represent the rotating Earth within the ecliptic. The cruciform or cross is significant for several reasons: symbolically, it represents the Earth, the material world, including man and his activities. Practically, it represents the four cardinal directions (north, south, east, and west), as well as the four major angles (sunrise, noon, sunset, and midnight).

Pollux: One layer of meaning upon another.

Author: Yes, that's probably why astrology is referred to as an esoteric or occult science (although to non-believers, it's nothing more than a pseudo-science). Some of those layers are quite apparent—the cardinal directions and angles—but some of them aren't. They're hidden or more metaphysical in their meaning. For instance, east or sunrise refers to birth, to the reincarnation of a soul; noon or south…

Castor: South? Don't you mean north?

Author: Here's another confusing idea. Although the birth chart can be "read" like a map, it is a bit different in its orientation. Whereas a road map, which you're probably familiar with, orients with north at the top, the birth chart, which is a celestial map of an individual's life potentialities, orients with south at the top. Think of it this way: you're standing in the northern hemisphere (the dominant perspective for astrologers in the Western world), looking toward the equator. Where is east?

Pollux: On your left.

Author: And west?

Castor: On your right.

Author: So if east is to your left and west is to your right, then where is south?

Castor: In front of you.

Author: Another way of saying that is, it's above you at the top of the chart.

Pollux: Which puts north at the bottom of the chart.

Castor: I still don't get it.

Author: Okay, let's see what astrologer Robert Hand has to say about this. He begins by having you imagine that you are lying down in the middle of a field, imagining the Earth beneath you and the sky all around you: "You're lying in a field, face up with your feet pointed to where the Sun would be at noon. In the Northern Hemisphere, this would be toward the south. Planets will rise to the left of you in the east, and set to the right of you in the west. When the Sun is exactly due south of you, it will be exactly halfway between its rising and setting, and therefore on the upper part of the meridian circle. At midnight, if you could see through the Earth, you would realize that the Sun is behind you, below the horizon exactly due north, halfway between its setting and rising, and therefore on the lower part of the meridian circle. The horoscope is a schematic diagram of this view of the celestial sphere."[4]

Castor: I think I get it.

Author: In other words, the birth chart is a map, just not a map of the Earth. Here are the associations with each major angle on the chart, moving clockwise from one angle to another: on the left side of the chart, east or sunrise refers to birth and to new beginnings; at the top of the chart, south or noon refers to life, maturation, and vitality; on the right side of the chart, west or sunset to death and decay; and at the bottom of the chart, north or midnight to the soul's return to the cosmic stream (for some, that means preparation for the soul's reincarnation).[5] When it comes to the natus, the one born, the four points of the cross represent the four most important points or "angles" in the birth chart—Ascendant, Midheaven, Descendant, and Imum Coeli.

Castor: Imum...*what?*

Pollux: Imum Coeli, doofus. Didn't you study Latin?

Author: Yes, it's Latin, meaning "Lowest Heaven." Before we get to that, let's back up and start at the beginning— literally— and talk about the Ascendant. At birth, when an infant draws his or her first breath, a sign of the zodiac is creeping over the eastern horizon. This is the Rising sign. It is also called the Ascendant. But the two are not exactly the same even though many astrologers use them interchangeably. I like the distinction Amy Herring draws between them: "The rising sign refers to the entire sign that was rising over the horizon in the place and time of your birth, whereas the Ascendant refers to the specific intersection at which that rising sign and the horizon meet."[6] That's why a birth chart will indicate the exact degree and minute of the Ascendant. Take my chart for instance. While my Rising sign is Gemini, my Ascendant is 2° 31' from the cusp or beginning of Gemini because that's where my horizon line crossed the ecliptic at the moment of my birth. The Ascendant is so important that many years ago astrologers believed it was more important than your Sun sign, perhaps the single most important point in a chart.

Pollux: Why?

Author: Because many other calculations in a chart are based upon the Ascendant. It's like the dial on a compass: once you set it for "true north" all of the other directions just fall into place. Before we explore more of the meanings associated with each of the four angles, let's look at more of the celestial mechanics involved. The very name of a birth chart refers to the Ascendant, i.e., horoscope, meaning "hour-watcher," which is the English translation of the Latin *horoscopus* based on the original Greek term.[7]

Castor: What does "hour-watcher" have to do with anything?

Author: Everything, Castor. Let's say you were a shepherd living thousands of years ago. When you weren't watching your flock, you were probably watching the sky, the movement of the clouds, the slow progression of the Sun, and, at night, the flickering stars overhead. In fact, you counted the hours by watching the stars. Probably one reason that the first zodiac was composed of 36 of the brightest stars, one rising over the horizon every 40 minutes or so. It makes perfect sense: if it takes 40 minutes for each bright star to appear over the horizon, then to complete a full revolution around the ecliptic, it would take 1,440 minutes.

Castor: Wait, I'm lost.

Author: Okay, I forgot to tell you that it takes four minutes to travel one degree. That's something astrologers have known for quite some time. Knowing this, all you have to do is multiply 40 (how many minutes it takes one of the bright stars to move 10°) times 36 (the number of bright stars you're watching) and you get 1,440 minutes, or 24 hours (which is 1,440 divided by 60, the number of minutes in an hour).

Castor: Isn't there a simpler way to do this?

Author: Yes, throw out the 36-star zodiac and replace it with a 12-sign zodiac. Then the math is much easier. Since there are 24 hours in a day, it takes each sign about two hours to clear the horizon.

Pollux: Which means that for a shepherd watching the night sky it would be a lot easier to keep track of the passing hours.

Author: Indeed, it would.

Castor: Is that why there are 12 signs of the zodiac?

Author: There are probably a few reasons, one being that it's easier to track 12 signs than 36 stars. Another is that 12 is a rather magical number, being the smallest number divisible by six factors—1, 2, 3, 4, 6, and 12. The number 12 also correlates with the lunar cycle, since there are approximately 12 lunations, i.e., full moons, in a solar year. But I digress. Back to being a shepherd. You watch your sheep in the daytime and you watch the stars at night, which means that you're both a "sheep-watcher" and an "hour-watcher."

Castor: A horoscopus?

Author: Yes, a horoscopus. The birth chart is you at the moment of your birth, and the horoscopus is that "freeze-frame snapshot" of the cosmos around you, including what was coming up over the horizon when you took your first breath of life.[8]

Castor: Cool.

Author: Let's return to the four angles of a natal chart, in particular to the Ascendant. According to Yasmin Boland, the Ascendant is "the most personal point on your chart because it's dictated by the exact time and place and date you were born."[9] April Elliott Kent calls it the "sunrise" angle of your chart, that represents your physical identity and appearance, and, as the point of new beginnings, "where you begin and others end."[10] Of all the descriptions of the Ascendant, I prefer one offered by Rae Orion...

Castor: Rae Orion? That can't be her real name.

Author: Nope, but then Alan Leo isn't his real name either. Here's what Rae Orion (whatever her name is) has to say about the matter: "The Ascendant describes the surface of your personality. It's your image, your persona, your mask, your vibe. Or think of it this way: Your Rising sign is like the clothes you wear; those outfits aren't exactly you, but they aren't irrelevant either. They convey a powerful, unspoken message to others—and even you may come to associate them with your deeper self."[11]

Pollux: That's easy to remember. The Ascendant is a mask.

Author: Quite often it is, but, according to Jodie Forrest, it's more than that: it's not just a mask, but an interface with the wider world. In her book *The Ascendant*, Forrest makes this claim: "The Ascendant is a channel for that inner world to express itself in an authentic way while still being able to interact with the environment's demands. By the same token, it can also serve as protection for that inner world, for the rest of the chart, to keep the world from trampling unheeded through our vulnerable insides."[12]

Pollux: It sounds like the Ascendant is a very important part of your chart.

Castor: More important than your Sun sign. At least that's what you said a minute ago.

Author: Whether or not it is, the two are quite different. Generally, whereas your Sun sign is your true, deeper self, your Ascendant is the outer mask you wear, the face that you show the world until you're ready—that is, feel safe enough—to drop the mask and show people who you really are. I like the way Stephen Arroyo looks at the Ascendant, more as a gateway or portal than a mask: "The Ascendant always indicates something essential about the person that is at once deeply inner and also outer. It is virtually impossible for a person to act in the world or express himself or herself without bringing the Ascendant into play. In many ways, it is the gate through which we most directly confront the outer world. It symbolizes our individual approach to life itself. It represents the way one actively merges with life in the outer world when one's energy is flowing spontaneously."[13]

Pollux; So it's not as simple as it appears.

Author: Not in the least, and I'm sure I'll have more to say about it later. For now, however, let's move on.

Castor: To the Medium Coeli?

Author: Well, not exactly. I mean, if we were to move in a clockwise fashion around our imaginary clock, I'd say you're right. But our clock is a celestial clock, so we follow it counterclockwise for that's how the signs and the houses move (at least, that's how they are placed around the birth chart).

Pollux: So next up is the Imum Coeli at the bottom of the chart.

Author: Correct, and if you remember, Imum Coeli means...

Castor: Lowest Heaven, or whatever.

Author: Each of the four angles carries a specific association. However, and this is a big however, not only do the associations vary according to the frame of reference we choose, but also the direction we choose to move around the birth chart.

Pollux: I don't think I'm following you.

Author: If we choose the twelve houses of the natal chart as our frame of reference, then we travel around the natal chart counterclockwise with these associations: sunrise, birth and infancy; midnight, childhood and family life; sunset, coming-of-age issues and relationship-building; and noon, work and career aspirations.

Pollux: It's the cycle of life, from infancy to old age.

Author: Yes, but that's only one way of looking at it. Alan Leo offers another way of looking at it, using the 24-hour axial rotation of the Earth as the frame of reference. In

Leo's scheme of things, as I hinted at before, the movement is clockwise with the following associations: *sunrise*, birth; *noon*, life and vitality; *sunset*, death and decay; and *midnight*, immortality (the "space" between physical death and a person's next incarnation). However, if we look closely, we see that Leo is following the apparent movement of the Sun, Moon, and planets as they parade across the sky each day. But it's all an illusion because it's really the Earth's counterclockwise axial rotation that causes this appearance, and it's why the four major angles of the birth chart, with their house subdivisions and zodiacal sign correspondences, are laid out in a counterclockwise manner, which means that after the Ascendent we come to the...

Castor: Imum Coeli.

Author: Well, I see someone is still listening. According to Judy Hall, the Imum Coeli is the root of the innermost self: "it symbolizes base security, what a person needs to feel safe."[14] As such, according to April Elliott Kent, it sheds light on a person's home, family, and personal history. Kent calls it the "midnight angle," the angle that represents "privacy, rest, and the security of the home."[15]

Castor: I like "midnight angle." Kind of spooky.

Author: After another quarter turn, we arrive at the Descendant. This is the "sunset angle," which marks the point where individuals begin to reach out, to extend themselves beyond the confines of home and family, and take their rightful place in society. It is the angle of relationships, whether they be personal or professional. It's interesting to note, as Kent has, that the Descendant is associated with the weakest hour of the day, when the Sun disappears slowly over the western horizon. But then embedded in the idea of any relationship is the giving up of some measure of independence in order to merge or blend with another. Some people do this better than others.[16]

Pollux: I'll say.

Castor: Why are you looking at me?

Author: Here's something else to think about. Each of the angles has a complementary pole, one balancing the other. Whereas the Ascendant is about the primacy of individual identity, the Descendant is about submitting to the demands of a relationship. When you look at a natal chart, you'll notice that they are diametrically opposite each other, like two ends of an axis, one marking the cusp of the first house, the other the cusp of the seventh house.

Pollux: But we haven't talked about houses yet.

Castor: We haven't even talked about the signs of the zodiac.

Author: I know, but we will. Before we do, we have one more angle to talk about.

Castor: The Medium Coeli.

Author: Yes, Castor, the Medium Coeli, also known as the Midheaven, which we find at the extreme southernmost point of the natal chart.

Castor: Which means it's at the top of the chart.

Author: It's kind of goofy, isn't it? But just as the Ascendant and Descendant represent complementary poles, the Imum Coeli and Midheaven represent complementary poles. So let me ask you, if the Imum Coeli symbolizes home and family life, what do you think the Midheaven symbolizes?

Castor: Going to college?

Author: Not exactly.

Pollux: Work and career.

Castor: I knew that.

Author: You both should have known that because I mentioned it earlier. The Midheaven is all about the pursuit of success, about recognition among one's peers, about making an impact or a lasting impression. Another way of thinking about it is this: the Midheaven marks both the highest point of the birth chart and an individual's highest worldly ambitions. Or, as Kent emphasizes, the Midheaven symbolizes the work you are called to do here on Earth. It's what you want to do or be in this life.[17]

Castor: I want to be a pilot.

Pollux: I want to be a mathematician.

Author: I want to leave you with another way to think about the four angles. Each pair of angles forms a line that cuts the celestial sphere into two equal hemispheres, each with its own set of meanings. Whereas the line from the Ascendant to the Descendant (horizon) divides the celestial sphere into a southern and northern hemisphere, the line from the Midheaven to the Imum Coeli (meridian) divides the celestial sphere into an eastern and western hemisphere. In her chapter on houses, Boland notes, "A person with a lot of planets in the top half of their chart lives their life quite openly—they are 'seen', they are out in society and they tend to be more outgoing and social. Conversely, someone with lots of planets in the lower half of their chart will be more private, perhaps more guarded, more subjective."[18] Robert Hand says just about the same thing when he observes that the horizon lines marks the fundamental division between subject and object, with the upper (southern) hemisphere associated with those aspects of life that are more "objective," that is, less personal and more social. According to Hand, if an abundance of planets populate this hemisphere, the individual will tend to be more outer-directed than inner-oriented.[19]

Pollux: Is that what you are?

Author: Oh, no. Most of my planets—in fact, almost all of them—are in the lower (northern) hemisphere, making me much more introspective and self-oriented than outer-directed.

Castor: What about the other line?

Pollux: The meridian.

Castor: I was just about to say that. What does it do?

Author: As I said earlier, the meridian divides the birth chart into an eastern and western hemisphere. According to Boland, people who have more of their planets on the left or eastern side of their chart tend to be self-starters. They're motivated individuals who tend to show a lot of initiative. On the other hand, people with a lot of planets on the right or western side of their chart are less self-focused, as they take their cues from the relationships they have with the surrounding environment. The reason for this, according to Hand, is that while the energies in the eastern hemisphere are moving from inner to outer, from the private to the social, the energies in the western hemisphere are doing the reverse, moving from outer to inner, from the social to the private.

Pollux: It's kind of like the Chinese Yin-Yang symbol.

Author: That's a great analogy, Pollux. Like the light and dark energies of the Yin-Yang symbol, the energies of the opposing east and west hemispheres in a natal chart are related, yet different at the same time. According to Hand, in my mind one of the most perceptive astrologers around, the two types of energies represented by the eastern and western hemispheres determine whether people will be "actors" or "experiencers."[20]

Castor: Actors or experiencers?

Pollux: We certainly know which one you are.

Castor: Hey, I resent that.

Author: Okay, settle down, let me finish. The difference comes down to this: whereas "actors" tend to act first and think later, "experiencers" tend to think first and act later. In other words, like most dualities in the natal chart, there is no inherently "good" or "bad" qualities, just ways to think about differences and how they can possibly manifest themselves.

Castor: Which one are you?

Author: What do you think?

Castor: Well, you do seem to take the lead in all of our conversations. I'd say that you were an actor.

Author: And you would be right. Seven of my "planets" are in the eastern hemisphere, which means that I tend to act first and think later (not to mention that I seriously considered a career in acting when I was younger). Let's take this idea one step further: let's put the horizon and meridian lines into the birth chart at perpendicular angles to each other so they make an equal-armed cross. Instead of hemispheres, what do we get?

Castor: Four really large pieces of pie.

Author: Exactly, only astrologers don't call them pie pieces (well, some do); they call them "quadrants."

Castor: Like a fire quadrant?

Pollux: That's fire hydrant, dodo bird.

Author: Actually, Castor is on to something, because each of the four angles is related to one of the four elements (i.e., fire, earth, air, and water), and the first angle (the Ascendant), perhaps the most important of the four, is related to fire. So I guess you could say that there is a "fire quadrant." Just like the four angles are laden with meaning, so too are the four quadrants: the first quadrant (Ascendant to Imum Coeli) addresses self-awareness; the second quadrant (Imum Coeli to Descendant) self-expression; the third quadrant (Descendant to Midheaven) self-expansion and social identity; and the fourth quadrant (Midheaven to Ascendant) social expression and self-transcendence.[21] Unfortunately...

Castor: This doesn't sound good.

Author: Like any endeavor, there are multiple viewpoints. So, as I was saying, unfortunately, not every astrologer holds the same understanding of the quadrants. For instance, most astrologers agree with what I said above, that the four quadrants begin with the large pie slice between the Ascendant and Imum Coeli, and move counterclockwise around the natal chart, ending with the fourth quadrant or pie slice between the Midheaven and the Ascendant. This makes sense from the point of view of how the signs and houses are placed in a birth chart. However, Robert Hand sees it entirely different.

According to Hand, the more common sense way of counting the four quadrants is to begin at the Imum Coeli at the bottom of the chart and progress clockwise around the natal chart. Beginning at the Imum Coeli is like starting the day at midnight rather than at sunrise. Of course, this seasoned and insightful astrologer has a rationale for starting the day at midnight. In doing so, the native will see "the upward sweep of energies from their most secret and private to their most public manifestations, and back down again."[22] This establishes a certain circularity of energy that flows from the inner energy of the Imum Coeli through the Ascendant to the outer energy of the Midheaven and, conversely, from the outer energy of the Midheaven through the Descendant to the inner energy of the Imum Coeli, returning to its origin.

Pollux: Like the Yin-Yang symbol.

Author: Yes, very much so, from inner to outer, from receptivity to action, from private to public, and back again. A never-ending cyclical process.

Pollux: May I ask you a question?

Author: Shoot.

Pollux: We know that when it comes to the upper and lower hemispheres most of your planets are in the lower hemisphere. And we know that when it comes to the eastern and western hemispheres most of your planets are in the eastern hemisphere. What about the four quadrants? Does one quadrant have more planets in it than the others?

Author: That's a great question. It shows that you're starting to think about the birth chart as a dynamic place where celestial bodies are activated in different ways according to their location. To answer your question, I'll have to list the planets in my chart. I say this because, when it comes to planets in a birth chart, not every astrologer uses the same *number* (anywhere from nine to 15) or *types* (planets, asteroids, comets, midpoints, mathematical points, etc.). The chart I had cast in the 1980s has twelve planets, though they may not all seem like planets to you. There's the Sun and the Moon...

Castor: The Sun and the Moon? They're not planets.

Author: I thought this might be a problem. Let's just say that years ago astrologers considered any moving celestial body, moving against the backdrop of "fixed" stars, a planet. Knowing this, we count the Sun and the Moon and the five visible planets (visible to the naked eye, that is), which include Mercury, Venus, Mars, Jupiter, and Saturn.

Castor: That's only seven.

Author: Next up we have the three "modern" planets— Neptune, Uranus, and Pluto.

Castor: That's ten.

Author: Here's where it gets a little sketchy. As far as I can tell, the last two "planets" my computer-analyst-qua-astrologer counted are my Ascendant and Midheaven, which would account for the totals on my chart.[23] But we were talking quadrants, not planets, so back to Pollux's question, Does one of the quadrants in my natal chart have more planets than the others? The answer is yes, the first quadrant, with the second quadrant a close second. I have five planets in the first quadrant and four in the second quadrant, with the five planets in the first quadrant "stronger" than the four in the second quadrant.

Pollux: What do you mean?

Author: In the second quadrant, I have Pluto, Saturn, Neptune, and the Moon, only two of which (Saturn and the Moon) are considered part of the seven visible or "classical" planets. On the other hand, Mercury, Mars, Venus, Uranus, and the Sun—not to mention my Ascendant—populate the first quadrant, making this quadrant full of intense, personality defining energy. In order to fully understand this, we're going to have to touch upon two other domains of the birth chart—the signs of the zodiac and the twelve mundane houses.

Castor: Signs of the zodiac, okay; but "mundane houses?" Sounds rather boring.

Pollux: *Castor.*

Notes

1. Kent, April Elliott. *The Essential Guide to Practical Astrology*, Chpt. 8, "Houses."

2. Although circular birth charts appeared with some frequency during the earliest days of the Roman Empire (often made of wood with moveable tokens to represent the planets), by the late Middle Ages the birth or natal chart had taken on a square format, influenced by Islamic astrology (which, in turn, was influenced by Indian or Vedic astrology). With the rediscovery of the Greco-Roman world during the European Renaissance, the birth chart reverted to its circular form, a direct influence of the resurgent interest in neoplatonic philosophy.

3. Leo, Alan. *Symbolism and Astrology*, Chpt. 6, "The Symbol of the Horoscope."

4. Hand, Robert. *Horoscope Symbols,* Chpt. 12, "The Horoscope Angles."

5. *Ibid.*

6. Herring, Amy. *Essential Astrology,* Chpt. 3, "The Natal Chart Map."

7. Kent, Chpt. 1, "The Language of the Stars." Robert Hand also addresses the topic of the horoscopus in *Horoscope Symbols*, calling the horoscopus the "watcher of the hour," indicating that its original meaning referred only to the Ascendant, and only later, during the European Renaissance, did it come to refer to the entire natal chart cast for the natus for a specific time and place. See Robert Hand, *Horoscope Symbols*, Chpt. 12, "The Horoscope Angles."

8. Herring, Chpt. 3, "The Natal Chart Map."

9. Boland, Yasmin. *Astrology,* Chpt. 6, "The Angles."

10. Kent, Chpt. 8, "Houses."

11. Orion, Rae. *Astrology for Dummies*, Chpt. 11, "What You See versus What You Get: The Rising Sign (And More)."

12. Forrest, Jodie, as cited in Herring, Chpt. 8, "The Houses."

13. Arroyo, Stephen. *Stephen Arroyo's Chart Interpretation Handbook,* Chpt. 6, "The Ascendant (or Rising Sign) & the Midheaven."

14. Hall, Judy. *The Astrology Bible*, Chpt. 5, "The Houses and Angles."

15. Kent, Chpt. 8, "Houses."

16. *Ibid.*

17. *Ibid.*

18. Boland, Chpt. 7, "The Houses."

19. Hand, Chpt. 12, "The Horoscope Angles." Hand describes the physical mechanism of the horizon and meridian in an earlier chapter, stating the following: "The horoscope angles are in part a device for expressing the horizon and meridian planes in terms of degrees along the ecliptic. The Ascendant and Descendant are the two points where the ecliptic crosses the horizon. Planets rise, or pass from below the horizon to above it, at or near the Ascendant. They set, or pass from above the horizon to below, at or near the Descendant. These two points are always exactly 180° from each

other. Similarly, the Midheaven and I.C. are always exactly opposite each other. These angles are where the ecliptic crosses the local meridian. The Midheaven (English for the Latin medium coeli) is where these two circles cross above the horizon, and the I.C. (short for imum coeli, or "lowest heaven") is where they cross below the horizon." See Hand, Chpt. 2, "The Symbol Systems of Astrology."

20. *Ibid.*

21. Boland, Chpt. 7, "The Houses."

22. Hand, Chpt. 15, "The Houses: Two Alternative Views." I would also direct the reader to ARHAT Media, Robert Hand's personal website for the distribution of his books, pamphlets, lectures, and other media. [URL] https://arhatmedia.com.

23. A close examination of my natal chart reveals a few inconsistencies, namely the number of planets in each of the four elements. When you look at my chart replicated in the front matter, you'll see that it lists the number of planets in each of the four elements: *fire* (3), *earth* (1), *air* (6), and *water* (2). Whereas fire (Jupiter, Venus, Pluto) and earth (Saturn) are pretty straightforward, air and water are not. Five of the six air planets are Mercury, Mars, Sun, Neptune, and the Moon. But what about the sixth air planet? It's either the Midheaven in Aquarius (air sign) or the Ascendant in Gemini (air sign). The aspect grid below the circular chart lists both the Midheaven (MC) and the Ascendant (ACS). My guess is that the sixth air planet is my Ascendant as it is the most important angle of the four major chart angles. But what about the two water planets? One of them is Uranus in Cancer (water sign), but what about the other one? The only glyph left unaccounted for in the circular chart is the North Lunar Node in Pisces (water sign). But if the North Lunar Node is counted as one of the twelve "planets" on my chart, why doesn't it appear in the aspect grid below the circular chart? It's all very mysterious to me (and perhaps to you, too).

5

The Great Pattern-Matching Game

The zodiac signs can be thought of like tick marks on the face of a clock, but instead of marking the hours of a day, they serve to mark the Sun's progress during the year. Each day, the Sun advances a little on its yearly orbit along the ecliptic to a new position within one of the zodiac constellations.[1]
Alexander Boxer, *A Scheme of Heaven*

For the third day in a row I'm up at 7 o'clock in the morning. Not because I want to, but because my neighbors have decided to rebuild their back deck. The workman arrive shortly before 7 a.m. and are soon pounding away, which means that for the last three days I haven't seen our feral cat. The reason: she sleeps beneath our neighbor's deck, now a construction site, and she's disappeared—it's not the first time. A couple of weeks ago she disappeared for several days. I thought perhaps she had met an alley cat who persuaded her to hitchhike to Canada. When she returned several days later, I figured they had a little spat on the way and she decided to head home. Now, however, there is no home to return to, so she'll just have to wait it out.

Meanwhile, I woke up with the same thought I had the other day: while the ecliptic in the sky represents a 365-day solar year, the ecliptic on my birth chart represents a 360-degree circle. To me, that's still a bit problematic. But after thinking about it, I decided that it's not. Here's why: while the ecliptic in the sky measures time (how long it takes the Earth to revolve around the Sun in the course of a year), the ecliptic on my birth chart measures distance, not *linear* distance (how far Mercury is from Venus, or some other heavenly body), but *angular* distance (how many degrees apart Mercury is from Venus, or Neptune, or Pluto, or some other body). If there is any mechanism that adds dynamism to a birth chart, it's the angular distance between two heavenly bodies, which is called their "aspect." More than anything else, aspects determine the personal qualities and behavioral tendencies of an individual. Before we get to that, we need to look at my birth chart as we proceed circle-by-circle to the inner core. And the next circle is the "Circle of Animals."

Castor: Circle of Animals?

Pollux: The Signs of the Zodiac, Castor. Don't you know anything?

Castor: I know more than…

Author: May I continue? It's true that the word zodiac derived from the Greek language means "circle of animals," but why do astrologers call it this in the first place?[2]

Castor: Because there are animals in the sky?

Author: Well, yes, but some very specific types of animals. Pollux, do you know why?

Pollux: The zodiac is a circle of constellations that appear in the distance behind the apparent pathway of the Sun, many of them named after animals, like Aries the Ram, Taurus the Bull, Cancer the Crab, Leo the Lion, and so forth.

Castor: Many of them? Not all of them?

Pollux: Not all of them, Castor. Think about us, we're kids, I mean humans—well, half human anyway.

Castor: Half human?

Pollux: Well, I am, you're not. Don't you know who your parents are?

Castor: I sure do. My mother is Leda, who became a queen after she married our father, Tyndareus, the king of Sparta.

Pollux: My mother is Leda also, only my father isn't Tyndareus.

Castor: He isn't?

Pollux: No, he isn't. My father is the all-powerful Zeus, god of gods, who disguised himself as a swan and seduced Leda. As a result, I was born—half-mortal, half-god.

Castor: So then you're only my half-brother?

Pollux: Something like that. Half-human or half-god, when it comes to astrology, we're known as the "heavenly twins," the two stars that give the constellation Gemini its name (which, after all, means twins in Latin).

Castor: And I'm the smarter of the two, right?

Pollux: Wrong. Not only am I smarter, but I burn brighter, and while I'm a warm golden glow, you're a cool, distant bluish-white.

Castor: *Rats.*

Author: A very interesting conversation, but let's get
back to the circle of animals, i.e., the signs of the zodiac. As I
mentioned earlier, when it comes to the apparent pathway of
the Sun, there are three interrelated concepts that we need to
grasp: (1) the ecliptic, which is the apparent pathway of the
Sun around the Earth (using the "highway" analogy, it is the
center line), (2) the zone of planetary orbits determined by
each planet's orbital inclination to the ecliptic (the highway's
paved roadway that extends a little more than seven degrees
on either side of the centerline, that is if you don't include
Pluto and other trans-Neptunian objects), and (3) the zodiac
made of twelve constellations—or thirteen, depending upon
who's counting—that you see in the distance behind the
planetary orbits (think of the zodiac as the shoulders of the
highway, a bit broader than the road itself). When it comes to
the zodiac, we first have to understand what a constellation is.

Castor: It's a group of stars.

Author: Yes, but that's just one part of the answer. Excuse
me while I grab my astronomy dictionary. When it comes to
constellations, the dictionary entry says that it is an officially
recognized group of stars, 88 in all, that populate the northern
and southern celestial skies.[3] Although many of them bear
names dating back thousands of years, each star group
represents a patch of fabric that when sewn together make up
the entire quilt of the sky.

Castor: *Quilt of the sky*—I like that.

Author: Yes, but within the patches of this quilt is another
type of star group called an "asterism." According to the
dictionary, an asterism is a miniature constellation; that

is, it's a group of stars, like "The Plough," that lies within a constellation (in the case of the "The Plough," it lies within the constellation Ursa Major).[4]

Castor: Why are there groups of stars in the first place? Aren't these just figments of people's imagination?

Author: Ultimately, yes, but they're not completely arbitrary. When our earliest ancestors looked up at the night sky they actually saw bears and whales and archers and chariots, all sorts of things that they experienced on Earth. They even saw the gods that they believed in (most of the planets are named after Greco-Roman gods). As time went on though, these star groups or constellations came in handy as a way of "navigating" the night sky. Think of it this way. There are millions of stars staring down at you at night. Actually, that's a bit of an overstatement: some of the first star charts cobbled together by our ancestors listed only a few thousand stars. But even a few thousand stars would be hard to remember. So what did our ancestors do?

Pollux: They divided the sky into star groups.

Author: According to Alexander Boxer, our ancestors grouped the stars into clusters and gave them names so they could remember them. I used to do this every Saturday morning after breakfast when I was a child. I'd go outside, lie down in the grass in the front yard, and stare up at the clouds. What did I see? Horses. Cows. Battleships. Dragons. Soldiers. Bathtubs. Well, maybe not bathtubs. In other words, all sorts of things that my fertile imagination could conjure up. Of course, unlike constellations in the night sky, my morning cloud formations never returned. They vanished just as quickly as they appeared. But the psychological mechanism is the same: group unfamiliar items into a whole and give it a name, not just any name, but something meaningful, or at least familiar. After all, that's how we're hardwired: we're fascinated by patterns. Boxer underscores this when he says, "we humans are pattern-matching animals, and astrology is the universe's grandest pattern-matching game."[5]

If we had started that pattern-matching game within the last fifty years, the constellations would carry names like "spaceship," "automobile," "wedding cake," "baby carriage," and "hamburger." Fortunately, the constellations were named many thousands of years ago and carry more mysterious names closer to the interests of our agrarian forefathers and mothers, names like Cygnus the Swan, Taurus the Bull, Orion the Hunter, Bootes the Herdsman, and Cetus the Whale. Mysterious to us, but not to our ancestors.

Castor: Are there really 88 constellations, or is that made up, too?

Author: There are 88 "official" constellations that the International Astronomical Union (IAU) adopted in 1930, the same group that demoted Pluto to a minor planet three-quarters of a century later. This is our current celestial map. Of course, there could have been more—or less—constellations. Eighty-eight is just the number they settled on at the time. Like we did with the tropic zone earlier, let's take the celestial map and flatten it out on a table. What we'd see roughly resembles the state of Iowa with all of its county boundaries drawn in, each one a bit different from the others both in size and shape. Now as we did with the flattened map of the tropic zone, let's trace the path of the ecliptic through the constellations. The first thing you notice is...

Castor: Hey, it makes that funny undulating wave through the middle of the map.

Pollux: That's a sine wave, Castor.

Author: Yes, a sine wave, also called a sinusoid wave, which cuts through some of the constellations, but not all of them. How many of them does it cut through?

Castor: Twelve of them. No, wait, thirteen of them.

Author: That's if you count Ophiuchus, the Serpent-Bearer.

Castor: Ophiuchus!

Author: Ophiuchus, who dips his toe across the line of the ecliptic between Scorpio and Sagittarius. Some astrologers count Ophiuchus, most don't. The reason: what is 360 divided by 13?

Castor: Ah.

Pollux: That's a hard one.

Author: It's hard because it's not a pretty number, at least it's not a whole number. That's why astrologers count 12 constellations along the ecliptic. And without him, the math's a heck of a lot easier. What's 360 divided by 12?

Castor: Thirty.

Author: Yes, thirty. But what does thirty stand for?

Castor: Thirty star groups?

Author: More like the number of degrees a constellation takes up within the 360° circle of the ecliptic. But here's where astronomy and astrology part company. You see, for an astronomer, constellations vary in size. Just look at the constellation map before you. It's not hard to miss that. But for an astrologer, each constellation or sign of the zodiac takes up exactly 30 degrees of the ecliptic.

Castor: Wait. You keep saying constellations and signs. Which one is it? Are they constellations or are they signs?

Author: Both.

Castor: Both?

Author: While astronomers prefer to talk about constellations, astrologers prefer to talk about signs—in particular, the "signs of the zodiac."

Pollux: The twelve signs of the zodiac that make up the undulating sine wave on the celestial map before us.

Author: Exactly.

Pollux: Who came up with the twelve signs of the zodiac in the first place?

Author: As I said before, the earliest zodiac didn't have twelve constellations; it had 36, but not 36 constellations, rather 36 major stars. According to Isabel Lasch-Quinn's entry in *Astrology Through History*, the earliest known zodiac appeared in Mesopotamia in the eighth century BCE and was formed on the basis of 36 stars that correlated with the twelve months of the Mesopotamian calendar. It was only later that the Babylonians introduced the idea of constellations, limiting the zodiacal constellations to twelve. At the same time, the Babylonians introduced the idea of the "tropical zodiac," which is based on the seasons and begins with Aries, the first sign of the zodiac, that appears—or at least did—at the spring or vernal equinox.[6]

Pollux: What do you mean "or at least did?"

Castor: This is very confusing.

Author: I know it's confusing, especially why the constellations that make up the zodiac are called "signs." As you might expect, this gets at the heart of things. First of all, whereas a "constellation" is a group of stars recalled by an association to something familiar to us (i.e., a whale, a hunter, a horse, a fish, etc.), a "sign" takes it a step further: it is a stand-in for something with a deeper, and often hidden, meaning. In other words, whereas the constellation Leo resembles a lion in its pattern of stars, the sign Leo refers more to the qualities that a lion exhibits, i.e., fierce, determined, dominating, and prideful. If there is something that astrology is, especially today's humanistic astrology, it's about revealing the latent personality characteristics and behavioral tendencies of an individual, characteristics and tendencies that remain dormant until we align the zodiacal signs with the planets and houses in the birth chart. Before we get to that, we need to look a bit closer at my sign wheel, which starts not with Aries, but with Gemini the Twins. The question is, Why does my birth chart begin with Gemini on the eastern horizon at sunrise and not with Aries?

Castor: 'Cause you're an early riser.

Author: Not exactly, but it does have to do with sunrise. But first, let's name the twelve signs of the zodiac, beginning with Aries. Let's do it together. Here we go: Aries, Taurus, Gemini, Cancer, Leo, Virgo, Libra, Scorpio, Sagittarius, Capricorn, Aquarius, and Pisces. We call this the "natural" zodiac. It's the default zodiac we use when we lay out a birth chart, and we do so because of Claudius Ptolemy, a Roman citizen living in Alexandria, Egypt, during the second century CE. This polymath (he was also an astronomer, geographer, mathematician, and cartographer) wrote two important books: the *Almagest* on the principles of astronomy and *Tetrabiblios* on the principles of astrology. Leaning on one of the greatest minds of Greek philosophy before him, Aristotle of Stagira, Ptolemy laid out a view of the world that would remain in place for more than a millennium.

Castor: What does this have to do with the zodiac?

Author: Everything, because Ptolemy had to make a choice: use a zodiac based on the seasons (which is called the "tropical" zodiac) or use a zodiac based on the actual movement of the stars (which is called the "sidereal" zodiac). Ptolemy chose the former—the tropical zodiac. What that means is that he focused his attention on the spring equinox, using the lineup of zodiacal signs listed above that starts with...

Pollux: Aries.

Author: Yes, even though Aries no longer appears on the horizon on the day of the spring equinox.

Castor: *What?*

Author: Today, the sign peeping over the horizon at the moment of the spring equinox is Pisces.

Castor: Pisces? Why not Aries?

Author: Because everything in the solar system—indeed, the universe—is moving, subtly, imperceptibly, but moving nonetheless. Remember what I said about the Earth being tilted on its axis 23.5 degrees.

Pollux: Yes.

Author: Well, because of that tilt and the elliptical orbit of the Earth around the Sun, as well as the Earth's bulging midriff or equatorial zone, the Earth "wobbles" on its axis.

Castor: Wobbles?

Author: Yes, wobbles, causing it—the spring equinox—to slip backwards through the zodiacal signs. When Ptolemy created his celestial system, the sign on the horizon at the time of the spring equinox was already approaching Pisces. According to Ptolemy, the equinox slips backwards 1° every 72 years. This is called the "Precession of the Equinoxes," which was first noted by the Greek philosopher Hipparchus several centuries before Ptolemy. Knowing this, how many years does it take for the spring equinox to return to its original position in Aries?[7]

Castor: Pollux, I think he's asking you.

Pollux: Let's see, there are 360° in the ecliptic, and if the spring equinox moves 1° every 72 years, then the answer would be the product of 360 times 72, which is 25,920.

Author: That's right. It takes approximately 25,920 years for the spring equinox to travel through all of the signs of the zodiac. Astrologers call this a Great or "Platonic" Year. Castor, your turn, How many years does the spring equinox take to travel through one sign of the zodiac?

Castor: Me?

Pollux: You can do it.

Castor: Let's see: since there are twelve signs of the zodiac (not counting Ophiuchus, my favorite sign), and a complete loop through the zodiac takes 25,920 years, then you'd divide 25,920 by 12 and get 2,160 years.

Author: Precisely, and this—the time it takes the spring equinox to travel through one sign of the zodiac—we call an "age."

Castor: What age are we currently in?

Author: Let me answer that question with this question, What is one of the most important events in Western civilization in the last 2,100 years?

Castor: The invention of the elevator?

Author: No, something much more important and influential.

Castor: We landed on the Moon?

Author: Not exactly. It is the rise of Christianity. Although this may not be the most important event for everyone, there is no denying that Christianity has been one of the most influential factors in shaping Western civilization over the last two millennia.

Castor: Why is this important?

Author: Because that's the "age" we're in, an age shaped by the life of Jesus of Nazareth, who, in his "Christhood," is known as a fisherman of men's souls. Do you know what symbol Christians use to indicate their faith?

Castor: A cross.

Author: Well, yes, but something else. You often see this image on car bumpers.

Pollux: A fish!

Author: Exactly. So, to answer your question, Castor, we are in...

Castor: The Age of Fishes.

Author: Yes, but let's call it the Age of Pisces. Actually, we're nearing the end of the Age of Fishes, I mean, Pisces, and soon (when precisely, astrologers don't agree) we'll be in the Age of Aquarius.

Castor: *This is the dawning of the...*[8]

Author: A bit out of tune, but we get the point. Here's another question, If the Age of Aquarius comes after the Age of Pisces, what age came before the Age of Pisces?

Pollux: The Age of Aries?

Author: As we travel back in time, we reverse the process and follow the natural order of signs: Aquarius, Pisces, Aries, and so forth. And it makes sense. What preceded the New Testament and the rise of Christianity?

Pollux: The Old Testament.

Author: Which is where we find a variety of stories about Judaism, one of the most important being the story of Abraham. Do you remember a story that involves Abraham?

Castor: He climbed a mountain and received some tablets from God?

Pollux: That was Moses, numbskull. To show his faith in God, Abraham was prepared to sacrifice his son Isaac as an offering to God. But he didn't.

Author: No, he didn't. Pleased with Abraham's act of faith, God instructed Abraham to sacrifice a ram that was caught in some brambles nearby.

Castor: And did he?

Author: He did, and it's very significant that it was a ram, for what animal do we associate with Aries?

Castor: A ram.

Pollux: Aries the Ram.

Author: Exactly, you see every age has an iconic image that sets it off from others. Let's go back one more age, to the Age of Taurus. What was it that the Jews refused to do in

Moses's time? They refused to worship what their captors, the Babylonians, worshipped. Do you know what they worshipped?

Castor: Turtles?

Author: They worshipped a golden bull.

Pollux: Taurus the Bull.

Author: Now you see the connection. Often the most dominant image of an age has to do with the sign of the zodiac that the Sun is moving through during that age.[9]

Castor: This is fascinating.

Pollux: So if the Sun will be moving through the sign of Aquarius soon, what will be the dominant image of the Age of Aquarius?

Author: That's a really good question, and quite frankly I don't know. Aquarius is the water-bearer, so probably the image will have something to do with water, or, sadly, the lack thereof. Enough of the so-called "ages." Let's try to visualize the zodiac from the perspective of someone standing on Earth. To do this, let me bring someone else into the conversation—Christopher Crockett, an astronomer who's written for *Scientific American* and *Science News*. Crockett uses the analogy of an amusement park carousel to help us understand what we see from Earth in relation to the Sun and the backdrop of stars. Here's an excerpt from a page on his website:

"Sitting on a wooden horse, your hands clasped around a cool, brass pole, you are swung around and around as the sights of an amusement park blur past your vision. As you circle around, your eyes begin to wander and become fixated on the central pillar of the carousel. The pillar goes out of focus as you begin to notice what's on the other side. The ticket booth goes by, then a food vendor. There's a family posing for a picture, then some benches with people resting their feet. Around and around, the scene drifting behind the center column of the carousel changes until you have come all the way around and are looking at the ticket booth again...

Now replace the horse with Earth, the column with the Sun, and the background panorama of an amusement park with the distant stars. As Earth flies around the Sun at 67,000 m.p.h. (108,000 kilometers m.p.h.), the "scenery" behind the sun changes. For example, if we could see the stars during the day, we would notice that in late March and early April, the constellation Pisces (the Fish) is on the other side of the Sun...

As the days and weeks went by, the Sun would appear to drift eastward across Pisces until moving in front of Aries, the Ram, in the second half of April. One month later, the Sun would be flanked by the stars in Taurus, then Gemini, Cancer, Leo, and so on. Roughly every month or so, as Earth moves in orbit, a different constellation sits behind the Sun."[10]

Castor: So it takes the Sun about a month to pass through one of the twelve signs of the zodiac, precession or no precession of the equinoxes.

Author: That's right, but that's not all.

Castor: I didn't think so.

Author: What you just described is the orbit of the Earth around the Sun. That's its annual movement. But there is also a diurnal or daily movement as well. This is a bit different since in this case the Sun and the sign that it's currently in parade across the sky together in the course of a 24-hour period, which means that it takes about two hours for a sign of the zodiac to clear the horizon. That's why you have a Sun sign and a Rising sign, and it's not just a matter of what time you were born. It really has to do with the two movements of the Earth, with your Sun sign related to the Earth's revolution around the Sun, and your Rising sign related to the Earth's rotation on its axis.

Castor: This really is fascinating.

Pollux: I'll say.

Castor: But where does the carousel begin? I mean, in what sign?

Author: Most astrologers place Aries at the head of the list, followed by Taurus, Gemini, Cancer, Leo, and so forth. This is the zodiac that Ptolemy laid out almost two thousand years ago. But things have changed, I mean moved. Now, as I mentioned earlier, Pisces shows up on the first day of the spring equinox, the point at which the tropical zodiac begins (and in the not-so-distant future Aquarius will peer over the horizon on the first day of the spring equinox). So, technically, the answer to your question is Pisces, but Ptolemy decided that it would be just a bit too much to recalculate the positions of the stars—and by association, the signs of the zodiac—every year, so that's why the sign of Aries (rather than the constellation) shows up every year on the first day of the spring equinox.

Pollux: Whether or not Aries is actually there?

Author: Correct.

Castor: This must have driven people crazy.

Author: Yes and no. Ptolemy was a very logical thinker. He knew he had to make a choice between paying attention to the actual movement of the stars or to the regular appearance of the seasons each year. He chose the latter, the seasons. That's why in Western astrology the sign of Aries appears at the time of the spring equinox. In short, Aries, the beginning of Ptolemy's tropical zodiac, is a marker; it marks the first day of spring each year even though another constellation might be rising over the horizon on that day.

Earlier, I asked you to hold on to a question about the names of the two tropics—the Tropic of Cancer and the Tropic of Capricorn? I think I can answer that question given what we've been talking about. Let me direct you again to Christopher Crockett's amusement park carousel analogy. You're sitting on one of the wooden horses of the carousel swinging around the outer edge of the carousel. Your gaze focuses on images beyond the center pole, images of the ticket booth, a food vendor, a family posing for a picture, and so on. Imagine, as Crockett wants you to, that the horse you're riding is the Earth, the center pole is the Sun, and the images beyond the center pole are the signs of the zodiac. As you ride around the carousel you notice that your horse bobs up and down exactly two times in one full circle around the carousel.

Now, replace the ticket booth, the food vendor, and the family posing for a picture with the signs of the zodiac. When the carousel begins, your horse is halfway into its upward cycle and the zodiacal sign you see beyond the center pole is Aries. By the time your horse arrives at the uppermost point of its upward cycle the zodiacal sign beyond the center pole is Cancer. Halfway down its downward cycle Libra is beyond the center pole. Finally, at the lowest point of its downward cycle, Capricorn is beyond the center pole. But you're really not riding a horse; you're standing on the Earth which is tilted on its axis causing this undulating up-and-down movement as the Earth (the carousel horse) revolves around the Sun (the center pole), and the four signs that you see in this up-and-down movement are the four seasonal points: Aries (spring equinox), Cancer (summer solstice), Libra (fall equinox), and Capricorn (winter solstice).

Castor: But what does this have to do with the names of the tropics?

Author: Everything. If Aries and Libra represent the zodiacal signs that the Sun is traveling through at the time of the spring and fall equinox, when the Sun is exactly halfway between to two terrestrial poles, then Cancer and Capricorn represent the zodiacal signs that the Sun is traveling through at the time of the summer and winter solstice. In other words, at the Sun's northernmost advance (summer solstice) and the Sun's southernmost advance (winter solstice), the sign of the zodiac seen behind the Sun when it pivots or turns on its way to either the spring or fall equinox is Cancer and Capricorn respectively.

Castor: Two equinoxes, two solstices.

Pollux: Each one at the cusp of one of the four natal chart angles.

Author: Bravo, Pollux. How did you figure that out?

Pollux: Well, if there are two equinoxes and two solstices, I just divided the twelve signs of the zodiac by four and got three, which means that there is either an equinox or a solstice every third sign of the zodiac. Then I remembered what you said above regarding the up-and-down movement of the carousel horse, that the two midpoints plus the upper and lower points represent the four seasonal points or angles.

Castor: But what about the birth chart angles? You haven't explained that.

Pollux: I'm getting there. When you list the twelve signs of the zodiac in order and highlight the four seasonal angles— *Aries*, Taurus, Gemini, *Cancer*, Leo, Virgo, *Libra*, Scorpio, Sagittarius, *Capricorn*, Aquarius, and Pisces—you'll notice that they divide evenly into four sets of three signs each.

Author: Now, instead of a line, make a circle out of them (which is what the zodiac is) and what you notice are two axes: the equinoctial axis (Aries/Libra) and the solstitial axis (Cancer/Capricorn), which represent the Line of the Horizon (Aries/Libra) and the Line of the Meridian (Cancer/Capricorn) respectively. Put them together and they make...

Castor: A cross.

Pollux: A cross with the cusp of each of the four major angles marking one of the four arms of the cross.

Author: Which, when we consider quadrants and cardinal directions, gives us the following:

1st quadrant: Aries, East, Spring Equinox, Ascendant

2nd quadrant: Cancer, North, Summer Solstice, Imum Coeli

3rd quadrant: Libra, West, Fall Equinox, Descendant

4th quadrant: Capricorn, South, Winter Solstice, Midheaven

Castor: Wow, it's like a great interlocking puzzle where everything relates to everything else.

Author: Indeed, it does. Unfortunately...

Castor: Why did I know this was coming.

Author: Unfortunately, Aries doesn't stay at the head of the line for long because the zodiac is recalibrated based on the newborn's Ascendant at the moment of birth.

Castor: Recalibrated?

Author: If you look at a dozen birth charts, you quickly realize that each one of them has a different sign of the zodiac in the first house on the left-hand side of the chart signifying sunrise. That's because the first sign of the zodiac—your personal zodiac—is "set" to the sign that was peeping over the horizon at the moment of your birth.

Castor: Didn't we cover this earlier?

Author: We did, but let's explore this a little further. Even though Aries may not be in the first house of your birth chart (because your Rising sign is, say, Scorpio), it doesn't go away completely.

Castor: Now I'm really lost.

Author: There's a medieval term that can help us here—*palimpsest*. Before paper was readily available, our ancestors used to write on specially prepared animal skins called parchment, which was made from the skins of young goats, cows, and sheep. It was very soft and could be bleached almost white. In lieu of paper, it made a terrific writing surface, except for the fact that it couldn't be erased entirely. Unfortunately, the thick oak-gall ink that medieval monks used in their monastic writing room, their *scriptorium*, mixed with the fine oils of the animal skins, which meant that there was always a trace of the original writing left over no matter how hard they tried to remove it. And they tried to remove it when they needed another sheet of parchment since it was a lot easier to reuse an old sheet of parchment than to make a new one.

Castor: But what does this have to do with palimpsest?

Author: A palimpsest is a sheet of parchment that has been reused in which the original writing still shows through. And that's what the zodiac is. It's two zodiacs: the "natural" or tropical zodiac peering through your "personal" or birth zodiac once the natural zodiac has been recalibrated to your Ascendant.

Pollux: So your Ascendant might be Virgo, but there is still some Aries lingering about.

Author: That's right. No matter what your Rising sign is, the energy of Aries—along with Mars, its ruling planet—will always be there.

Castor: Ruling planet?

Author: I'll explain that later when we get to planets. For now, it's enough to know that there are two zodiacs: your personal or birth zodiac calibrated to your Ascendant, and the natural or tropical zodiac that begins with Aries, both of which exert influence over your personality.

Pollux: What is your Ascendant?

Author: I think you know that.

Castor: You're a Gemini.

Author: That's right. I mean why else would I invite you to join this conversation. Besides, it says so right here on my birth chart. Look in the lower part of my chart, on either side of the planetary aspect grid. Can you read what it says?

Castor: June 15, 1951, 4:15 a.m., Jersey City, New Jersey.

Author: Excellent.

Pollux: But June 15 makes your Sun sign Gemini, not your Ascendant.

Author: Yes, so you have to look at the time I was born.

Pollux: 4:15 a.m.

Castor: So you are an early riser.

Author: Remember, your Ascendant is about the Earth's rotation on its axis in a 24-hour period, which means that we divide up the 24 hours into 12 two-hour segments, each segment representing one of the 12 "houses" of the birth chart. The first segment or house is between 4:00 and 6:00 a.m., or sunrise. We know from my birth date that my Sun sign is Gemini, and now we know, since I was born at sunrise, that my Rising sign/Ascendant is also...

Castor: Gemini.

Author: That's right. I'm known as a double Gemini, or, as some astrologers prefer, a Gemini Rising.

Castor: A double Gemini? Does that mean instead of two of you, there are four of you?

Author: Not exactly, but since my Ascendant and my Sun sign are both in Gemini in the first house of my birth chart, a house that is all about one's identity, it means that I exhibit all of the characteristics of a Gemini and then some. We'll look at the Ascendant in more depth a little later on. For now, just know that I'm a double Gemini with the Sun and my Ascendant in the first house, along with a few other celestial bodies.

Pollux: You keep mentioning "houses." When will you get to them?

Author: As we continue exploring my natal chart circle by circle, at some point we will have covered the signs, planets, and houses in my chart, along with a few other things. However, it's really hard to talk about signs and planets unless we know where in your chart they appear. And that's what houses represent, of which there are twelve.

Castor: Twelve? That number keeps reappearing.

Author: There's a good reason for that. But back to houses. The twelve houses in your birth chart represent twelve major areas of your life, namely childhood experiences, family life, relationship-building, work, career, and so forth. You might say that whereas signs and planets are celestial in origin, houses come from the terrestrial or "mundane" world.

Castor: *Mundane?*

Pollux: As in everyday or ordinary.

Author: But also, "earthly."

Notes

1. Boxer, Alexander. *A Scheme of Heaven*, Chpt. 1, "To Everything There Is a Season."
2. Bobrick, Benson. *The Fated Sky*, Chpt. 2.
3. Dainith, John and William Gould. *Collins Dictionary of Astronomy* (Aylesbury, England: Market House Books, 2006), "Constellation."
4. *Ibid.*
5. Boxer, Chpt. 1, "To Everything There Is a Season."
6. Lasch-Quinn, Isabel. "Zodiacs" in William E. Burns (ed), *Astrology through History*. Robert Hand offers this useful description: "Tropical 0° Aries marks the intersection of two fundamental planes: the plane of the ecliptic, along which secondary motion takes place, and

the plane of the equator, along which primary motion takes place. As defined above, the ecliptic is the plane of the Earth's orbit around the Sun, or, as seen from the Earth, the plane of the Sun's apparent path through the fixed stars. The equator, on the other hand, is the plane of the Earth's daily rotation on its axis. Tropical 0° Aries marks the beginning of the Sun's yearly cycle: on the first day of spring, the Sun is directly overhead at the Earth's equator, midway between its extreme north and south declinations." Robert Hand, *Horoscope Symbols*, Chpt. 2, "The Symbol Systems of Astrology."

7. Bobrick, Chpt. 2.

8. Although many of us associate Castor's song "The Age of Aquarius" with the musical *Hair*, we might not realize that it was released later as a medley of two songs with the less-than-catchy, and somewhat obscure, title "Medley: Aquarius/Let the Sunshine In (The Flesh Failures)," with lyrics by James Rado and Gerome Ragni, music by Galt MacDermot, and recorded by the popular R&B band The 5th Dimension for their 1969 album *The Age of Aquarius*.

9. Boxer, Chpt. 1, "To Everything There Is a Season." For a very unusual take on the different astrological ages, see Rudolph Steiner's *Astronomy and Astrology*, Chpt. 19, "The Cultural Epochs and the Passage of the Equinox," in which he explains five "post-Atlantean epochs" beginning in the very distant past with the age of Cancer. Also worth reading are excerpts on Jung's ideas about the precession of the equinoxes and the various "ages," especially the Christian era under the sign of Pisces, found in Rossi, Safron and Keiron Le Grice, *Jung on Astrology*, Chpt. 7, "The Symbolic Significance of the Precession."

10. Crockett, Christopher. "Ecliptic Traces the Sun's Path," *EarthSky* [January 27, 2017], https://earthsky.org/space/what-is-the-ecliptic/. For another explanation of the Earth-Sun-Zodiac relationship, see Alexander Boxer, *A Scheme of Heaven*, Chpt. 3, "A Quick Spin Around the Celestial Sphere."

6

A Battlefield in France

Serving as the lens to focus and personalize the planetary blueprint onto the landscape of actual life, the houses bring the chart down to earth. And yet the meanings and functions of the twelve houses are usually the least understood of all the basic astrological factors.[1]
Howard Sasportas, *The Twelve Houses*

We now come to the twelve houses of the birth chart. To put them in context, let me start by paraphrasing April Elliott Kent: If life were a dramatic play, the planets would be the actors, the signs would be the costumes they wear, and the houses would be the set and props where various scenes of the play are acted out. In other words, in the dramatic structure of your life, the houses of your chart indicate where the action is taking place: is it taking place in "a parapet, a battlefield in France, a ship?"[2]

Castor: I'll take the battlefield in France.

Pollux: I'll take the parapet.

Castor: What do parakeets have to do with anything?

Pollux: *Parapet*, Castor. You're so infuriating.

Castor: Whatever.

Author: As I was saying, to help us understand the nature of houses, let's revisit the work of British astrologer Howard

Sasportas. According to this seasoned astrologer, whose books are touchstones for any serious student of astrology, the difference between signs and houses can be attributed to the two motions of the Earth. We know that the Earth moves in two basic ways: while it's rotating on its axis, it's also orbiting the Sun. Of the two motions of the Earth, it's the first motion—axial rotation—that gives us the twelve houses of the natal chart. According to Sasportas, "The early astrologers had to find some way to correlate the celestial phenomenon of planets moving through the signs to the terrestrial phenomenon of the daily rotation of the Earth on its own axis."[3] The most obvious way of doing this was to divide the 24-hour rotation of the Earth into sections based on how long it took the Sun to move from sunrise to noon, noon to sunset, sunset to midnight, and midnight to sunrise. In other words, according to Sasportas, while signs are subdivisions of the zodiac based on the apparent annual revolution of the Sun around the Earth, houses are subdivisions of the Sun's apparent daily trek around the Earth, the result of the Earth's axial rotation.

Pollux: *Sunrise. Noon. Sunset. Midnight.* Aren't these the major angles of a birth chart?

Author: Yes, but like everything in astrology, there are multiple meanings and perspectives. So not only are they the four major angles, they're also the dividing lines between the four six-hour "watches."

Castor: Can we go back to the acting stuff? You know, the battlefield in France?

Pollux: You're such a pest, Castor.

Castor: But I like this acting stuff. Do we get to wear costumes?

Author: In many respects you already are. These are the signs that appear in the houses of your natal chart.

Castor: I'll need a coat of armor if I'm going to do battle in France.

Author: Since Mars, the god of war, is in your first house along with the Sun, you just might get your wish. But, as usual, we're getting ahead of ourselves. There are several things I need to establish regarding the houses of a birth chart before we move on. First of all, there are twelve houses in a natal chart. Secondly, unlike the planets and signs, they don't move. Finally, and perhaps most importantly, astrologers disagree on where the cusp or leading edge of each house begins.

If you look at my birth chart, you'll notice a circle of numbers very close to the center that label the various pie slices of the chart—the so-called "houses." Moving counterclockwise, we begin with the first house in the 9 o'clock position and end with the twelfth house in the 10 o'clock position. The numbered wedges or pie slices are the twelve houses of the birth chart. Notice also that the houses are separated by radials emanating from a central point, extending almost to the outer edge (with the four major angles extending slightly beyond the rest of the radials).

Pollux: It reminds me of a clock.

Castor: But a clock that starts at 9 o'clock, not at noon.

Author: That's because the signs and houses of the birth chart begin at sunrise in the 9 o'clock position.

Castor: But why do you count the houses counter-clockwise around the chart?

Author: Which way does the Earth rotate?

Castor: Counterclockwise?

Author: Exactly. Try this: hold out your fist out and turn it slowly counterclockwise. The other way, Castor. It's the same direction in which the numbers of the houses in the inner circle move (of course, they don't actually "move," it's just the direction they're oriented toward when you follow them sequentially around the chart). Remember, according to Sasportas, the houses are derived from the axial rotation of the Earth. That's why they're placed counterclockwise around the birth chart. Now imagine that the Sun is passing overhead. As your fist—the Earth—rotates counterclockwise which way does the Sun "appear" to be moving.

Pollux: Clockwise.

Author: That's right. If the Earth was still and the Sun was moving it would appear that the Sun was moving clockwise, which is the way it appears to move each and every day, from sunrise in the east to sunset in the west. It's also why the house circle starts with the first house in the 9 o'clock or sunrise position rather than at noon.

Castor: Because 9 o'clock on a birth chart is really 6 o'clock on a clock clock?

Author: That's one way of saying it. Now, about the houses being fixed in place. The first house will always be at 9 o'clock, the second house at 8 o'clock, the third house at 7 o'clock, and so on. This doesn't mean that each house cusp will be exactly at 9 o'clock, 8 o'clock, and 7 o'clock. That's because third on my list is the fact that astrologers slice up the natal chart differently so that houses are not all the same size, nor do they even start in the same place. It all depends upon which house system you use.

Castor: Pollux, do you know what he's talking about?

Pollux: Kind of, sort of—not really.

Author: Hang in there. I'm sure you'll get it. Although I must admit, astrologers can't even agree on how to talk about house systems. Do you talk about space-based vs. time-based house systems? Do you talk about quadrant vs non-quadrant house systems? Or do you talk about ancient vs modern house systems? In other words, when it comes to house systems, it's more about *what* you divide than *how* you divide it.[4] For most astrologers, it's really a matter of what "great circle" you divide to arrive at the twelve houses of the birth chart.

Let's start with the most obvious circle—the ecliptic. Two of the earliest approaches to house divisions are Whole Sign and Equal House. In Whole Sign, the ecliptic is divided into twelve equal sections, each section measuring exactly 30 degrees, with the cusp or beginning of each subsequent house starting at the first degree of that sign. In this house system, the signs and houses each take up the same amount of degrees of the ecliptic in a one-to-one correspondence. In other words, if you know what house you're in, you know what sign you're in (this is also why some astrologers overlap the meaning of a house and its respective sign, i.e., Aries shares the same qualities as the first house, Taurus the second house, Gemini the third house, and so on). Here's another way of thinking about this: the first house is the entire sign in which the Ascendant is located, regardless of which degree in that house the Ascendant is located.

One of the earliest modifications of Whole Sign was introduced by the second-century Hellenistic astrologer Vittius Valens, a contemporary of Alexandrian astrologer Claudius Ptolemy, who used Whole Sign to determine the area or sphere of life a planet would affect, but then switched to a quadrant system to determine the strength of the planet. This is an important observation because it points to the two main functions of houses in the first place: on the one hand, they highlight an area or sphere of life (for instance, the second house deals with money, possessions, and personal assets); on the other hand, they determine the strength of a planet (Is it in a strong "angular" house, or is it in a weaker "succedent" house, or is it in an even weaker "cadent" house?).

Pollux: *Angular? Succedent? Cadent?*

Author: I know, we're getting ahead of ourselves. Hopefully, by the time we're through, all of these pieces will make sense in the grand scheme of things. So let's forge ahead and let me talk about Equal House. This house system also divides the ecliptic into twelve 30° sections, but instead of each house beginning on the cusp of a new sign, each one starts at the degree of the Ascendant of the Rising sign. Let's say that you were born with 12° of Leo rising, your second house would begin with 12° of Virgo rising, your third house with 12° of Libra rising, and so on. Of the early house systems, Equal House is one of the more accurate and easy to use.

Pollux: In both of these systems then each house is always 30 degrees; they just start at different places within a sign?

Author: The distinction between the two approaches lies in the fact that in Whole Sign the cusp of the first house is the beginning of the sign that contains the Ascendant, while in Equal House the degree of the Ascendant is itself the cusp of the first house. This is not insignificant. In Whole Sign, you always have one sign per house, whereas in Equal House, a house can—and usually does—straddle two signs.

Pollux: Who developed the first house system?

Author: Astrologers believe that early Babylonians established the concept of house division, more than likely using the Whole Sign approach. But it wasn't until the Hellenistic period, around the second century BCE, that house systems began to emphasize the Ascendant in the construction of house divisions, which is still the basis for most modern approaches to house systems.

Pollux: Are there any other ecliptic-based house systems?

Author: One more worth noting. It's called Porphyry, named after the third-century Platonic philosopher Porphyry of Tyre, which arose slightly later than the two systems discussed above. In her entry for *Astrology Through History*, Bernadette Brady discusses this quadrant-based, ecliptic house system in which the cusps of the major angles divide the ecliptic into four sections or quadrants with the Line of the Horizon (Ascendant/Descendant) defining the first and seventh house cusps and the Line of the Meridian (Imum Coeli/Midheaven) defining the fourth and tenth house cusps. After this initial division, the span of the ecliptic contained within each quadrant is trisected to produce three houses, but due to the unequal quadrant sizes (a function of birth

latitude, time of day, and birth month and year), the size of
houses in the first quadrant (houses 1-3) are usually different
from the size of houses in the second quadrant (houses 4-6), a
difference that is reflected diagonally across the birth chart in
the houses above the horizon.[5] The three ecliptic-based house
systems were popular well into the European Renaissance,
at which point other house systems began to emerge. One of
these systems, which also yielded houses of unequal size, was
developed by the fifteenth-century German mathematician,
astronomer, and astrologer Johannes Müller of Königsberg,
also known as Regiomontanus.[6]

Castor: How on earth do you get Regiomontanus from
Johannes Müller?

Author: It's a pseudonym, as he often wrote under the
Latinized name of Ioannes de Monteregio, which he also
spelled Monte Regio and Regio Monte. Despite his odd
pen name, Regiomontanus was a prolific author who wrote
about various aspects of mathematics, including algebra
and spherical trigonometry. He also calculated extensive
astronomical tables for yearly ephemerides, crafted scientific
instruments, including an astrolabe and portable sundial, and
co-founded the world's first scientific printing press. But what
we remember him for most is his astrological house system.
In a two-step process, Regiomontanus first divided the
celestial equator—rather than the ecliptic—into twelve equal
segments. Then, using the twelve segment points, he drew
great circles from the zenith to the nadir, using the points
where the circles intersected the ecliptic to determine the

house cusps, which typically resulted in houses of different sizes. The main point, however, is that instead of dividing the ecliptic directly, Regiomontanus first divided the celestial equator and then projected those divisions back unto the ecliptic in order to find the cusps of the twelve houses.

Castor: Sounds like a lot of work.

Author: It is. However, since each house system usually has a shortcoming, astrologers are always trying to come up with a more perfect way of creating the cusps and dimensions of the natal chart houses.

Pollux: Are there any other systems that divide the celestial equator?

Author: Yes, several. One system that divides the celestial equator is called Morinus, named after the seventeenth-century French mathematician Jean-Baptiste Morin. An opponent of Italian scientist and astronomer Galileo and a critic of French philosopher and mathematician René Descartes, Morin is best known for his multi-text work on astrology known as *Astrologia Gallica* ("French Astrology"), which covers various uses and traditions of astrology, as well as specific techniques to enhance the predictive nature of natal astrology. A contentious personality, Morin challenged much of classical astrological theory, including that of Claudius Ptolemy. Morin's house system starts where the local meridian crosses the celestial equator, the latter of which is divided into twelve 30° sections, with the points where it intersects the horizon and the meridian among the subsequent divisions. However, instead of projecting the

twelve celestial equator points onto the ecliptic from the pole
of the equator, they are projected from the pole of the ecliptic.
Unlike quadrant systems,...

Castor: Stop! You lost me at "pole of the equator."

Author: Right. But I'm almost through. Unlike quadrant
systems, the Ascendant and Midheaven do not appear on
the cusp of the first and tenth houses. Moreover, Morinus
house cusps do not depend on the birth location's latitude,
a shortcoming of several house systems, which makes them
less effective the closer the birth place is to the north and
south poles.

Castor: Not only is it a lot of work, it's also very confusing.

Pollux: But fascinating nonetheless.

Author: And we're not through. There are dozens of house
systems. Before moving on, let's look at one more system that
divides the celestial equator. This is the Meridian system, also
known as the Axial or Equatorial system. Similar to Morinus,
the Meridian system divides the celestial equator into twelve
30° sections starting at the local meridian, hence its name.
The resulting points are then projected onto the ecliptic along
the great circles containing the north and south celestial
poles, with the intersections of the ecliptic with those circles
providing the house cusps. In this system, the Ascendant is
determined by the intersection of the horizon and the ecliptic,
from which all other house cusps issue, with the Midheaven,
as one would hope, situated on the tenth house cusp.

Castor: *Ecliptic. Horizon. Meridian. Equator.* Can we please
move on?

Author: I understand your frustration, Castor. I know this is a bit pie-in-the-sky, but astrology is a pragmatically oriented philosophical system supported by a complex mathematical system.

Castor: As you say, pie-in-the-sky.

Author: That's exactly what the celestial sphere is: it's a three-dimensional "pie in the sky" that astrologers represent as a two-dimensional birth chart. Having said that, let's do a quick recap: We've seen that house systems can start with divisions of the ecliptic directly, or they can start with divisions of the celestial equator that are then related back to the ecliptic. But there's another approach that's somewhat similar, only this approach divides the prime vertical.

Castor: What's that?

Pollux: That's the line directly over your head, numbskull.

Author: Think of it this way. You're standing on the surface of the Earth. In front of you is due south, to your left is east, to your right west, and behind you north. These are the four cardinal directions. Now look straight up. The point in the celestial sphere that is directly above you is the zenith (and by inference the point directly below you is the nadir). Your meridian (not the Prime Meridian that runs through Greenwich, England, but your local or birth meridian) is a great circle that begins at your zenith, runs through the north cardinal point, through your nadir, then through the south cardinal point, only to return to the zenith.

Castor: But what does this have to do with the prime vertical?

Author: I was just about to get to that. The prime vertical is the great circle that runs perpendicular to the local meridian.

Castor: *What?*

Author: Perhaps a simpler way of saying this is that it's the circle perpendicular to the horizon that links the due east and due west points on the horizon, made possible (or at least a bit easier) by the astrolabe that provided an alternative method of dividing the four quadrants by using the prime vertical, which is reflected on the latitude plate of the astrolabe as the circle of unequal hours.

Castor: I thought you said, "a simpler way of saying this."

Author: Nothing in astrology is ever that simple. In any case, it was the eleventh-century Islamic scholar Al-Biruni who first described how to use the astrolabe to construct the twelve natal chart houses using the prime vertical. However, it wasn't until the thirteenth century that two brothers, Joseph and Matthew Campanus, published Al-Biruni's house system as a set of easily referenced tables, making it widely available to astrologers during the Renaissance. It became popular in Western astrology, and remained so, as a quadrant-based system that divided equally the local space around an individual and represented this spatial division on the ecliptic. Like spatial systems before it, the Campanus house system created three houses in each of four quadrants with the Ascendant the cusp of the first house and the Midheaven the cusp of the tenth house.[7]

Castor: Stop, my head is spinning.

Pollux: Mine, too.

Castor: Can't you just tell us what system your astrologer used to cast your birth chart and leave it at that?

Author: Sure. But first, take a moment and look at my birth chart, and tell me which approaches we can to eliminate.

Pollux: Whole Sign and Equal House.

Author: Why?

Pollux: Because the houses in your chart aren't equal in size.

Author: We can also eliminate a fairly recent approach I've not touched on called Solar for the same reason. We can also eliminate Morinus and Meridian because both approaches result in houses that are equal—or, at least, near equal—in size.

Castor: So what house system did your astrologer use?

Author: We're getting there. As you can probably tell, he used a system that we haven't discussed yet. Moreover, in order to discuss it, we're going to have to talk about several other systems.

Castor: Do we have to?

Author: I'm afraid so. And they may not be as easy to understand as the earlier systems we discussed because instead of being divisions of space, they're divisions of time.

Castor: Speaking of time, isn't it time for a break?

Author: We'll take one, but not until we finish this discussion. We start with the tenth-century Islamic astrologer Al-Qabisi, also known as Alcabitius, who worked as the palace astrologer of Sayf al-Dawla in Aleppo, a main trade route situated between the Mediterranean Sea and the Euphrates River in modern-day Syria. Al-Qabisi used a quadrant-based system used by sixth-century astrologer Rhetorius of Egypt, the author of a compendium written in Greek of the techniques of previous Hellenistic astrologers. Rhetorius's work is an important link between the earlier Hellenistic tradition and the Arab and medieval practices that followed him, in this case those of Al-Qabisi. Similar to Porphyry's house system, Al-Qabisi divides the four quadrants into three equal parts, but not based on a division of the ecliptic, rather on a division of the equator.

Castor: But we covered this. I mean, equator-based house divisions.

Author: Yes, but this is just a lead-in to the house system I believe my astrologer used to create my natal chart. Back to Al-Qabisi. At the time, Al-Qabisi's method was the earliest known system to divide the equator instead of the ecliptic. This is an important observation since it signaled a shift from the yearly cycle of the ecliptic (the Earth's annual revolution around the Sun) to the diurnal cycle of the equator (the daily rotation of the Earth on its axis). Remember Howard Sasportas: the houses are the heavens brought down to Earth. Given this observation, Al-Qabisi's approach to house division is quite logical as it abandons the idea that houses are a division of the ecliptic (i.e., celestial in origin), and replaces it with the idea that houses are better understood as a division of the equator (i.e., terrestrial in origin). As a result of trisecting the four equatorial quadrants, Al-Qabisi's houses are of unequal size.

Pollux: So your astrologer could have used Al-Qabisi's approach.

Author: Perhaps, except for the fact that by the fifteenth century Al-Qabisi's house system, which had more or less replaced the earlier Porphyry house system, had been superseded by other approaches, including Regiomontanus. Two centuries later, Regiomontanus was superseded by another house system that is still in use today.

Pollux: And that is?

Author: Placidus.

Castor: Did you say platypus?

Author: Not exactly. Placidus is a house division system named after the seventeenth-century astrologer and mathematician Tito de Placidus (though he may not have originated the system). Placidus's innovation is that instead of trisecting the quadrants of the ecliptic by spatial units (i..e, degrees), he trisected the diurnal rotation of the Earth (the time it took for the Ascendant to move from the first house in one quadrant to the first house in the next quadrant), with the resulting house cusps related back to the ecliptic. It is a quadrant-based system resulting in unequal-sized houses based on the division of time and space.[8]

Castor: I was just about to say that.

Pollux: Sure you were, Castor.

Author: In many ways, Placidus beat Einstein to a view of the universe as a space-time continuum. To understand this, however, we'll have to look a little more at the mechanics of the Placidus system. Instead of focusing on great circles—horizon, equator, ecliptic, etc.—the Placidus house system focuses on portions—semiarcs—of the prime vertical. Since six houses make up the top or diurnal (daylight) portion of the natal chart, the arc is divided into sixths according to how long it takes the Ascendant in its diurnal motion across the sky to move 1/6 of the arc (marking the cusp of the twelfth house), 2/6s of the arc (marking the cusp of the eleventh house), 3/6s of the arc (marking the cusp of the tenth house and Midheaven), and so on.

Pollux: That accounts for houses 7-12, what about houses 1-6?

Author: The nocturnal houses in the bottom portion of the chart? Since Placidus is made up of unequal houses, the nocturnal houses (1-6) are merely reflections of the top six houses, with the following pairs of houses forming an axis: 1-7, 2-8, 3-9, 4-10, 5-11, 6-12, with axis 1-7 marking the Ascendent/Descendant, and axis 4-10 marking the Imum Coeli/Midheaven. The problem is...

Castor: I knew this was coming. There's always a problem.

Author: It's not insurmountable, but it needs to be considered. If you were born within the north or south polar circle, you couldn't use this system.

Castor: Why not?

Author: Within the arctic or antarctic circle, portions of the ecliptic are not visible as the curvature of the Earth blocks their appearance. That means that some zodiac signs never rise above the horizon (and conversely, some never set). If they don't, then how do you determine the four angles of the natal chart.

Pollux: So the zodiac would be missing some signs.

Castor: That's weird.

Author: Weird and impractical for an astrologer. Here's how Kevin Guan, a physics student at the National University of Singapore, puts it: "Inside the polar regions, a part of the zodiac never rises above the horizon. Hence, certain signs can never be Ascendant there. Examples are northern Alaska or Siberia. In these two places, the signs of Sagittarius and Capricorn never rise above the horizon, while the opposite signs, Gemini and Cancer, [never fall] below the horizon. Therefore, people born there cannot have these four signs as their Ascendant."[9]

Pollux: Because two of them are always below the horizon (Sagittarius and Capricorn) and two of them are always above the horizon (Gemini and Cancer).

Castor: Which means you weren't born in Siberia.

Author: You're both correct. Returning to the Placidus house division system, despite this particular shortcoming (which it shares with several other house systems), Placidus remains one of the most popular house systems in Western astrology, and the house system that my computer-analyst-qua-astrologer probably used.

Castor: Probably used?

Author: As I said, there are close to two dozen house division systems, and Placidus shares many elements with several of them. The only way to really know is to dig out books and tables and charts and recalculate the cusps of each house in my chart and compare them to the original.

Pollux: Won't that take a long time?

Author: No, it won't take long at all—not with the computer. All I have to do is go to horoscopes.astro-seek.com, fill in my birth data using the "house systems calculator," and we can compare up to four house systems at a time based on my birth data.[10]

Castor: Awesome.

Author: Let's see, enter the data—June 15, 1951, 4:15 a.m., Jersey City, New Jersey—click submit, and—*presto!*—there it is. But wait. What's this? The cusps of the houses on my chart don't match up to Placidus. They're close in some instances, but way off in others.

Pollux: Now what?

Author: Fortunately, the Astro-Seek calculator offers comparison data for over a dozen approaches. I guess we'll have to go system by system through the calculator to find the one that matches my house cusps. Or,...

Castor: Or what?

Author: Or I could let you do the comparing, but not to house cusps. I want you to focus on the location of my planets. In particular, I want you to look at the planets in my fifth house. You'll find three planets there. Castor, can you tell us which ones?

Castor: Saturn, Neptune, and the Moon.[11]

Author: That's right. So as we flip through the various birth charts, each one representing a different house division approach, watch them. Do the planets move? Do they stay within the fifth house? Or do they "jump" to another house, either before or after the fifth house? Okay, first up, Regiomantanus.

Castor: The Moon's in the sixth house now.

Author: So we can eliminate Regiomontanus. Next up, even though we talked about it earlier, Morinus.

Pollux: Now the Moon and Neptune have jumped to the sixth house.

Author: So, again, we can nix Morinus. Since Meridian and Campanus house systems divide the houses in a similar manner, we can nix them as well.

Pollux: What about Porphyry?

Author: What do you think?

Pollux: The Moon has moved, but not completely out of the fifth house. It's the same for Venus in the third house, which has moved right to the cusp of the fourth house.

Author: So the Moon has moved, but not completely out of the fifth house. Let's hold on to Porphyry. Next up, an approach we haven't talked about yet—Topocentric.

Castor: *Topo...what...tric?*

Author: Topocentric. It's a popular house system invented by astrologers Wendell Polich and Nelson Page (the approach is also known as the Polich-Page house system). First published in 1961, the approach is a refinement of the Placidus house system, so quite expectedly Topocentric house cusps are quite close—within a degree or two depending on geographic latitude—to Placidus house cusps.

Castor: Why is it called Topocentric?

Author: The term "topocentric" refers to a point or location on the surface of the Earth, that location being the native's place of birth. Here's how Graham Bates from the Urania Trust describes this approach: "To get a feel for what the Topocentric house system is about, consider the Earth, turning on its axis. This axis is called the Topocentric axis.... The Geocentric Horizon passes through the centre of the Earth, and is the horizon normally used in astrology. If we rotate the geocentric horizon about the Topocentric axis we get a cone of rotation. It is the cone that is used to construct the Topocentric house cusps."[12]

Castor: You can stop there. My head is spinning, much like your cone of rotation.

Author: Well, we won't spin it, but we will use it to derive the twelve house cusps. But maybe it's a bit too much now, and, anyway, it won't help answer our question. The question is answered quite easily by looking at the house location of the Moon.

Pollux: It's in the sixth house.

Castor: And Neptune's not far behind.

Author: Which means...

Castor and Pollux: We can nix Topocentric.

Author: Precisely. That brings us to the last house approach on my list—Koch.

Castor: Koch! I thought that was a popular drink.

Author: It is, but it's spelled differently. In this case, Koch refers to a house system named after... I know you're expecting me to say, George or Thomas or Bernard Koch, or some other person with the surname Koch, but I'm not, because the system was invented by Friedrich Zanzinger and Heinz Specht.

Castor: I can see why it's not named after them. Sounds like they repair watches.

Author: Walter Koch, for whom this approach is named, was a mid-twentieth-century German mathematician and astrologer, who refined and published the work of Zanzinger and Specht in the early 1970s. Also called the Birthplace House System, the method is a modification of the house system created by Islamic astrologer Al-Qabisi, only the method is reversed. In Al-Qabisi's system, the semiarc of the Ascendant (how long it takes for the Ascendant to reach the Midheaven) is trisected, beginning with the time it takes to reach 1/3 of the distance (twelfth house cusp), 2/3s of the distance (eleventh house cusp), and 3/3s of the distance (the Midheaven and tenth house cusp).

In the Koch house system, we reverse the process, as well as modify it, and start at the Midheaven, working backwards to the Ascendant. The difference is that in the Koch system only the diurnal semiarc of the Midheaven is trisected (the time it takes to rise from the horizon to the ecliptic). The Midheaven is then rotated backwards through its diurnal semiarc to the horizon to determine the eleventh house cusp, and then again to determine the twelfth and so on.

Castor: Pollux, do you know what he's talking about?

Pollux: Afraid not.

Author: That's okay, because what we really want to know is the placement of my chart's planets in the Koch house system. Any ideas?

Pollux: Well, Saturn, Neptune, and the Moon are in the fifth house, and Pluto is in the fourth house, and Venus is in the third house...

Castor: And the Sun, Mercury, and Mars are in the first house. So far, so good.

Pollux: Not only that, but the four major angles are the same in both charts.

Author: And the house sizes?

Castor: Identical.

Pollux: So your chart was created using the Koch house system.

Castor: It's a Zanzinger-Specht self-winding astrological natal chart.

Author: Yes, well, sort of... To recap, let me say that in all of these house systems it really comes down to which fundamental plane (great circle) is the object of the initial division, and whether the divisions represent units of time or degrees of space, or some combination of the two. In addition to this, regardless of the different approaches, all house systems in Western astrology share certain commonalities: they all project the twelve house cusps onto the ecliptic; they all place the cusp of the first house near the eastern horizon; and they all utilize the uniformity of 180° house axes (i.e., first house opposes seventh house, second house opposes eighth house, third house opposes ninth house, and so on). And that brings us to the end of this discussion on the various natal chart house systems.

Castor: Thank goodness.

Pollux: What's next?

Castor: How about a milkshake?

Author: How about a deeper dive into the meaning of houses?

Pollux: I'd like that.

Castor: I'd like a milkshake.

Notes

1.   Sasportas, Howard. *The Twelve Houses*, Chpt. 1, "Basic Premises."
2.   Kent, April Elliott. *The Essential Guide to Practical Astrology*, Part 3, "A Place for Everything: Houses."

3. Sasportas, Chpt. 2, "Space, Time, and Boundaries."

4. For a concise yet thorough discussion of house systems, see
    Michael R. Meyer, *A Handbook for the Humanistic Astrologer*, Part II,
    Chpt. 11, "Systems of House Division."

5. Brady, Bernadette. "House Systems" in William E. Burns's (ed.)
    *Astrology through History: Interpreting the Stars from Ancient
    Mesopotamia to the Present.*

6. The subsequent discussion on the history of house systems is
    synthesized from the following sources: Bernadette Brady's "House
    Systems" in William E. Burns's (ed.) *Astrology through History*;
    Graham Bates's "The Astronomy of Houses," *Urania Trust*, Dec.
    2014 & March 2015, [URL] https://www.uraniatrust.org/astrology/
    astronomy-of-houses; Howard Sasportas's *The Twelve Houses*, and
    Michael R. Meyer's *A Handbook for the Humanistic Astrologer.*

7. Brady, "House Systems."

8. *Ibid.*

9. Guan, Kevin Heng Ser. "The Mathematics of Astrology: Does
    House Division Make Sense?" Republic of Singapore: National
    University of Singapore, 2000-2001, p. 28.

10. "House Systems Calculator," *Astro-Seek*, [URL] https://horoscopes.
    astro-seek.com/astrology-house-systems-calculator.

11. This observation is based on a reading of my birth chart calculated in
    1984, which, as it turns out, used the Koch system of house divisions.
    However, after generating several charts using Astro-Seek's chart
    calculator, I've come to prefer the Placidus system of house divisions,
    which keeps the planets relatively stable but shifts the sizes of the
    4th, 5th, and 6th houses (and their axial counterparts), enough at
    least to shift the Moon from the fifth house to the sixth house and
    the North Lunar Node from the tenth house to the eleventh house.

12. Bates, Graham. "The Astronomy of Houses," *Urania Trust*, Dec. 2014
    & March 2015, [URL] https://www.uraniatrust.org/astrology/
    astronomy-of-houses.

7

A Turn of the Kaleidoscope

> Every symbol in the chart can and often will manifest
> at all levels of the personality and environment. But
> some symbols work better at certain levels than at
> others. Every indication in the chart has a positive role
> to play, yet it can also be made to play a difficult one.[1]
> Robert Hand, *Horoscope Symbols*

Our previous discussion focused on how astrologers
think through the process of dividing the birth chart into
sections, including what to divide and how to project those
divisions back to the ecliptic in order to arrive at the cusps of
each of the twelve houses. In this discussion, we'll look more
closely at each house and how they relate to each other. But
first, some general comments. Open any popular book on
astrology and the authors usually begin their chapter on birth
chart houses with a list of the twelve houses and the areas
of life they address. Amy Herring captures this sentiment in
the introduction to her chapter on houses when she writes:
"Each house corresponds with a categorization of different
types of activities and behaviors that human life is made up
of. Anything you do can be categorized in a particular house
in the natal chart. Visiting your therapist? That's the territory

of the eighth house. Talking on the phone? You're in the third house now. Spending time at home? That's the shelter of the fourth house."[2]

To the uninitiated, the list of houses and their associated attributes can appear rather haphazard. Here's the beginning of Rae Orion's list of house characteristics: House #1 - your appearance and apparent disposition; House #2 - income possessions, and values; House #3 - communication, writing, short journeys, brothers and sisters; House #4 - home, roots, one parent, circumstances at the end of life....[3] April Elliott Kent, on the other hand, puts a little more meat on the bone in her house descriptions: "The first house addresses first impressions, the self and appearance, leadership, new initiatives, fresh starts and beginnings... The second house covers all matters related to your immediate material and physical environment taste, smells, sound, touch, sights; it also rules income, money, and self-esteem... The third house rules all forms of communication—talking, thinking, gadgets and devices; it also covers siblings, neighborhoods, local travel, libraries, schools, teachers and community affairs....[4]

From these and other lists it should be apparent that the twelve natal chart houses address the human condition— life on planet Earth with all of its complexity. But where is the rhyme and reason in all of it? Why does the first house address identity and appearance, while the fourth house addresses family origins and home life? Why is the third house about communication, while the fifth house is about creativity and children? What's the connection? Perhaps that's the problem with popular books on astrology: they've lost the connection and are happy just to list the usual litany of house characteristics without really thinking about them. What it means is, we've lost context...

Castor: Oh, excuse me, I must have dosed off.

Pollux: *Castor.*

Author: It's all right, Pollux. I was starting to get carried away with myself anyway. Nonetheless, I am interested in the origins and deeper meaning of birth chart houses, so let's pull back the curtain and take a look. And, believe it or not, it has to do as much with mathematics as it does with linguistics.

Castor: What do you mean?

Pollux: I think he means that we're in for some math problems.

Author: Remember our earlier discussion about the number twelve? We said it was the smallest composite number with exactly six divisors.

Castor: 1, 2, 3, 4, 6, and 12.

Author: We also determined it was the smallest abundant number, a number for which the sum of its proper divisors is greater than itself.

Castor: $1 + 2 + 3 + 4 + 6 = 16$.

Author: Moreover, we noted that is was a sublime number, a positive integer with a perfect number of positive factors, all of which add up to form another perfect number.

Castor: $1 + 2 + 3 + 4 + 6 + 12 = 28$.

Author: I'm impressed, Castor.

Castor: Pollux might remember his Latin and Greek, and know how to do higher level math problems, but of the two, I have the better memory.

Pollux: I hate to say it, but he does,

Author: Logic, memory, thinking—all fine qualities of a Gemini Sun sign. Now back to the number twelve. Our first equation or problem is quite simple: we simply divide twelve by one.

Castor: Which is twelve.

Author: I told you it was going to be easy.

Castor: But what does this have to do with anything?

Author: In order to understand the relationship among the birth chart houses, we have to understand the twelve houses themselves. My question, in other words, is rhetoric: since we know that the natal chart contains twelve houses, dividing the twelve houses by one yields what we already know—that there are twelve sections or houses in the birth chart. This is just our starting point from which all other equations emanate. All we have to do is divide twelve by its divisors to reveal a kaleidoscope of rich associations. In fact, the analogy of a kaleidoscope is quite apt for this discussion.[5]

Castor: Kaleidoscope? I got one of those for my birthday last year.

Pollux: And you promptly broke it.

Castor: It was an accident.

Pollux: Sure.

Author: Whether or not it was an accident, Castor has what we call "prior knowledge," which means that I don't have to explain how a kaleidoscope works.

Castor: You just turn the cylinder to get new pictures.

Author: Or, in the case of astrology, configurations. So let's turn the cylinder and see what configurations we get.

Castor: May I turn it first?

Author: Certainly, although you do know we're talking figuratively.

Castor: *Fig-ur-a-tive-ly?*

Pollux: There's no kaleidoscope, dummy. It's all in your imagination.

Castor: There's no kaleidoscope?

Author: No, but it's a useful analogy. So let's turn the kaleidoscope, this time we factor twelve by its first proper divisor—two—and get six.

Castor: Six what?

Author: When we look at a natal chart, we notice that each house is mirrored by an opposing house. This is the consequence of the six diagonals that divide the chart into twelve sections, which in turn produce six house axes (the result of two diagonals crossing each other to produce a wedge, pie slice, or "house" of equal proportion on either side of the chart's center point). Beyond their similar physical size, they also share common objectives; it's just that they approach these objectives from opposite points of view. Here's how April Elliott Kent describes the shared attributes of each house axis:[6]

The axis of *boundaries* between self (1) and other (7)

The axis of *resources* between what's mine (2) and what's yours (8)

The axis of *knowledge* between learning (3) and teaching (9)

The axis of *stability* between home (4) and career (10)

The axis of *creativity* between individual (5) and group (11)

The axis of *helping* between self-interest (6) and altruism (12)

But the six house axes are just one way of looking at the birth chart, so let's give the kaleidoscope another whirl and see what we get with another equation. This time we factor twelve by three which yields the number four. Although we learned earlier that there are four quadrants, in this case "four" refers to four elements—fire, earth, air, and water—and their associated houses. When it comes to the four elements and how they relate to the twelve houses, let me once again turn to April Elliott Kent for her insight:[7]

Fire, the Houses of Life (1, 5, and 9)

Earth, the Houses of Substance (2, 6, and 10)

Air, the Houses of Relationships (3, 7, and 11)

Water, the Houses of Endings (4, 8, and 12)

Castor: The Houses of Endings? Sounds gruesome.

Author: Could be, except that endings come in a variety of ways: the end of a job, the end of a relationship, the end of a long journey, the end of a book, and, yes, the end of a person's life. For now though, let's look at the "air" houses—the Houses of Relationships. The third house involves your relationships with your family, especially your siblings; the seventh house involves marital or intimate relationships (as well as business partnerships); and the twelfth house deals with wider social relationships. In other words, even though the three houses have slightly different foci, they are bound together by the central concept of relationships.

Pollux: I think I understand.

Author: Let's take it a step further. Let's say that you have a preponderance of planets in your first, fifth, and ninth houses, the "fire" houses. More than likely your energy and focus throughout your life will be on your place in the world; that is, on your identity (first), your creativity, (fifth), and your personal philosophy and spiritual life (ninth).

Castor: Kind of like your chart.

Author: Yes, where the first and fifth houses have six out of twelve planets, that is if you count the Ascendant and North Lunar Node as "planets."

Pollux: That's a lot.

Author: Quite a lot. What it means is that self and identity are a strong pull in my life. Let's hold that thought and think about the four elements in relationship to the four major points or angles in a chart. What do you notice?

Pollux: They're all different.

Author: How so?

Pollux: Thinking about what you said above, the Ascendant is in the first house, a fire house; the Imum Coeli is in the fourth house, a water house; the Descendant is in the seventh house, an air house; and the Midheaven is in the tenth house, an earth house.

Author: Each of the major angles represents one of the four elements, which brings to that angle and house, a different vibration or tone. It also shades or colors the entire quadrant. It's also in keeping with the nature of a kaleidoscope: there's a structure and logic to how the individual parts move. They may seem random to the uninitiated, but when you look deeply and carefully at them you begin to realize that everything is intricately related.

Castor: *As above, so below.*

Author: Indeed. On to our next math problem. If above we factored twelve by three, what do you think we'll do this time?

Pollux: Factor twelve by four, which equals...

Castor: Three, as in...

Author: Three house modalities.

Castor: *Modalities?* Do you mean like musical scales?

Author: That's not a bad analogy. Each time we turn the kaleidoscope we get a new musical scale. I like that. And just as music—sound—is vibrational, so too is everything in the birth chart and in the universe for that matter. When it comes to house modalities, astrologers recognize three: houses that are angular, succedent, or cadent.

Castor: You mentioned these earlier.

Author: Yes, I did, and now we can appreciate them. Like house axes and house elements, house modalities are spread equidistantly around the natal chart. So the first group, the angular houses, are the 1st, 4th, 7th, and 10th houses.

Castor: The houses of the four major angles.

Author: Imagine that. But then what else would you call the houses that contain the four major angles, but *angular*? Kind of makes sense, doesn't it?

Castor: I'll say.

Pollux: What about the next group, the succedent houses?

Author: What does it mean to succeed?

Castor: To win or to come out on top.

Author: Yes, but it has another meaning. Pollux?

Pollux: Something that comes after something else?

Author: Precisely. So the succedent houses are...?

Pollux: The 2nd, 5th, 8th, and 11th houses, which come after the 1st, 4th, 7th, and 10th houses.

Castor: Which means that the 3rd, 6th, 9th, and 12th houses are the cadent houses.

Author: Now you're catching on. I told you it's not that difficult.

Castor: But why is the third modality called "cadent?"

Author: If the angular house starts or initiates something, for that's what that house does, and the succedent house that follows it tries to maintain that initiative rather than start its own activity, the cadent house tries to wind down the initiated activity and prepare for the start of a new cycle in the next quadrant.[8]

Pollux: I notice that each of the four quadrants contains three houses: one angular, one succedent, and one cadent.

Author: Everything is interlocked, which means that when it comes to house modalities you can look at them in two different ways: as separate entities (four angular, four succedent, and four cadent houses) or as unified blocks (four quadrants, each one containing a three-house sequence of modalities). Like everything in astrology, there's usually more than one way to look at something. Again, let me tap April Elliott Kent's understanding of the three house modalities and what they bring to the natal chart. In angular houses "you define yourself (first house), create a tribe to provide security and nourishment (fourth house), join forces with equal partners (seventh house), and pursue your calling (tenth house)." In succedent houses "you gather resources (second house), use them to create things (fifth house), combine your resources with the personal resources of others close to you (eighth house), and bring together community resources for the larger work of society (eleventh house)." In cadent houses "you exchange information (third house), analyze it and apply it to practical tasks (sixth house), synthesize it into knowledge and beliefs (ninth house), and use it to explore hidden and even mystical realms (twelfth house)."[9]

Castor: Ready for the next equation?

Author: Not yet. Before we move on I want you to visualize something. I want you to see in your mind's eye the twelve houses of the birth chart spread equally around the chart. Focusing on the angular houses, draw a line to connect all of them. What pattern do you get?

Castor: A square.

Pollux: That makes sense since there are four equally spaced houses for each of the three modalities.

Author: Let's do this for the four elements. Focus on the fire houses and do the same thing: draw a line that connects them. What do you get?

Castor: A triangle.

Pollux: Which also makes sense since there are three equally spaced houses for each of the four elements. But what do you get if you connect the six house axes?

Castor: A real mess.

Author: Try a twelve-pointed star. Not only that, but taken as a whole the three modality squares also give you a twelve-pointed star, as do the four elemental triangles.

Pollux: Wow, it really does look like a kaleidoscope.

Castor: Awesome.

Author: Yes, awesome. On to the next equation, where we factor twelve by six to get two.

Castor: Two really big houses.

Author: Otherwise known as hemispheres. If you recall, we touched upon this earlier when we talked about the two sets of hemispheres in a birth chart, each set created by dividing the natal chart in half, first by the horizon and then by the meridian.

Castor: *Which* forms a cross, *which* determines the major angles, *which* create the four quadrants, *which* contain the three house modalities, *which*...

Author: I think you get it, Castor, and it's a perfect segue to our last math problem. What do we get when we factor twelve by itself.

Castor: Is this a trick question?

Pollux: Twelve divided by twelve is one, Castor. Any numbskull knows that.

Castor: Hey, I'm not a...

Author: No, you're not. But Pollux is right: twelve divided by twelve is one. And we end where we began many sessions ago—with wholeness, completion, unity, totality, the ouroboros, the microcosm and the macrocosm, the adage "As above, So below," and the Nitty Gritty Dirt Band's refrain "May the circle be unbroken." I'd like to end this discussion with a quotation, one of my favorites from humanistic astrologer Dane Rudhyar: "The development of consciousness begins with the realization of duality. The whole to which a man belonged by birth and which enfolded him like a womb must be sundered. The circle of unconscious prenatal wholeness must be divided into two halves; and this division must be directly perceived, felt, experienced: I and the other; I and the world."[10] The act of sundering is the act of dividing. We divide the twelve houses of the horoscope—the birth chart—by its divisors, by 1, 2, 3, 4, 6, and 12. In doing so, we find a myriad of combinations, a plethora of relationships, a stunning kaleidoscopic view of the living, breathing universe around us.

Castor: And within us.

Author: Yes, and within us.

Pollux: Now what do we do?

Author: What do we do? I think we should take a break.

Castor: Now you're talking.

Notes

1. Hand, Robert. *Horoscope Symbols*, Chpt. 1, "The Horoscope: A Map of the Psyche."
2. Herring, Amy. *Essential Astrology*, Chpt. 8, "The Houses."
3. Orion, Rae. *Astrology for Dummies*, Chpt. 12, "The Sun, the Moon, and the Planets in the Houses."
4. Kent, April Elliott. *The Essential Guide to Practical Astrology*, Chpt. 8, "Houses." As a point of reference, here is a list of the twelve houses and the areas of life they address gleaned from several sources:
   1st House: Self, Appearance, Body Type, Impressions

2nd House: Priorities, Habits, Work Ethic, Possessions

3rd House: Communication, Thinking, Siblings, Early Education

4th House: Home, Family, Foundations, Emotions

5th House: Creativity, Self-Expression, Romance, Fertility

6th House: Health, Fitness, Work Habits, Organization, Service

7th House: Marriage, Partnerships, Contracts, Social Relations

8th House: Assets, Inheritances, Joint Ventures, Shared Finances

9th House: Religion, Philosophy, Travel, Learning, Ethics

10th House: Career, Profession, Social Status, Reputation

11th House: Groups, Friends, Social Awareness, Hopes, Dreams

12th House: Closure, Solitude, Spirituality, Endings, Afterlife

5.   I borrow the term "kaleidoscope" from Alan Leo, who uses the term when discussing the two motions of the Earth—axial rotation and solar revolution—suggesting that the two motions "produce a kaleidoscope with an infinite number of patterns, each pattern never repeated in an individual horoscope within a cycle of thousands of years." Leo, *Symbolism and Astrology*, Chpt. 6, "The Symbol of the Horoscope."

6.   Kent, Chpt. 8, "Houses."

7.   *Ibid.*

8.   According to Joanna Martine Woolfolk, the term "cadent" comes from the Latin cadere, meaning "to fall." In this scheme of things, cadent houses, the third and last of the threefold house system, "fall away" from the angular and succedent houses (Woolfolk, Chpt. 8, "The Houses of Astrology"). Alexander Boxer supports this view when he writes, "Houses Three, Six, Nine, and Twelve were called 'falling' or 'cadent' Houses," implying, like Woolfolk, that the term "cadent" is derived from the Latin *cadere* (Boxer, Chpt. 8, "When You Wish Upon a Star, Which Algorithm Should You Use? Guido Bonatti's Astrological Wheel of Fortune"). Yasmin Boland extends the meaning of cadent with this interpretation: "Succedent [houses] are effectively 'on the rise' while the word 'cadent' means 'fallen' and is the root of the word cadaver, meaning corpse"

(Boland, Chpt. 7, "The Houses"). Technically, the root of the word "cadent" is *cadere*, the present infinitive of *cado* meaning "I fall" (from which we derive the word "corpse"). April Elliott Kent, on the other hand, gives "cadent" a very different—and somewhat misleading—interpretation: "To modern ears, 'cadent' is an odd, archaic-sounding word. It's related to 'cadence,' or rhythm in dance or music; in music, a cadence is a progression of chords moving toward resolution. These are the houses of resolution, then, but even more interesting is the part about rhythm. In the cadent houses, you learn to dance with life by attuning yourself to its rhythms." Kent, Chpt. 11, "Where You Dance: The Cadent Houses."

9. Kent, Chpt. 8, "Houses."
10. Rudhyar, Dane. *Person Centered Astrology*, Chpt. 14, "The Geometrical Principles of Formation of Aspect."

8

Suspended in Air

Each of the four elements manifests in three vibrational modalities: cardinal, fixed, and mutable. Combining the four elements with the three modalities produces the twelve primary patterns of energy called the Signs of the Zodiac.[1]
Stephen Arroyo, *Stephen Arroyo's Chart Interpretation Handbook*

Although today astrology aligns itself with the therapeutic arts, the practice of astrology is still undergirded by a dense matrix of mathematical calculations (fortunately for us, this is carried out by computers). No matter how you slice it, astrology is a game of math based on the geometric relationship among its various and sundry parts. In our last discussion, we talked about some of those relationships, especially how they pertained to the twelve houses of the natal chart, i.e., the six house axes, the four elemental houses, the three modalities, and the two sets of hemispheres.

Castor: It's the kaleidoscope thing.

Author: Yes, Castor, it's the kaleidoscope thing, and today we're going to use the analogy of the kaleidoscope again, just with a new set of information—the signs of the zodiac. Just like the houses of the birth chart, the zodiacal signs divide into several categories based on the division of twelve by its divisors. Of course, we know rhetorically that twelve divided by one equals twelve, twelve signs of the zodiac, so we can skip the first equation and focus on twelve's proper divisors, which means that the first math problem is twelve divided by two...

Castor: Which any nincompoop knows is six.

Pollux: *Castor.*

Author: When we applied this equation to the houses of the natal chart, we identified six house axes; that is, axes between the 1st and 7th houses, the 2nd and 8th houses, the 3rd and 9th houses, and so on. It's the same with the signs of the zodiac, except when we divide the twelve signs of the zodiac by two we don't get six sign *axes*, we get six sign *dualities*.

Castor: Why not sign axes?

Author: House axes are created by the lines of two adjacent house cusps crossing at the center of the natal chart to form two houses of comparable size on the either side of the chart. Depending upon which house system is used, the size of the houses vary, except for the axial houses (i.e., the houses directly opposite each other). They're always the same size given their geometric relationship. It's different in the case of signs because the size of each sign around the perimeter of the birth chart is always 30°. In other words, signs are not related through an axis point in the same way that houses are. As such, we give the two signs that stand on opposite sides of the birth chart a different name: we call them dualities.

Pollux: Are they that different from house axes?

Author: They're related in that both are based upon complementary forces or energies. With house axes, each pair revolves around a particular theme. For instance, the 1st and 7th houses deal with the theme of *boundaries* (between self and others); the 2nd and 8th houses deal with the theme of *resources* (between what's mine and yours); the 3rd and 9th houses deal with the theme of *knowledge* (between learning and teaching), and so on. It's the same with sign dualities, only instead of houses, our concern is with zodiac signs: Aries and Libra deal with the theme of *relationships* (between self-assertion and compromise); Taurus and Scorpio deal with the theme of *change* (between steadfastness and transformation); Gemini and Sagittarius deal with the theme of *mental development* (between information-gathering and knowledge), and so on.

Castor: But what does this mean practically?

Author: If you have planets in each sign of a duality, you'll need to learn how to balance the two dimensions (since planets draw our attention to the house and sign they are in). For instance, Aries and Libra deal with relationships, specifically the push-pull between the ability to assert yourself when necessary and the alternate ability to compromise. Learning how to balance these contradictory forces is part and parcel of the Aries/Libra duality. Does this make sense?

Castor: I think so. But what if you have planets in only one sign of the duality, the way you do in your Gemini/Sagittarius duality?

Author: Excellent question, Castor. Think of it as a seesaw. When you have planets in both signs of a duality, they tend to balance each other. In other words, they both have the power to pull in their direction; you just have to learn how to maintain the balance between the two. On the other hand, when you have one sign loaded with planets and the other empty of planets, then the seesaw is weighted toward one end, the end with all of the planets. In that situation, you really have to struggle to find the balance between the two signs of the duality.

Castor: So with your three planets in Gemini (Mercury, Mars, and the Sun) and none in Sagittarius, you're heavily weighted toward first-house Gemini's energy to the exclusion of poor old, empty-planet, seventh-house Sagittarius.

Author: I guess you could say that. There's two things at work here: the 1st-house/7th-house axis of relationships between self-assertion and compromise, and the Gemini/Sagittarius theme of mental development between information-gathering and knowledge. In my case, since my first-house Gemini contains Mercury, Mars, and the Sun and my seventh-house Sagittarius is absent any planets, I have to watch that I don't overpower people with the information that I collect (a sure sign of Mercury in Gemini) and take care to develop relationships beyond my personal interests and needs.

Castor: Which appears to be hard for you.

Author: Moving on to the next equation, What is twelve divided by three?

Castor: Easy-smeasy. It's four, as in four elements.

Author: Just as there are four elemental houses, there are four elemental signs. This is a throwback to an earlier age, when astrologers used the Whole Sign house approach in which houses and signs aligned themselves in a one-to-one correspondence, i.e., first-house Aries, second-house Taurus, third-house Gemini, etc.[2] Since the two—houses and signs—

aligned themselves so closely, they often shared the same qualities. In this case, the four elements shine their light on both the house and its associated sign. However, once we recalibrate the signs based on the moment of birth, the sign/house relationships are disturbed, which means, at least theoretically, that a water sign can inhabit a fire house, an air sign can inhabit an earth house, a fire sign, a water house, and so on.

Castor: Just turn the kaleidoscope.

Author: That's right, just turn the kaleidoscope. In this scheme of things, three signs are assigned to one of the four elements with each group of signs called a *triplicity*, or, as some astrologers prefer, a *trigon*, which translates "three-cornered" as in a three-cornered hat.

Castor: We made a three-cornered hat in school.

Author: What do you remember about it?

Castor: It's like a big triangular slice of pizza.

Author: With the corners spread equidistantly around the circumference of the pizza slice. The same is true for a birth chart, which means if you connected them with a continuous line, each three-sign element would form an equilateral triangle. Moreover, if you placed all four elemental triangles within the birth chart, they would form a twelve-pointed star.

Castor: Just like the houses.

Author: Think multi-layered kaleidoscope. Everything is related, just turn the kaleidoscope to get a new configuration. Since our current configuration is focused on elemental signs, let's look at their respective qualities:

Fire: Aries, Leo, Sagittarius (active and enthusiastic)

Earth: Taurus, Virgo, Capricorn (practical and stable)

Air: Gemini, Libra, Aquarius (intellectual and communicative)

Water: Cancer, Scorpio, Pisces (emotional and intuitive)[3]

These are the signs that make up the four elemental triangles, the triplicities, each one with a different flavor or characteristic. When planets appear in different signs of the same element, that is significant as they reinforce the theme of that triplicity.

Pollux: How does that translate to your chart?

Author: In my case, I have a preponderance of planets—five to be exact—in air signs: three planets in Gemini and two planets in Libra. If you look in the four corners of my chart, just outside the main set of concentric circles, the computer-analyst-qua-astrologer indicates the number of planets in each sign: fire (3), earth (1), air (6), and water (2).

Castor: Wait a minute. You said that you have five air planets, but your astrologer lists six. What gives?

Author: It's a good question. I've long thought about this because when you count the planets in my chart there are only five planets in air signs (the Sun and Moon, Mercury, Mars, and Neptune). So what is the sixth planet?

Pollux: Maybe he counted the Midheaven in Aquarius, which is the third air sign?

Author: Possibly. However, when it comes to the four major chart angles, the two most important are the Ascendant and the Midheaven—in that order. It's more likely that he counted my Ascendant in Gemini as the sixth planet. But five or six, it really doesn't matter because in either case half or more of my chart's planets are in air signs.

Castor: I guess you could say that you're an airhead.

Pollux: *Castor.*

Author: That's okay, Pollux. Castor's right: I'm an airhead, a person who lives in his head, and one without too many practical skills (only one earth sign) or deep levels of emotion (just two water signs); yes, an airhead, but one driven by passion (three fire signs). I can tell you the exact moment I realized how much of an air sign I am. My wife is always trying to get me to walk, with or without her. She just thinks walking is good for you, and I'm sure it is. But I prefer to ride a bicycle, so I'm always turning her down, preferring instead to ride my bike. One day I was riding along on my bicycle thinking about this and looked down and saw my feet pedaling away. There they were, going round and round, never once touching the ground. In other words, I was fully suspended in air. That's when it dawned on me, I mean really hit me, how much air is in my chart. No wonder I don't want to walk; I'd rather be suspended in air riding a bicycle. By the way, my wife is all fire and earth, so walking comes natural to her, and not just walking, "power walking"—that's the fire in her.

Pollux: You keep mentioning the four elements, but aren't there more than that?

Author: The current periodic table of elements lists 118, but we're not talking about chemical components in an external, scientific way. The use of elements in astrology dates back to a time when our ancestors experienced everything as one of four primal forces. However, these are not descriptions of external realities as much as they are subjective realities. As Robert Hand puts it: "Modern people ask what is the objective reality of a substance's makeup, whereas the ancients asked what is its subjective reality, that is, what are the components of the experience one has of a substance."[4] Although we identify four classes of elements, astrologers often combine them into two sympathetic groups: fire/air and water/earth.

Castor: What do you mean?

Author: Again, it's about our experience of these elements. When you make a fire, where does the smoke go?

Castor: It rises.

Author: Yes, it rises and mixes with the air. The opposite is true of water: it runs down a mountain and mixes with the earth. That's why astrologers say that there's a sympathetic relationship between fire/air and water/earth. Since my chart favors fire and air (nine out of twelve planets are in these elemental signs), let me add another insight from Robert Hand: "Fire rises, whereas wind moves horizontally. Fire strives to go higher, away from ordinary reality toward an ideal or abstraction, whereas air moves about horizontally relating everything it encounters in the physical world to everything else." It is precisely because of air's association with horizontal motion that the element of air is connected with the transport of ideas.[5]

Pollux: Which is why you are always saying that you live in your head.

Castor: Ah-ha, so you are an airhead.

Author: An airhead in the sense that logic and reasoning are my natural go-to functions (and why I have very few practical skills). But it doesn't mean that I live isolated from others. Unlike fire, which is more about personal drive and will power, air has a social aspect to it. In this way, according to Hand, air is similar to earth: both are primarily concerned with a reality external to the self, whereas fire and water are more concerned with personal, inward truths or realities. Moreover, the strong social quality of air is true for its triplicity, the three signs it defines. All of them—Gemini, Libra, and Aquarius—have to do with relating to others, just in a different sort of way: "Gemini to the immediate world through mind and speech, Libra through achieving perfect balance within a one-to-one relationship, and Aquarius through group consciousness and interaction."[6]

Castor: But you don't seem social to me. You've always got your head in a book or your computer.

Author: Although air is very social, it doesn't always handle intimacy that well. The reason for this is because air operates "extensively" rather than "intensively," trying to cover as much ground as possible in order to gain an understanding of the whole. In short, close personal relationships get in the way of the information-gatherer, of which I am. Not only that, but getting involved with a person on a deep, intensive level runs the risk of interfering with the need to experience many people and situations extensively.

Castor: It's kind of like you're trading intensity for extensity.

Pollux: I don't think "extensity" is a word.

Author: Me neither, though I do get Castor's point, for I see this in my own life: I have many acquaintances, as I am fast to connect with people in any situation, but in terms of deep, intensive relationships, I have only one—my wife. In many ways, she's my lifeline to the world of being fully human. Without her, I'd float off into space like an untethered balloon.

Castor: What about us?

Pollux: I'm not sure we count.

Author: You do, but not in this case. But you do point to the challenge that all airheads face: the need to develop sensitivity to the internal, emotional worlds of other people. In other words, airheads are really good at processing information. We observe, plan, and organize very quickly. We see the whole before others do. More than any other elemental type, we move faster and more efficiently through the world of information. But we're not so good at reading the deep undercurrents of other people's emotions. It's probably why I'm attracted to my wife: she's a fire/earth combination, with a strong need to connect on a deep emotional level.

Castor: So you're good for nothing but thinking?

Author: Another way of saying it is that in this lifetime I need to slow down and consider the emotional side of life as I tend to run over my emotions in order to get to "the answer" as fast as possible (whether the question be about things or people). But enough of that, at least for now. Let's talk about the signs and elements in relationship to seasonal change. For this, let me turn to the work of Dane Rudhyar who's written about this in *The Astrology of Personality*. We call the elemental signs triplicities for the simple reason that each element is associated with three different signs, each one equally spaced around the birth chart. We know from earlier discussions that the most distinguishing aspect within the birth chart is the cross, or quadrature, made from the intersection of the horizon and meridian lines, which divide the circular chart into four sections or quadrants, the beginning of each one defined by its relationship to a point of seasonal change, i.e., first-house Aries (spring equinox), fourth-house Cancer (summer solstice), seventh-house Libra (fall equinox), and tenth-house Capricorn (winter solstice). Now let's assign to each of these seasonal signs their respective element: Aries (fire), Cancer (water), Libra (air), and Capricorn (earth).[7]

Pollux: They each represent a different element.

Author: And given their axial relationship, i.e., Aires (fire)/ Libra (air) and Cancer (water)/Capricorn (earth), you can see why fire/air and water/earth are sympathetic to each other. But we also see something else: there is a certain "momentum" the four chart angles and their respective elements generate around the circumference of the natal chart as they alternate from one element to the next. This momentum will become more apparent in the next equation.

Castor: Which is what happens when we divide twelve by four.

Pollux: Which is three.

Author: But three what?

Pollux: When we did this with houses, we got four houses in one of three modalities, i.e., angular, succedent, or cadent. I assume it's the same for signs?

Author: Similar, but not the same. With signs, we get four signs in one of three *qualities*, i.e., cardinal, fixed, or mutable. These are the "quadruplicities," a reference to the four signs associated with each quality. The term is related to "quadrature," from the Latin *quadratura* meaning "to square".

Castor: I thought *quad* meant "four."

Author: It does, but it has two meanings: *four* as in four signs per quality and *four* as in four angles of a square. That's the shape the four signs of a quality make when you connect them within the circle of the birth chart.

Pollux: Just the way we connected the house modalities to make three squares of four houses each.

Author: Returning to sign qualities, according to Joanna Woolfolk, each quality signifies the sign's interaction with the outside world:

Cardinal: Aries, Cancer, Libra, Capricorn (initiators and entrepreneurs)

Fixed: Taurus, Leo, Scorpio, Aquarius (perfecters and consolidators)

Mutable: Gemini, Virgo, Sagittarius, Pisces (adjusters and transformers)[8]

As with the triplicities, planets that congregate in one of the three sign qualities influence you more than the other qualities. In my case, I have four planets in cardinal signs (Jupiter, Uranus, Neptune, and the Moon), two planets in fixed signs (Venus and Pluto), and four planets in mutable signs (Mercury, Mars, Saturn, and the Sun).

Castor: Wait, let me get this straight. You have five air planets, four of which are mutable. That means you're not just an airhead, you're a scatterbrain.

Pollux: Castor, stop it.

Author: It's okay, Pollux, Castor is on to something. He's starting to see a larger slice of the natal chart, combining various signs, planets, and houses. After all, that's what chart interpretation is. In terms of my being a scatterbrain, my four cardinal planets (and, to a lesser degree, two fixed planets) offset my four mutable air planets, making me an airhead (someone who likes to think), but one with focus and drive.

Castor: You mean you're not a scatterbrain?

Author: No, I'm very focused, although I do live most of my life in my head. Having said that, let's look more closely at the three sign qualities, starting with the cardinal signs. When Woolfolk says that cardinal signs are entrepreneurial, she means that the signs are concerned with initiating change. Another way of saying this is that they set things in motion. In general, cardinal signs are the most active, enterprising, and vigorous. In short, cardinal personalities are leaders, not followers; they're assertive almost to the point of aggression. According to Judy Hall, a natal chart showing four or more planets within cardinal signs indicates "a strong will and a powerful desire to command."9

Castor: Is that you?

Author: I think so, although I wouldn't say that I have a powerful desire to command. But put a planet in a cardinal sign and the cardinality of the sign "energizes" the planet, making its expression more forceful. For me, that means Jupiter, Uranus, Neptune, and the Moon, which are all in cardinal signs. Except for the Moon, none of these are inner planets, which means that they have less impact on my "commanding" personality than Mercury, Venus, and Mars would have in a cardinal sign. Of the ten planets, the Sun and, to a lesser extent, the Moon are effected by being in a cardinal sign. But for all its self-starting assertiveness, a cardinal personality is often not very persistent, having a hard time sustaining the activities they initiate.

Pollux: But you don't seem to have that problem.

Author: No, but then I'm not a dominant cardinal personality; given the fact that many of my inner planets are in mutable signs, I have more of a mutable personality, which means that I try to adapt to changing situations. Before we discuss mutable signs, let's talk about fixed signs. These are signs—Taurus, Leo, Scorpio, and Aquarius—that often resist change, preferring the stability of a predictable routine. If the signature attribute of cardinal signs is to initiate, the signature attribute of fixed signs is to continue or persist. The downside of a fixed personality, however, is that their persistence devolves into an intractable stubbornness, which can become a barrier to progress.[10]

Castor: Fortunately, you only have two fixed planets: Venus and Pluto.

Pollux: Both in fire signs.

Author: Which brings out their character even more. As for planets in mutable signs, I have four, three mutable/air signs (Mercury, Mars, and the Sun) and one mutable/earth sign (Saturn). What's interesting about mutable signs is that three of the four are "dual" signs (Gemini, Sagittarius, and Pisces, but not Virgo).

Pollux: I understand that Gemini the Twins and Pisces the Fish are dual signs, but why is Sagittarius considered a dual sign?

Author: We often forget that Sagittarius the Archer was, at least in mythical times, a centaur, half-man, half-horse. Astrologically, the two symbols represent the search for knowledge, truth, and adventure as well as new, innovative thinking. The dual nature of three of the four mutable signs underscores a mutable personality's ability to remain flexible and adaptable, especially amid changing realities. With four or more planets in mutable signs, an individual revels in exploration and change, finding it difficult to stick to the same routine. They are often restless, bounding with nervous energy, and can be irascible, unpredictable, even unstable. But if properly channeled, mutable personalities can develop exceptional skill at multitasking.[11]

Castor: You're a mutable personality, are you good at multitasking?

Author: I think so. The test for me, at least recently, has been riding my bicycle. I have a mirror attached to my handlebar that I often look into to see what's coming up behind me. At the same time, I have an eye on the road ahead of me, especially on the parked cars to my right. I find this a very easy task. My wife, on the other hand, finds it quite difficult. The reason: she can't look in the mirror, i.e., look backwards, and maintain her gaze forward at the same time. To me, this is an indication that she's not a multitasker: her concentrated Leo energy is so intensely focused that it's hard for her to "split" her attention between two or more stimuli. Not so for me.

Castor: Better not give her a mirror for her birthday.

Author: No, not a good idea. Now, let's take this one step further and relate the above to the cycle of seasons. According to Robert Hand, each season can be divided into thirds, with each third defined by one of the three sign qualities, i.e., cardinal, fixed, and mutable. Here's how Hand describes this relationship: "The first third of each season is a cardinal sign: in this period the qualities of that season are asserted strongly. It is a period of dynamic change as the new season takes hold upon the Earth. The new season is often in conflict with the one that preceded it, but eventually it triumphs. The second third of each season is a fixed sign. Here we have the qualities of that season stabilized and most perfectly represented. The weather has settled down and is reasonably predictable. The last third of each season is the mutable sign. Here the qualities of the season are giving way to those of the next. Again, we have dynamism, but it is the dynamism of something giving way to something else, rather than that of something asserting itself."[12]

This description goes along with Dane Rudhyar's understanding of how the sign qualities unfold, one into the other, with cardinal signs addressing the *generation* of power, fixed signs addressing the *concentration* of power, and mutable signs addressing the *distribution* of power. For instance, during the spring season, Aries generates power, Taurus concentrates it, and Gemini distributes it. Likewise, in summer, Cancer generates power, Leo concentrates it, and Virgo distributes it, and so on.[13]

Pollux: It's one never-ending cycle of change.

Castor: It certainly is never-ending.

Author: We'll end soon enough. We have just one more equation to complete. What is twelve divided by six?

Castor: Two, as in two hemispheres.

Author: Not exactly, but I like your reasoning. Dividing twelve by six yields two sign *polarities*, which alternate—positive and negative—around the twelve signs of the birth chart. Since sign polarities alternate around the chart, with six positive and six negative signs, they don't form hemispheres (six contiguous signs); rather they form two groups of six signs spread equidistantly around the twelve-sign perimeter. Pollux, let's see if you can list the positive signs, starting with Aries.

Pollux: Aries, Gemini, Leo, Libra, Sagittarius, and Aquarius.

Author: And the negative signs, Castor?

Castor: Taurus, Cancer, Virgo, Scorpio, Capricorn, and Pisces.

Author: Excellent.

Castor: It's kind of like the ouroborus snaking around the perimeter of the birth chart.

Author: Imagine that. Before we look at the "snaking" quality, let's dwell a little longer on the nature of the polarities. First of all, I want you to study the positive signs and tell me how do they relate to the four elements?

Pollux: They're all fire and air signs. While Aries, Leo, and Sagittarius are fire signs, Gemini, Libra, and Aquarius are air signs.

Castor: Which means that the negative signs are made up of three water signs (Cancer, Scorpio, and Pisces) and three earth signs (Taurus, Virgo, and Capricorn).

Author: Once again we see the sympathetic relationship between fire/air and water/earth. Here's how Stephen Arroyo puts it: "The elements have traditionally been divided into two groups, fire and air being considered active and self-expressive, and water and earth considered passive, receptive, and self-containing."[14] In one sense, sign polarity can be seen as the result of the changing of the elements around the circumference of the birth chart (the zodiac), where fire and air (positive) alternate with earth and water (negative). But what does it mean for a sign to be positive or negative?

Castor: It's either good or bad.

Author: That's often the traditional way of describing polarities. But in astrology, where all things are relative (and dependent upon multiple factors), there is no inherent "good" or "bad." We have to look beyond these descriptors to find their core or essential meanings. Robert Hand describes the polarization of signs this way: "The positive signs are usually more objectively oriented and more outgoing, assertive, and interested in what is going on around them. The negative signs are more likely to be inwardly directed and concerned with subjective experience."[15] Joanna Woolfolk says the same thing when she argues that positive signs are "outer-directed, energetic, and strong through action," while negative signs are "receptive, magnetic, and strong through inner resources."[16]

Castor: Where are your planets?

Author: Mine? Well, I have a preponderance of planets in positive signs, namely, Mercury, Mars, the Sun, Venus, Pluto, Neptune, the Moon, and Jupiter.

Castor: Wow, that's eight out of ten planets!

Pollux: Only Uranus and Saturn are in negative signs.

Author: Which means, according to Judy Hall, that I tend to be dominant and forceful in my self-expression, regardless of my Sun sign.[17]

Castor: And is that the case?

Author: Well, that's what my wife is always telling me. But that's neither here nor there. Let's return to the idea of energy "snaking around" the perimeter of the natal chart. We see this most dramatically in the alternating sign polarities that alternate around the birth chart like an electric current: Aries (+), Taurus (-), Gemini (+), Cancer (-), Leo (+), Virgo (-), Libra (+), Scorpio (-), Sagittarius (+), Capricorn (-), Aquarius (+), and Pisces (-). Such a configuration energizes the relationship between neighboring signs. Now add element and sign quality and you can easily see that the vibrational energy of the birth chart is pushed along by the unique characteristics of each sign:

Aries: positive, cardinal, fire

Taurus: negative, fixed, earth

Gemini: positive, mutable, air

Cancer: negative, cardinal, water

Leo: positive, fixed, fire

Virgo: negative, mutable, earth

Libra: positive, cardinal, air

Scorpio: negative, fixed, water

Sagittarius: positive, mutable, fire

Capricorn: negative, cardinal, earth

Aquarius: positive, fixed, air

Pisces: negative, mutable, water[18]

And it's all based on the number twelve's proper
factors—2, 3, 4, and 6—which resolve themselves once we've
completed the twelve-sign cycle of the zodiac as expressed
in the birth chart. Each sign is different in the same way that
each house is different, which means that as you recalibrate
the birth chart based on your birth data, there are 144 (12
houses x 12 signs) possible combinations of house and sign
characteristics.

Castor: That's a lot.

Author: But that's not all. Let's throw in the ten planets.
Unlike the signs and houses which come as a package in the
respect that they're locked into a particular sequence, each
planet is on its own, defined by its orbital period around the
Sun. With this information we can calculate the chance of
repeating the same house, sign, and planet configuration in
the birth chart of any two individuals. Let's see, it would be
something of the order of 12^{12} power (12 houses x 12 signs x 12
possible house/sign locations of the Sun, 12 possible house/
sign locations of the Moon, 12 possible house/sign locations
of Mercury, and so on), which means that there's almost a
one-in-ten-trillion chance of two people having the same
birth-chart configuration unless they were born in the same
place, in the same year, in the same month, on the same day,
and at the exact same time.

Pollux: It certainly gives new meaning to the word
"individual."

Castor: That's for sure.

Author: Let's run with that concept and think about it
the way Dane Rudhyar does. According to Rudhyar, there is

"Man," i.e., the unique individual, and there is "Mankind,"
i.e., the collective and generic human being. Here's what this
deep-thinking astrologer has to say about the two (excuse
the sexist language; like all of us, Rudhyar is a product of his
time): "As men live on the whole surface of the Earth, and not
merely at one spot on the globe, the Earth as a whole has to
be considered the symbol of Man. The rhythms of the Earth
motions will be used to symbolize the rhythms of the generic
human being. On the other hand, an individual man is born
at a particular point of the Earth surface; and therefore, while
generic mankind is not affected by the axial rotation of the
Earth, the individual selfhood of a particular man will be
determined in function of this very axial rotation."[19]

Castor: I'm not sure I follow this.

Pollux: It sounds like Rudhyar equates "Man" with the
Earth, or, at least, the Earth is a symbol for man.

Author: Let's go back to the three basic glyphs used in the
language of astrology: the circle, the semicircle, and the cross.
If the Sun is represented by a circle with a dot in the center,
and the Moon is represented by a crescent or semicircle, how
is the Earth represented?

Castor: By a cross.

Pollux: By an equal-armed cross or quadrature.

Castor: I was just about to say that.

Author: In Rudhyar's scheme of things, the Earth and
Mankind are both represented by the cross. It's how Rudhyar
distinguishes between "Man" and "Mankind" that I find
extremely insightful: "There is no day or night (the results of
axial rotation) for Mankind as a whole, as it is always day for

one half of Mankind and night for the other half. But there is day and night for a particular Man occupying a particular place on the surface of the globe. On the other hand, the relationship (aspects) of the Earth to the other planets of the system have exactly the same significance for collective man and for any individual man, except that the position of the individual man on the globe's surface will focalize these aspects in a section of his own heavens either below or above the horizon, and more precisely in what astrology calls one of the houses."[20]

Castor: I'm still not sure what this means.

Author: That's okay. Sometimes you have to read something many times before the words sink in. Perhaps this is a good place to stop and do just that: let Rudhyar's words sink in.

Notes

1. Arroyo, Stephen. *Stephen Arroyo's Chart Interpretation Handbook*, Chpt. 3, "The Four Elements and the Twelve Signs." In the same chapter, Arroyo elaborates on the "twelve primary patterns of energy," symbolically represented by the signs of the zodiac. According to Arroyo, each sign is a combination of characteristics consisting of one of four elements (fire, earth, air, water), one of three qualities (cardinal, fixed, mutable), and one of two polarities (positive, negative). According to this insightful astrologer, it is the unique combination of these factors that produce the twelve signs of the zodiac, which in their essence are unique vibrational patterns, i.e., manifested forms of consciousness.

2. In chapter nine of *Stephen Arroyo's Chart Interpretation Handbook*, titled "Guidelines to Chart Synthesis," Arroyo lists twelve "letters" of what he calls the "astrological alphabet." In this alphabet each

letter is made up of more than just sign and house; it's made up of a unique combination of sign, planet, and house. This is Ptolemy's tropical or natural zodiac (updated to include the three modern planets), with the addition of each house/sign's ruling planet:

Letter 1: Aries, Mars & 1st House

Letter 2: Taurus, Venus & 2nd House

Letter 3: Gemini, Mercury & 3rd House

Letter 4: Cancer, Moon & 4th House

Letter 5: Leo, Sun & 5th House

Letter 6: Virgo, Mercury & 6th House

Letter 7: Libra, Venus & 7th House

Letter 8: Scorpio, Pluto & 8th House

Letter 9: Sagittarius, Jupiter & 9th House

Letter 10: Capricorn, Saturn & 10th House

Letter 11: Aquarius, Uranus & 11th House

Letter 12: Pisces, Neptune & 12th House

3. Hall, Judy. *The Astrology Bible*, Chpt. 2, "The Elements." In the same chapter, see the chart titled "Elemental Combinations" for an interesting look at how the four elements pair up in either a harmonious or discordant manner.

4. Hand, Chpt. 10, "The Signs: An Introduction."

5. *Ibid.*

6. *Ibid.*

7. Rudhyar, Dane. *The Astrology of Personality*, Chpt. 7, "The Signs of the Zodiac."

8. Woolfolk, Joanna Martine. *The Only Astrology Book You'll Ever Need*, Chpt. 1, "Sun Signs." In chapter ten of *Horoscope Symbols*, in the section titled "The Crosses and Quadruplicities," Robert Hand provides several interpretations of the four "crosses" (the result of each modality—cardinal, fixed, and mutable—composed of four equally spaced signs, thus forming a quadrature or cross within the natal chart). Most interesting is his understanding of the three crosses as "modes of reaction" when events or circumstances are

initiated from outside: "Cardinal reaction is counteraction, the making of a second initiative to counter the first. Fixed reaction is resistance, the effort to endure in the face of external initiative, and to avoid change. Again, the emphasis is on stability. Mutable reaction does not actively resist what is happening, but tries to alter it indirectly by bending the course of events onto a desired path." Hand, Robert. *Horoscope Symbols*, Chpt. 10, "The Crosses and Quadruplicities."

9. Hall, Chpt. 3, "The Qualities and Polarities"
10. Hand, Chpt. 10, "The Signs: An Introduction."
11. Hall, Chpt. 3, "The Qualities and Polarities."
12. Hand, Chpt. 10,"The Signs: An Introduction."
13. Rudhyar, Chpt. 7, "The Signs of the Zodiac."
14. Arroyo, Chpt. 3, "The Four Elements and the Twelve Signs."
15. Hand, Chpt. 10, "The Signs: An Introduction."
16. Woolfolk, Glossary.
17. Hall, Chpt. 3, "The Qualities and Polarities."
18. Orion, Rae. *Astrology for Dummies*, Chpt. 1, Table 1-2, "An Astrological Overview: The Horoscope in Brief." These are nothing more than Stephen Arroyo's "twelve primary patterns of energy" described above.
19. Rudhyar, Chpt. 4, "A Key to Astrological Symbolism."
20. *Ibid.*

9

Fields of View

If we want to know a person as a whole, we must therefore
approach his birth chart in a whole act of perception. What
strikes us at first is the gestalt (or overall configuration) of
the chart: i.e., how it looks as a whole. If we learn to look
intently enough the chart-as-a-whole may "speak" to us.[1]
Dane Rudhyar, *Person Centered Astrology*

I woke up today thinking about a film I saw many years ago
called *Powers of Ten*. Charles and Ray Eames created it in 1971
while working as project designers at IBM Corporation's
Chicago headquarters.[2] The film starts with a couple having
a picnic on Chicago's lakefront on a gorgeous day in early
October. The narrator tells us that the first camera shot is
taken one meter above the couple, creating a one-meter-
square field of view, and that every ten seconds the camera
will withdraw above the couple by a power of one, creating
a field of view ten times wider. So we go from a one-meter-
wide field of view at 10 meters away, to a 10-meter-wide field
of view at 10^1 meters away, to a 100-meter-wide field of view
at 10^2 meters away, and so on, until we reach a field of view
that is 10,000 million light years wide at 10^{24} meters away. As
the camera withdraws farther and farther, not only does the

couple on the blanket disappear, but so does the Earth and the Moon, the Sun and its orbiting planets, indeed the entire Milky Way galaxy, which becomes just one more speck among billions of other galaxies.

What happens next is what got me thinking about this film in the first place: the camera begins to retrace its steps back to Earth and to the couple on the blanket, only with a twist. The camera doesn't stop at the couple on the blanket, but continues another 10^{24} meters into the subatomic molecular structure of their bodies. The re-entry process is quite speedy, and what's really interesting about this is that whether you're 10^{24} meters above the couple or 10^{24} meters inside of them, it all looks the same.

Pollux: It's the macrocosm/microcosm thing.

Author: Yes, it's the macrocosm/microcosm thing. Or another way of saying it is there are two "pictures" astrologers pay attention to when analyzing a birth chart: the "big picture" and the "little picture." In terms of the big picture, before astrologers dig into the information contained in a chart, they often view the chart at arm's length, so they can see it more holistically. This objective, holistic view helps them see the big picture, which is the overall configuration of a chart's planets distributed around its center. Astrologers give these configurations or "pictures" names.

Castor: Like cat, rabbit, and skateboard?

Author: Not exactly, more like bundle, bowl, seesaw, and splay. They're looking for very specific patterns, patterns that tell them something about the individual in question. These pictures are often referred to as unaspected chart patterns."[3]

Castor: What do you mean "unaspected?"

Author: In order to understand the term "unaspected,"
you have to know what an "aspect" is. Quite simply (though
nothing is simple in astrology), it is the number of degrees
between two planets, and by "planets" I mean any celestial
body or point that an astrologer deems important when
creating a natal chart. So an "unaspected chart pattern" is a
global or holistic view of the birth chart without any concern
for the angular relationships between two or more planets. In
short, the difference between an unaspected view (the "big
picture") and an aspected view (the "little picture") is the
difference between a view that is *aesthetic*, i.e., visual, and one
that is *angular*, i.e., mathematical.

Castor: I think that makes sense.

Author: Good, because it's just about to get a little more
complicated. There are really three pictures or views: *global*
views (unaspected chart patterns), *regional* views (multi-
planet aspect patterns), and *local* views (bi-planet aspects, the
building blocks of multi-planet aspect patterns).[4]

Castor: I think you just lost me.

Author: For instance, an unaspected chart pattern called
a bundle might have an aspect pattern within it called a
T-square, which in turn is made up of several bi-planet aspects.
In other words, whereas a bundle is primarily a visual pattern
made by all of the planets in a chart (i.e., the global "big
picture" perspective), a T-square is an aspect pattern made
up of a handful of planets within the larger unaspected chart
pattern (i.e., the regional "little picture" perspective). Aspect
patterns, in turn, are made up of individual aspects (i.e., the

local "little picture" perspective). In the case of a T-square, it is an "opposition" (180°) between two planets, bisected by another planet at a perpendicular angle that creates two "squares" (90°) to the planets in opposition. In other words, the opposition and two squares, each of which is an aspect, combine to make a larger multi-planet aspect pattern. Along with planets, signs, and houses, aspects and aspect patterns contribute to a fuller understanding of the natal chart. At least that's according to Rae Orion: "To comprehend the true complexity of an astrological chart, you need to know how the planets interact with each other. That information is revealed by the mathematical angles, or aspects, between the planets."[5]

Castor: It kind of makes sense. But where do we start?

Author: We start with global unaspected chart patterns.

Pollux: The "big picture."

Author: The big picture because that's where most astrologers start when they first pick up a birth chart. To understand this level of analysis, let me turn to astrologer Glenn Mitchell, author of *Discover the Aspect Pattern in Your Birth Chart*. A serious student of astrology who's studied with some of the best astrologers in the world, Mitchell explores the work of Marc Edmund Jones, Robert Jansky, and Bil Tierney, three noted astrologers who've done extensive work on planetary patterns. Mitchell underscores the importance of looking at the big picture when he writes, "A natal chart must be seen as a whole before an intelligent understanding of its parts is possible."[6] The "whole" that Mitchell is talking about is the different visual patterns that planets make around the natal chart, patterns that reflect basic psychological drives and motivations, and which, in their totality, suggest an individual's characteristic response to the world. Mitchell identifies eight such patterns, seven of which are original to Marc Edmund Jones's work in the early 1940s. Let's start with the "splash," which, according to Astro-Databank's natal chart database, is a chart pattern that appears rather infrequently.[7]

Castor: Splash? Are we going to a water park?

Author: Not this time of year, but let me ask you, What happens when water splashes about?

Castor: It gets all over the place.

Author: And that's what this planetary pattern does. A splash is created when planets are "splashed" all over the place; that is, they are distributed more or less evenly around the birth chart. Let's start, however, with Dane Rudhyar's generic definition of a shape or form: form is something that arises out of "the specific arrangement of the elements constituting, in their interdependent state of togetherness, a definite whole."[8]

Castor: Say what?

Author: Yes, I know, Rudhyar's not the easiest writer to understand, but let's keep going. Rudhyar adds the caveat that if the component factors in a group are found evenly distributed throughout the whole, something more ideal than realistic in a natal chart (probably why a splash is quite rare), then the whole has no internal pattern. According to Rudhyar, it is more a *plenum*, i.e., a fullness of interrelated activities with no accentuated parts, than a definable form. In other words, pattern emerges "when the distribution is uneven, and one or more zones of concentration is found, balanced in some manner by zones of emptiness."[9]

Castor: Ooh, "zones of emptiness." I like that.

Author: In a splash, however, there are very few zones of emptiness. According to Mitchell, you'll never find two empty houses or signs adjacent to each other (empty of planets, that is). But you will find a handful of oppositions with no more than one planet in the same house or sign. When we talk of planets, we're talking about ten basic celestial bodies: the Sun, the Moon, Mercury, Venus, Mars, Jupiter, Saturn, Uranus, Neptune, and Pluto (no asteroids, no parts, no midpoints, or nodes in this group). In the case of a splash, the order is irrelevant, since the somewhat equal distribution of planets around the chart precludes a leading or trailing planet, planets astrologers call "high-focus" planets. It's pretty apparent that my chart has no splash of planets, at least as defined above, so let's move on to the next picture: the "locomotive."

Castor: *Locomotive?* I thought we were talking about planets.

Author: We are, and how they distribute themselves around the natal chart. When it comes to the locomotive, this pattern is formed when planets are more or less perfectly spread across two-thirds of the chart, which is equivalent to nine consecutive signs. Think of it as a splash that has been squeezed into a smaller space, giving more form to the planetary lineup, a lineup that has an engine (the leading planet) and a caboose (the trailing planet), both of which are important indicators of the type of energy the individual might have. In general, however, it's the leading planet—the engine pulling the planetary train around the birth chart— that's of particular interest. When coupled with house and sign position, the leading or "high-focus" planet will show the part of the individual's personality that is the motivating force, as well as the type of experiences he or she is most likely to seek out. Which brings us to the question, Do the planets in my chart form a locomotive?

Castor: I don't think so, there are too many signs and houses without planets.

Author: Very observant, Castor, so let's move on to the "bowl."

Castor: Speaking of bowl, I'm hungry.

Pollux: Pay attention, Castor.

Author: That's all right, I think my stomach's growling as well. To get a bowl pattern, all we have to do is squeeze the locomotive pattern a little more, so the planets in a chart fall within five or six consecutive signs, or one half of the chart. In the most ideal situation, the bowl is "sealed" by an opposition of two planets on either side of the bowl's rim. Given the more tightly spaced planetary lineup, a bowl person is usually someone who is driven, who has intense energy, who knows where they're going and how they're going to get there.

Pollux: Didn't we talk about this pattern earlier?

Author: How so?

Pollux: Something about hemispheres?

Author: When a bowl pattern is rimmed by either the horizon or the meridian, we have a special type of bowl—a hemispheric bowl. When defined by the horizon, the horizontal axis of consciousness, an "upper bowl" person tends to be extroverted, social in nature, and career-driven, whereas a "lower bowl" person tends to be more self-contained, introverted, and private in nature, sometimes painfully so. On the other hand, when the bowl is defined by the meridian, the vertical axis of power, a person with an "eastern bowl" on the left-hand side of the chart often is strong-willed and assertive, whereas a person with a "western bowl" on the right-hand side of the chart is more relationship oriented, sensitive to the nuances of their environment. In either case, the rim of opposition runs through either the horizon (Ascendant/Descendant) or the meridian (Midheaven/Imum Coeli).

Pollux: Do you have a bowl chart?

Author: On first appearance it seems so, doesn't it? Nine of my planets are contained within five consecutive signs, that's approximately 150°. So, yes, it appears that I have a bowl, not only that, it's a hemispheric bowl in the lower part of my chart. But what about Jupiter that sits nearby, just outside of the bowl's rim in eleventh-house Aries? How do we account for that?

Pollux: Can't you just count it as part of the bowl?

Author: It depends on where you draw the bowl's rim. If you draw it from first-house Mercury to an "empty" seventh house to create a northern hemispheric bowl, then Jupiter is over 50° from the eastern edge of the bowl. That's way too far to consider Jupiter part of the bowl. But if you draw the bowl's rim following the opposition between eleventh-house Jupiter and fifth-house Neptune, then Jupiter becomes part of the bowl.

Pollux: But where does that leave fifth-house Moon which is slightly outside of that opposition?

Author: Excellent question. Since the Moon is just under nine degrees beyond Neptune and the bowl's western rim, the question becomes, Is the Moon "conjunct" Neptune?

Castor: Moon conjunct Neptune?

Author: Remember when we talked earlier about astrology being a language of symbols with a lexicon and a grammar or syntax. Think of "Moon conjunct Neptune" as a grammatical statement that says that the position of the Moon and Neptune in my chart are such that they form a conjunction, i.e., a relationship in which there is hardly any separation.

Pollux: But they are separated, by almost nine degrees.

Author: Which means we have to determine if nine degrees is an acceptable "orb of influence."[10]

Castor: Orb of influence?

Author: Think of it as the margin of error that statisticians talk about when they report the results of a survey. When they give you a statistic like, "Folks with Gemini Rising with Mars and Mercury in the first house talk 85% of the time"...

Pollux: Gee, I wonder who that could be?

Castor: Don't look at me.

Author: When you hear that, statisticians usually follow it up with something like "plus or minus 3," meaning that the number they're talking about isn't 85% exactly, it's really somewhere between 82-88%. It's the same with astrology. When we say that a bowl pattern can't exceed 180°, what we really mean is that it can't exceed 180° plus its "orb of influence," which are those extra degrees that astrologers allow as a kind of margin of error. In order for the Moon to

be part of the bowl, it would have to share the same space,
i.e., be conjunct, with Neptune, which means that we have to
look up the accepted orb of influence for a conjunction.[11] As it
turns out, the orb of influence for a conjunction is between 5°
and 10° (depending upon who's doing the counting), which
means that the Moon can be considered conjunct Neptune,
but just by a hair's breadth.

Pollux: Which means you have a bowl chart pattern.

Author: It appears that way, doesn't it. But let's hold off on
that assessment for a moment and let me talk about several
other planetary patterns. Next up, the "bundle."

Castor: Bundle? Isn't that a bunch of sticks tied together?

Author: In this case, it's planets. Think of a bundle as a
bowl of planets squeezed together even more tightly. In other
words, it's a group of planets that are squeezed together or
contained within 120° of each other, which is no more than
four consecutive signs apart.

Pollux: Wait a minute. With each new planetary pattern
you've introduced the amount of space that holds the planets
keeps getting smaller: *splash*, the entire chart; *locomotive*,
three-quarters of the chart; *bowl*, half of the chart; and *bundle*,
a third of the chart.

Author: Excellent observation, Pollux.

Pollux: What happens when you run out of space?

Author: What happens is what happens when you
squeeze something too tightly—things begin to pop out. But
first, a few words about people with a bundle chart pattern.
Whereas people with a bowl pattern can be intensely focused
and driven, people with a bundle pattern can be borderline

obsessive, since their range of focus is more limited in scope, confined to the spheres of life related to the third of the chart in which their planets reside. On a positive note, people with a bundled planetary distribution tend to be tenacious, single-minded, focused, and usually very self-contained, that is if their obsessiveness doesn't drive them—and others—crazy. Now let's move on. Remember what I said comes next?

Castor: Squeeze too hard and things pop out, but I'm not sure what you're talking about.

Author: If you squeeze something too tightly, something is bound to give, and when it does it often pops out, to free itself. That's the "seesaw."

Castor: I love seesaws.

Author: How does a seesaw work?

Castor: Well, there's a ...I think it's called a fulcrum, over which a board is balanced. A person sits at either end of the board and together they teeter up and down, sometimes fast, sometimes slowly.

Author: Which gives the seesaw its other name.

Pollux: Teeter-totter.

Author: The basic premise Castor has identified is that two groups of "things" balance each other. When it comes to your horoscope, a seesaw is composed of two groups of planets that balance each other on opposite sides of the chart. The two groups of opposing planets are separated by a couple of empty houses on either side of them. Because the two groups oppose each other, you can expect a number of oppositions (180° separation) among the opposing groups (and also a lot of personal contradictions within the individual). But as Rudhyar warns us, we should not think of the symbolic image of a seesaw "as implying necessarily a constant shifting of activity from one end to the other, though it may be what takes place within the consciousness of a person born with such a type of planetary pattern."[12] According to Rudhyar, it all depends on how the ten planets are divided. Are there five planets on one side and five on the other? Or three planets on one side and seven on the other? The distribution of planets on either side of the chart's midpoint will largely determine the amount of "seesawing" back and forth an individual does related to important issues in their life.

Castor: As much as I like seesaws, I don't think your chart is a seesaw.

Pollux: I don't think so either.

Author: You're both correct: no seesawing in my chart. But we still have three more planetary patterns to explore. Next up, the "splay." If when we squeeze the planets in a chart too tightly and get a seesaw, then all we have to do is squeeze it a little harder to get a splay. Any idea what a splay looks like?

Castor: Not a clue.

Pollux: When something's splayed, it means it's pulled or split apart.

Author: Yes, but in this case, instead of splitting into two groups (as in a seesaw), a splay is split into three groups. Technically, that's three groups of planets of two signs each with two empty signs in between. Of course, this is the ideal distribution; some charts might have a planet or two that stray from this ideal. Visually, a splay looks like the base of a tripod, generally a very stable pattern. However, with three tight planetary groups spread somewhat equally around the natal chart, this pattern has the effect of spreading out the interests of the individual, albeit within a confined amount of houses or areas of interest in the individual's life. In other words, the person has the propensity for being skilled at more than one thing, given the planetary intensity within each of the three tight-knit groups, but focus might be a problem.

Pollux: You're not a splay, are you?

Author: No, I'm not, and that leaves two more planetary patterns to consider, each one related to a pattern we've already discussed. The first is the "fan," which is nothing more than a bundle with one planet (or two in tight conjunction) opposing the midpoint of the bundled planetary group. In other words, it's a bundle with a handle. Even though it uses the basic bundle form, at least in its base, the energy of a fan is quite different from a bundle because the energy contained in the bundled planetary group (the fan's base) is released through the opposing planet (the fan's "handle"), which astrologers call a planetary "singleton."[13]

Castor: Since it stands by itself.

Author: Yes, but not only that: since it stands by itself, it's of particular interest to astrologers as a high-focus planet, a planet that demands attention. The singleton literally points to the area in life—to a specific chart house—that the individual needs to pay attention to and to which the bundled planets's energies are directed. In other words, the fan is one of the more intense planetary patterns of the whole group.

Castor: Speaking of intense, this is intense. When can we take a break?

Author: Soon. We only have one more chart pattern to discuss—the "bucket."

Castor: Sounds exciting.

Author: If a fan is a bundle with a handle, a bucket is simply a bowl with a handle.

Castor: *Bucket. Bundle. Bowl.* You're giving me a headache.

Author: Sorry, but we're almost through. Dane Rudhyar calls the bucket pattern a "funnel" since the isolated planet—the singleton—acts like a funnel channeling the energies of the opposing bowl planets. Rudhyar goes on to say that the image of a funnel is most appropriate when the isolated planet is in opposition to the midpoint of the bowl planets on the other side of the chart: "The power generated within the grouping of the nine planets is brought to a focus in a thin stream which is released through the narrow opening of the funnel."[14] In other words, the singleton is the object of intense focus because the power of all the other planets is concentrated and released at the point of the single, isolated planet. In an ideal bucket, the handle planet will make a Grand Cross (that's one of those regional aspect patterns we still have to discuss) with opposition planets on either side of the bowl's rim (assuming there is such an opposition). Furthermore, whereas the leading planet is the high-focus planet in a bowl pattern, the singleton or "handle" is the high-focus planet in a bucket pattern.

Pollux: What's a bucket person like?

Author: An individual with a bucket chart tends to be self-contained, as you might expect from the related bowl pattern. But unlike a bowl person who can compromise with others, a bucket person has a harder time of it. He or she tends to be extremely goal oriented, capable of focusing considerable energy on achieving specific aims with an uncompromising and single-minded determination. And watch the handle: the sign and house position will show you how and in what area of life this effort is likely too be directed.[15] Individuals with a bucket chart can be highly productive, unwavering in their focus, but they can also be very hard to deal with, especially if they resist compromise too strongly, by which they risk alienating those around them. This brings us to the end of our tour of unaspected chart patterns, i.e., the big picture. Before we move on, I wonder what you'd call the pattern in my chart—a splash, a locomotive, a bowl, a bundle, a seesaw, a splay, a fan, a bucket? Castor, how about you, any ideas?

Castor: Me? Can't Pollux go first?

Author: Pollux, what do you think?

Pollux: I think Castor should go first, that's what I think.

Castor: Okay, I'll take a stab at it. But I'd rather start by telling you what you're not. You're not a splash. You're not a splay. You're not a locomotive or a seesaw, and you're not a bundle, which means you're not a fan. So, you're either a bowl or a bucket.

Author: Excellent, Castor, I'm impressed. But which one am I? Pollux, your turn.

Pollux: Well, I think you have a bowl chart with a rim opposition between Jupiter and Neptune, allowable because Moon conjunct Neptune is within an acceptable orb of influence.

Author: Well done, both of you. To double check this assessment, I did a few things before we got started. First of all, I took out my natal chart and scoured it, looking for any hints from the computer-analyst-qua-astrologer who did my chart. Next, I emailed the chart to a friend of mine named Loren who teaches classes in astrology and asked her what she thought.[16]

Castor: What did you find out?

Author: I found out that astrology, like life, isn't an exact science: astrologers vary in their opinions like the rest of us. Regarding my chart, it took a while but on the second page I found the following note scrawled in the margin: "Bucket chart with Jupiter as handle (upper half)."

Castor: We were right. It's a bucket.

Author: Maybe, maybe not. The email I received from Loren contradicted this assessment. According to her, I have a bowl chart.

Castor: So which is it—a bucket or a bowl?

Author: Let's ring up Loren and see what she has to say about this… Hello, Loren, we have a question for you. Is the chart pattern in my horoscope a bucket or a bowl?

Loren: I think it's pretty clear that you have a bowl pattern, and here's why. You have a very strong rim opposition between eleventh-house Jupiter in Aries and a fifth-house Neptune/Moon conjunction in Libra. All of your other planets fall below this rim opposition, which is a sure sign of a bowl. According to Astro-Databank, one in ten people have a bowl pattern, which must meet these criteria: (1) all ten planets should be within 180° of the natal chart; (2) the two planets at the far edges of the pattern should form a rim opposition of approximately 180°; (3) the planets within the bowl should be spaced in a roughly even distribution, with none separated by more than 60° from the others; and (4) in most instances the leading planet should be considered the high-focus planet.[17] In terms of a rim opposition, when it exceeds 180° the planetary pattern will remain a bowl as long as the orb of influence for an opposition is not exceeded. However, when the accepted orb of influence is exceeded, then the bowl pattern begins to look like a bucket.

Pollux: Which is why the astrologer who originally cast your chart thought your chart pattern was a bucket.

Author: That's quite reasonable.

Loren: If the astrologer had drawn the rim opposition in your chart between Jupiter and Neptune (recognizing Moon conjunct Neptune), he would have quickly seen that you have a bowl chart. Individuals who have a bowl pattern tend to be rather self-contained, but that self-containment diminishes with the absence of a rim opposition. Fortunately, your chart has such an opposition, which helps you find balance in your life (theoretically, that is). How well balanced you are depends on how evenly distributed the planets are within the bowl portion of your chart. In your case, they are evenly spread out in five of six houses. Something else to consider: although, technically, you don't have a hemispheric bowl (all planets in either the top, bottom, left, or right half of your chart), you almost do. Nine of your ten planets are evenly distributed below the horizon line, with only eleventh-house Jupiter in Aries above it.

Pollux: What does that mean?

Loren: There's a couple of things to think about. First of all, let me address the nine planets below the horizon. As you learned earlier, individuals with a bowl pattern tend to be self-contained; that is, they make their own way in the world to their own satisfaction. The sense of self-containment is maximized when the planets are in the bottom of the chart, which is the northern portion of the chart. Think of it as a bowl that is upright and can't spill its contents, which makes the individual more self-contained and usually quite introverted. According to Robert Jansky, the individual is likely to be a "collector," one who goes about collecting experiences and storing them up.[18] For this individual, privacy is of upmost importance. Not only that, since the northern hemisphere involves the first six houses, the houses of early development and family, the individual has a higher chance of experiencing unfinished business from his or her childhood.

Author: Loren, could you talk about my eleventh-house Jupiter in Aries since it's the only planet above the horizon?

Loren: Think of the planets in your bowl as a parade with eleventh-house Jupiter the parade's lead planet. Since Jupiter leads the parade of planets clockwise around the natal chart, we give it more prominence among the family of planets. But that's not all, referring to Jansky again, if the leading planet is the only planet in a particular hemisphere, it becomes a "singleton in hemisphere" and gains quite an influence over the individual.[19] In your chart, Jupiter is a singleton in hemisphere since it's the only planet above the horizon line. When we combine the two—leading planet of your bowl pattern and singleton in hemisphere—Jupiter's influence is magnified. In short, it's one of your chart's high-focus planets, except...

Castor: Except?

Loren: Except the rim opposition of the bowl is part of a T-square with Uranus the squared planet.

Pollux: What does that mean?

Castor: It means it's time for a break.

Notes

1. Rudhyar, Dane. *Person Centered Astrology*, Chpt. 15, "The 'Signature' of the Whole Person."

2. Eames, Charles and Ray Eames. *Powers of Ten*, IBM Corporation of America, 1971.

3. While some astrologers use the term "unaspected chart patterns," I prefer "global non-aspected chart patterns," the difference being that "unaspected" could simply mean that there are no consequential aspected planets in the pattern, whereas "non-aspected" refers to the fact that no aspects are considered at all.

4. Following up on the last footnote, "global," "regional," and "local" are terms I employ to distinguish between unaspected chart patterns (global in nature) and aspected planetary patterns (regional multi-planet aspect patterns and local bi-planet aspects).

5. Orion, Rae. *Astrology for Dummies*, Chpt. 13, "Amazing Aspects: The Secrets of Cosmic Geometry."

6. Mitchell, Glenn. *Discover the Aspect Pattern in Your Birth Chart*, Introduction.

7. Astro-Databank is a freely accessible wiki website containing a collection of astrological data (i.e., birth details and associated birth charts of public figures and mundane events) that was started in 1971 by astrologer and astrological data compiler Lois Rodden. The

database rates eight planetary patterns from least to most frequently appearing: *splash* (0.59), *bundle* (1.54), *fan* (2.93), *bucket* (7.58), *bowl* (10.42), *seesaw* (13.89), *splay* (15.63), and *locomotive* (31.25), [URL] https://www.astro.com/astro-databank.

8. Rudhyar, Chpt. 15, "The 'Signature' of the Whole Person."

9. *Ibid.*

10. The "orb of influence" is a term applied to the exactness of an aspect. Orbs vary depending upon several factors: the planet, the aspect, and the astrologer. The entry for "Orb of Influence" in James Lewis's *The Astrology Book: The Encyclopedia of Heavenly Influences* reads: "Few aspects are ever exact (exact aspects are referred to as partile aspects). For this reason, astrologers speak of the orb—or the orb of influence—within which specific aspects are effective. For a sextile, or 60° angle, for example, many astrologers use a 6° orb in a natal chart, which means that if any two planets are making an angle (with respect to earth as the vertex) anywhere in the 54°-66° range, then they are regarded as making a sextile aspect with each other" (p. 503). The entry ends by noting that major aspects, as well as important celestial bodies like the Sun and the Moon, are given larger orbs than minor ones.

11. Robert Hand offers this guidance concerning acceptable orbs of influence: "Most traditional astrologers simply divide the aspects into major and minor. The major aspects, the conjunction, opposition, trine, square, and sextile, are all given the same, usually large orb, about 10°. Minor aspects, if used, are given varying orbs, commonly about 2°. The 10° orb is mainly a holdover from Renaissance astrology. Modern astrologers tend to cut orbs down to 7° or 8°, and a growing number now use even smaller orbs, 5° or less on the major aspects, 1° or less on the minors. Hand, Robert. *Horoscope Symbols,* Chpt. 6, "The Aspects: Introduction."

12. Rudhyar, Chpt. 15, "The 'Signature' of the Whole Person."

13. Mitchell, Chpt. 4, "The Fan."

14. Rudhyar, Chpt. 15, "The 'Signature' of the Whole Person."

15. Mitchell, Chpt. 6, "The Bucket."
16. Loren's part in this dialogue is an amalgamation of "voices" or perspectives gleaned from several sources. First of all, Sarah Pickett, who teaches astrology at Chicago's Discovery Center and offers private consultations under the name "Sarandipity," [URL] www.facebook.com/sarandipitythechicagoastrologer. Secondly, the results of several online websites that analyzed my natal chart using digital software. These include: *Astro Charts* [URL] astro-charts.com; *Astro Dienst* [URL] www.astro.com; *Astrolabe* [URL] alabe.com; *Astrology Cafe* [URL] www.astrologycafe.com; *Cafe Astrology* [URL] cafeastrology.com; and *Just Astrology Things* [URL] justastrologythings.com.
17. Mitchell, Chpt. 5, "The Bowl."
18. *Ibid.*
19. *Ibid.*

10

N/1, N/2, N/3, N/4, N/5

> Astrology deals with projective geometry, meaning distances
> to celestial bodies are inconsequential. Only their relative
> positions on the celestial sphere are important. In other
> words, only the angular differences from the Earth matter.[1]
> Kevin Heng Ser Guan, *The Mathematics of Astrology*

Unaspected and aspected patterns in a birth chart hinge
on the meaning of the word "aspect." We've seen that this
is the angular distance from one chart factor to another,
whether those factors be planets, points, nodes, or what have
you. This brings us to consider the difference between the
words "angle" and "aspect." For many astrologers there is no
difference: just as the Rising sign and Ascendant are often
used interchangeably, so too are the terms angle and aspect.
This doesn't sit too well with astrologer Robert Hand. He
suggests that the term "aspect" is more appropriately used to
denote one of the four principal mundane points in the birth
chart (i.e., Ascendant, Midheaven, Descendant, and Imum
Coeli), and that the term "angle" be applied specifically to
the angular or mathematical relationship between planets
on a chart.[2] I'm not sure I buy into this strict interpretation.
I don't mind using either term to represent the same thing

as long as we understand that in either case we are talking about a mathematical relationship and a relationship of meaning. For instance, when we say Mercury square Mars, what we are saying is that Mercury and Mars are at a 90° angle to each other *and* that their relationship can be characterized as hard or difficult. Because of this, I prefer the term "aspect" when talking about planetary angles, as it implies both a mathematical relationship and a relationship of meaning. Let's turn to a deeper understanding of these building blocks of chart analysis: aspects created by the angular distance between two planets.[3]

Castor: Two planets? How can you have an angle between two planets? Don't you need a third planet to make an angle?

Author: Excellent question, Castor. And what do you think that third planet might be?

Castor: The Sun?

Author: If we were using a Sun-centered or heliocentric system, I'd agree. But we're not. Astrology, like some forms of astronomy (for instance, how to land a spaceship on the Moon), uses an Earth-centered or geocentric system.

Pollux: So the third planet is Earth.

Author: Smack dab in the center of the birth chart, for that's what the center represents, planet Earth, and by implication the natus, the one born. It is the implied third factor in the relationship between two celestial bodies. This is an important point to remember because any cycle of relationship between two celestial bodies exists only in reference to Earth. The Earth is not only the endpoint or "vertex" where the rays emanating from two planets meet, but it is from Earth that planetary aspects not only are observed, but also become meaningful.

Pollux: What's the largest angle possible between two planets?

Castor: 360°.

Author: Why do you say that?

Castor: Because that's the number of degrees in a circle.

Author: You're right and you're wrong. You're right because there are 360° in a circle, which in astrology is the ecliptic represented by the outer circle or wheel of the birth chart. You're wrong because the largest angular distance between two planets (with Earth as the vertex) is 180° or half of 360°.

Castor: Why half?

Author: It's in the nature of the cyclical process of any planetary relationship. The entire process, which covers the 360° of the ecliptic is best understood as two related processes: what happens between 0° and 180° and what happens between 180° and 360°. In other words, what happens during the hemicycle—i.e., half-cycle—of conjunction to opposition and, conversely, what happens during the hemicycle of opposition to conjunction. The former being a process of expansion or potential (what Rudhyar calls the "involutionary" process); the latter, a process of contraction or release (what Rudhyar calls the "evolutionary" process).[4]

One of the most visible examples of this process is the lunation of the Moon as seen from Earth, from one New Moon to the next. Like any celestial cycle, lunation is a cycle of relationship. Rudhyar considers it the "archetype" of all cycles involving the relationship between two celestial bodies moving at different speeds.⁵ The reason lunation begins with the New Moon is precisely because it begins the expansion or waxing process experienced from Earth by the physical changes of the Moon's shape during the first of two hemicycles. The first lunar hemicycle includes New Moon, Waxing Crescent, First Quarter, Waxing Gibbous, and Full Moon. Once the Moon reaches culmination during the Full Moon phase, the process reverses itself and we experience the second hemicycle, the contraction or waning process, which includes Full Moon, Waning Gibbous, Third Quarter, Waning Crescent, and New Moon.

Pollux: It's kind of like breathing—in and out, in and out.

Author: Yes, very much so—expansion/contraction, expansion/contraction. The reason that Rudhyar and others use the lunation of the Moon as a visible example of the cyclical nature of a planetary relationship is because we clearly "see" the major aspects of the Sun/Moon relationship: New Moon (conjunction), First Quarter (square), Full Moon (opposition), Third Quarter (square), and New Moon (conjunction). Although we don't see these in every planetary pairing, they are implicit in every relationship. Unfortunately, understanding planetary aspects is a complicated affair. There are well over a dozen major and minor aspects. Here are a few in just the first 90° of the first hemicycle: conjunction (0°), semisextile (30°), decile (36°), semisquare or octile (45°), sextile (60°), quintile (72°), and square or quartile (90°). And this is just half of a hemicycle, or a quarter of the full cycle. How many aspects are there in total? Which ones are important? Which ones can we ignore?

Castor: I think you're starting to put me to sleep.

Author: I know, but this is an important topic. So let's start with one of the easiest ways to understand and remember planetary aspects—the "sign" continuum.

Castor: As in stop sign?

Author: As in signs of the zodiac. But first, we have to do a little math.

Castor: Of course.

Author: Let's take 180°—one hemicycle—and draw it as a line rather than a half-circle. Now let's mark off six equal segments. How many degrees would each segment have?

Castor: Thirty.

Pollux: Thirty as in 30° per zodiacal sign.

Author: Yes, so starting with 0°, let's count off the segments.

Castor and Pollux: 0°, 30°, 60°, 90°, 120°, 150°, 180°.

Author: You have just marked the cusp of the first six signs of the zodiac along with seven planetary aspects.

Castor: Seven?

Author: Yes, because we count 0° (conjunction) as the first aspect. Now using signs rather than angles, we can count seven important aspects: conjunction (same sign), semisextile (one sign apart), sextile (two signs apart), square (three signs apart), trine (four signs apart), quincunx (five signs apart), and opposition (six signs apart).[6]

Castor: You mean all we have to remember is how many signs one planet is from another?

Author: Yes, it's that easy. It's just not that accurate, because it doesn't allow for orbs of influence. Say you have a planet at the beginning of one sign and a second planet at the end of the sign adjacent to it? Are the planets one sign apart (semisextile) or are they two signs apart (sextile)?

Pollux: I see what you mean.

Author: Yes, so as you can see, the sign continuum is at best a handy instructional aid, which means that most astrologers don't use it in their natal chart interpretations. This brings us to the next approach—the "degree" continuum. It differs from the sign continuum in only one respect: instead of signs, the continuum uses degrees to define the limits of an aspect (which makes it more mathematically accurate). As we did above, we can identify seven aspects, each one defined by the degrees of separation between two heavenly bodies: conjunction (0°), semisextile (30°), sextile (60°), square (90°), trine (120°), quincunx (150°), and opposition (180°).

When asked what are the most important aspects in a birth chart, astrologers usually identify five: conjunction (0°), sextile (60°), square (90°), trine (120°), and opposition (180°). These are derived by dividing the 360° of the ecliptic by one, two, three, four, and six, which are the first five divisors of the number twelve. In doing this, we arrive at the "classical" or Ptolemaic aspects, codified in the second century CE by Claudius Ptolemy using the work of earlier Babylonian and Greek astrologers.[7]

Pollux: What about semisextile (30°) and quincunx (150°)? Why aren't they considered important aspects?

Castor: Probably because people couldn't pronounce them.

N/1, N/2, N/3, N/4, N/5

Author: That's a good guess. But let's return to our lineup of important aspects and do some math. We start with 360° divided by one, which equals...

Pollux: Three hundred and sixty.

Author: Or zero, since we're talking about the beginning of the zodiac. What this means is that the most important aspect is conjunction (0°). Let's do the next math problem. What is 360° divided by two?

Pollux: One hundred and eighty.

Author: Which means that the next most important aspect is...

Castor: Opposition.

Author: By extension, we can fill out the sequence: 360°/3 = 120° (trine), 360°/4 = 90° (square), and 360°/6 = 60° (sextile). This process gives us the five most important aspects in order of importance: conjunction (0°), opposition (180°), trine (120°), square (90°), and sextile (60°). We also have the answer to Pollux's question above, about the omission of semisextile (30°) and quincunx (150°).

Pollux: They're not derived by dividing 360 by one of twelve's divisors.

Author: It all boils down to math, doesn't it? But then numbers were seen as an expression of the universal Logos in the early days of astrology. And just as numbers express relationships, aspects do the same. According to Dane Rudhyar, each segment or step, from conjunction (0°) to opposition (180°), represents "a further stage of differentiation and complexification of the energy released at the beginning of the cycle." In other words, each subsequent aspect represents "a deeper advance of the creative will and idea into matter."[8]

Castor: I'm definitely falling asleep.

Author: Then let me wake you up with this. Returning to the number and types of planetary aspects an astrologer can work with, all of them are derived by dividing the 360° circle by small whole numbers, not all of them divisors of twelve. When we divide 360° by 1, 2, 3, 4, etc., we are establishing a mathematical progression. In this case, according to Robert Hand, a "harmonic series," the general form of which is as follows: N/1, N/2, N/3, N/4, N/5,...N/I, N/(I+1),..., where I is a series of integers or whole numbers from one to infinity. N can have any value, but in astrology it is 360.[9]

Castor: That didn't wake me up. It just made my eyes cross.

Author: What I'm trying to get at is the fact that beyond the five major aspects, based on dividing 360° by the number twelve's first five divisors, is that there are a number of other possibilities. By the Renaissance, astrologers began experimenting using different divisors. They divided by five, which yielded the quintile (360°/5 = 72°) and the biquintile (2 x 360°/5 = 144°). They divided by seven, which yielded the septile (360°/7 = 51°25'42.9"), the biseptile (2 x 360°/7 = 102°51'25.7"), and the triseptile (3 x 360°/7 = 154°17'08.6"). They also divided by eight, which yielded the semisquare or octile (360°/8 = 45°) and the sesquiquadrate or trioctile (3 × 360°/8 = 135°).

Castor: What do you divide by to get a crocodile?

Pollux: *Castor.*

Castor: Just kidding.

Author: Such divisions are also responsible for the semisextile (360°/12 = 30°) and the quincunx (5 × 360°/12 = 150°), which is why they are not considered as important as the other five aspects listed above.

Castor: But what does it all mean?

Author: Yes, I do think we are starting to get lost in the "hard-won glare of facts and indicators," so let's move on to the next continuum—the "major/minor" continuum. We already know the major aspects: conjunction, (0°) opposition (180°), trine (120°), square (90°), and sextile (60°). To that list, let's add the minor aspects: semisextile (30°), decile (36°), semisquare or octile (45°), quintile (72°), tridecile (108°), sesquiquartile or trioctile (135°), biquintile (144°), and quincunx or inconjunct (150°).[10]

Castor: What, no crocodile?

Author: As I said earlier, there is a wide array of aspects. Writing about what he calls the "Sabian symbols," early twentieth-century astrologer Marc Edmund Jones argued that there are 360 aspects, one for each degree in a circle.[11] Jones's thesis is expressed by Robert Hand in his book *Horoscope Symbols*: "The position of every point is usually projected onto the plane of the ecliptic and expressed as a particular degree and minute of celestial longitude. The horoscope is usually represented as a circle, with the person as the center, and the planets and other points...arranged around the circumference. Thus every point lies in some angular relationship to every other point in the chart."[12] Although true, to me it's a bit over the top, and also not necessarily helpful in the process of chart analysis.

Castor: Excuse me if I close my eyes for a minute.

Author: Stay with me a little longer; we're almost through. We have one more continuum to look at—the "attribute" continuum. This continuum classifies planetary aspects by their effect, separating them into two general categories: *harmonious* aspects (i.e., easy, flowing, or compatible) and *dynamic* aspects (i.e., hard, difficult, or challenging). Although several astrologers add a third category, i.e., *neutral* aspects, composed of only one aspect: conjunction. According to Yasmin Boland, a conjunction isn't an aspect, at least technically, because two planets standing side by side can't view each other. This is in keeping with the ancient idea that planets "glance" or "look at" each other (from which the word "aspect" is derived). Although most astrologers treat a conjunction as an aspect, what we really should be saying, according to Boland, is "conjunctions and aspects."[13]

Robert Hand would agree with Boland's point, only offering a different explanation. Hand divides aspects into three categories: conjunction, two-series aspects, and three-series aspects. Let's consider the last two categories first. The aspects in the two-series sequence, considered "hard" or "malefic," are derived by dividing 360° by multiples of two: $360°/2 = 180°$ (opposition), $360°/4 = 90°$ (square), $360°/8 = 45°$ (semisquare), etc. The aspects in the three-series sequence, considered "easy" or "benefic," are derived by dividing 360° by multiples of three: $360°/3 = 120°$ (trine), $360°/6 = 60°$ (sextile), $360°/12 = 30°$ (semisextile), etc. Although divisions by five, six, seven, etc., are also possible (and have been popular since Renaissance astrologers began experimenting with them), aspects in the two- and three-series sequences are the most important aspects in a birth chart. Notice, however, that conjunction starts, but is not part of, either series. According to Hand, this is because dividing 360 by one yields itself, i.e., a conjunction. Hence, according to Hand, conjunction should be considered a separate aspect, but not necessarily a neutral aspect, as it tends to signify "patterns of action rather than passive states of being."[14]

Castor: So there are three types of aspects?

Author: Theoretically, at least. However, since conjunctions are often lumped together with hard or difficult aspects given their inherent dynamic quality, most astrologers identify two broad types of aspects: easy, flowing, or harmonious aspects and difficult, dynamic, or hard aspects. The full range of harmonious aspects include the semisextile (30°), decile (36°), sextile (60°), quintile (72°), sesquiquartile (108°), trine (120°), and biquintile (144°). Stephen Arroyo says several things that might help us understand this type of aspect. First of all, harmonious aspects, especially sextiles and trines, tend to "correspond with spontaneous abilities, talents, and modes of understanding and expression" that an individual is able to utilize and develop with relative ease and consistency. According to Arroyo, these abilities constitute "a set of steady and reliable personal assets upon which the person may draw at any time."[15] The harmonious blending of the planetary energies involved demonstrates a sympathetic relationship, the one reinforcing the other within the individual's energy field, helping to foster a positive, sympathetic, and reinforcing tone. Of the two—trines and sextiles—Rae Orion suggests that the former is the more powerful aspect, and rightly so as it comes after conjunction and opposition in the lineup of five major planetary aspects.

Castor: What about hard or difficult aspects?

Author: Generally, hard aspects include opposition (180°), square (90°), semisquare (45°), sesquisquare (135°), and quincunx (150°), all of which are apparent in the lunation cycle. In the first hemicycle of that cycle we have New Moon to Waxing Crescent (45°, semisquare), New Moon to First Quarter (90°, square), New Moon to Waxing Gibbous (135°, sesquisquare), and New Moon to Full Moon (180°, opposition). It's the same for the second hemicycle, only with the phases of the waning Moon instead. In other words, in all of the major phases of the Moon, we have the expression of difficult or challenging aspects. Another reason why astrologers use the lunation cycle as a visual aid.

Pollux: What do dynamic aspects mean in terms of how they impact an individual?

Author: If you think about aspects in terms of vibration, you'd observe that dynamic aspects are those whose energies don't vibrate harmoniously. According to Arroyo, the planets involved tend to interfere with each other's expression, creating stress within their related energy field, "as if two energy waves were in a discordant relationship to each other, setting up what one might call an unstable or irritating tone."[16]

Castor: But what does it mean practically?

Author: Let's turn to Arroyo again, who offers this example: "A dynamic aspect between Mercury and Mars can manifest as an impatience (Mars) to communicate (Mercury), a strong drive (Mars) to learn (Mercury), the tendency to assert too forcefully (Mars) one's ideas and opinions (Mercury), an irritable nervous system, an overly critical nature, etc." However, if the inner tension is successfully controlled and directed, "such an individual may well be able to focus the tremendous drive toward learning into the development of exceptional skills which require keen intelligence."[17]

Castor: Like me.

Pollux: You certainly are challenging.

Author: According to April Elliott Kent, difficult or hard aspects symbolize an uneasy relationship between planets in signs that have little in common. The reason for this is that they're often in signs of the same quality (cardinal, fixed, or mutable), but of different elements (fire, earth, air, or water). In other words, they want some of the same things, but they go about them in very different ways, which means there are bound to be challenges, tensions, or inner conflicts, all of which need to be overcome.[18]

Pollux: Why is opposition the most difficult aspect?

Author: Think of an opposition as two planets looking at each other from opposite ends of a spectrum, vying for attention. Amy Herring sums up the dynamic of an opposition in this way: "Two planets opposing each other represent two parts of a person that may feel at odds with each other, contradicting each other or battling each other, each one sometimes trying to gain dominance but frequently caught in a tug of war or stalemate."[19] Although oppositions are generally challenging aspects, there is the potential for growth given that the oppositional planets are always in compatible elements:

air signs are always opposite fire signs, and water signs are always opposite earth signs. According to Yasmin Boland, although conflict is possible, even expected, "the potential for two planets in opposition is that, since they're in signs of complementary element, they can learn from each other how to develop the qualities they envy in one another."[20]

In *Essential Astrology*, Herring puts it in more concrete terms: "We've all felt the tension between knowing what we want and wanting to please ourselves, but also feeling an obligation to consider the desires of a person we care about. This is the very definition of compromise: we get a little of what we want, and the other person gets a little of what they want. When we have two planets in opposition in our natal chart, an internal compromise must be reached and continually revisited throughout our lives. It is the only way to ease the tension: by realizing that the tension is not the problem, but is only the warning signal..."[21] There's something else Herring says that I think is rather insightful. Although it might seem desirable to have more easy aspects than difficult ones, Herring asks us to consider this in terms of the impact on personal growth, noting that while it is human nature to ignore or take for granted what doesn't hurt or bother us, it is the dynamic or difficult aspects, while they may make us uncomfortable, that are more likely to compel us to decisive action.[22]

Herring relates this idea to Carl Jung's conflictual model of personal growth. Jung asks the question, How does consciousness arise? In Jung's scheme of things, it's when there are problems to solve. It's a cyclical process: a problem creates tension in the psyche, which in turn generates a creative response to solve the problem, which, then, relieves the mounting tension. Conversely, if there is no problem to solve, no intrapsychic tension, then we act naturally vis-a-vis instinct. In short, according to Herring's interpretation of Jung's dynamic model, "it is conflict, with its tendency to generate creativity and create consciousness, that drives our evolution, whereas instinct keeps things running smoothly but somewhat passively overall."[23]

Castor: Do you have a lot of conflict?

Author: I think you mean, Do I have a lot of dynamic aspects?

Castor: Isn't that what I said?

Author: Every chart has a combination of harmonious and dynamic aspects. Regarding my chart, I have over a dozen dynamic aspects (four conjunctions, five oppositions and five squares) and almost two dozen harmonious aspects (twelve trines and eight sextiles).[24]

Castor: Which means you're not going to grow?

Pollux: *Castor.*

Author: Which means that if I'm not careful, I tend to slide by on my...

Castor: Good looks?

Author: No, on my natural abilities. I'll give you an example from my experience as a writer. I've written many pieces over the last thirty years: essays, professional articles, academic books, fiction, nonfiction, as well as a number of children's books. Early in my career I worked on a book of poetry for the middle-grade reader. It was a series of poems that captured the ins and outs of professional baseball over the course of a year, from the first day

of spring training to the last out of the World Series. For each
"poem" I wrote a prose paragraph and then broke it up to look
like free verse. When I received the editor's letter of rejection,
aside from the usual niceties ("this isn't for us," "you might try
elsewhere," etc.), I noticed a handwritten note at the bottom of
the letter, which is usually a good sign—someone actually read
the piece. It said, rather succinctly: "No craft."

Pollux: What did she mean by that?

Author: She meant that I knew nothing whatsoever about
the "craft" of poetry. And she was right, I didn't. I had only
picked up a "sense" of poetry through various exposures to the
craft, but had never taken the time to learn the craft. In other
words, she saw right through me. Or, to put it in astrological
terms: she saw that I had a predominance of harmonious
aspects (trines and sextiles) in my birth chart and that rather
than taking the time to learn the craft of poetry, I simply relied
on my natural, God-given verbal talents (double Gemini
with Mercury and Mars in the first house) to get me through.
Great when you're at a cocktail party; not so great when you're
sending your work out professionally.

Castor: You mean, she didn't like it.

Author: No, she didn't like it.

Notes

1. Heng Ser Guan, Kevin. "The Mathematics of Astrology: Does
    House Divisions Make Sense?" An Undergraduate Research
    Opportunity Programme in Science, Department of Physics,
    National University of Singapore, Semester II 2000/2001.

2.   Hand, Robert. *Horoscope Symbols*, Chpt. 2, "The Symbol Systems of Astrology." I'm not sure I agree with Hand on this, for two reasons. First of all, the four points make up the major "angles" of the birth chart (i..e., they form the equal-armed cross within the ecliptic, each point—at least theoretically— 90° from the next point). Secondly, the first house of each quadrant is an "angular" house (rather than succedent or cadent) precisely because it is on the cusp of a major chart point. For these reasons alone, I would reverse Hand's assessment and use "angle" to describe the four major birth-chart points and "aspects" to describe the mathematical relationship between two or more planets. For the purposes of this document, I use "angle" when I'm describing the mathematical relationship between two or more planets, and "aspect" when I'm describing the attributes associated with a particular angular relationship.

3.   When we go back to the era of Hellenistic astrology, during the time of Claudius Ptolemy, an aspect was thought of as one planet "looking at" another planet (this is based on the archaic meaning of the word "aspect," to glance or look at). According to Joanna Martine Woolfolk, this is still a useful way of regarding aspects. For example, if there is a Sun-Jupiter aspect in your chart, you might ask yourself, "Does the Sun look at Jupiter in a friendly way (a good aspect) or an unfriendly way (an adverse aspect)?" Woolfolk, Joanna Martine. *The Only Astrology Book You'll Ever Need*, Chpt. 10, "Aspects and Synastry."

4.   Rudhyar, Dane. *Person Centered Astrology*, Chpt. 14, "The Geometrical Principle of Formation of Aspects." To put these two processes into context, Rudhyar discusses them in relationship to a trine (120°) aspect: "Real consciousness is always awareness (the opposition aspect) plus understanding and the sense of value; the trine is an aspect of growth in understanding. What has been 'seen' in the opposition phase, is now understood because it is related to a larger frame of reference. The vision or intuition becomes related

to the collective mind and to the values of the culture; it can then be expressed and formulated by appropriate symbols and words. When the trine is reached during the involutionary first half of the cycle, what is being established in concrete substance reaches the point at which it can be felt or comprehended as a whole; the general purpose of the instinctive impulse born of need and desire begins to be realized; an appreciation of beautiful proportions is emerging. The technician or mason can become, to some extent at least, philosopher and artist. Interpreted in terms of the evolutionary second hemicycle, the trine refers perhaps to the formal systemization of an intuition, or to the final harvest of a truly fulfilled relationship."

5. *Ibid.*

6. This concept is explicated even further by theosophist Alan Leo in *Symbolism and Astrology*: two planets same space or sign (conjunction); two planets one sign apart (semisextile); two planets one-and-a-half signs apart (semisquare); two planets two signs apart (sextile); two planets three signs apart (square, the "angle of sorrow"); two planets four signs apart (trine, the "angle of joy"); two planets four-and-a-half signs apart (sesqisquare or sesquiquadrate); two planets six signs apart (opposition) Leo, Alan. *Symbolism and Astrology*, Chpt. 12, "A Symbolic Aspectarian."

7. Hand, Chpt. 6, "The Aspects: Introduction."

8. Rudhyar, Chpt. 13, "The Aspects Formed During the Hemicycle of Spontaneous and Instinctual Action."

9. Hand, Chpt. 6, "The Aspects: Introduction."

10. Astrologers differ in their assessment of the quincunx. Judy Hall considers it a major aspect along with conjunction, sextile, square, trine, and opposition (Hall, Judy. *The Astrology Bible*, Chpt. 6, "The Aspects"). Following the ideas of Dane Rudhyar, Michael Meyer does the same, but provides a rationale for this placement, identifying it as the sixth step in Rudhyar's "involutionary" or time-factor series of aspects: conjunction, semisextile, sextile,

square, trine, quincunx, and opposition (Meyer, Michael. *A Handbook for the Humanistic Astrologer*, Chpt. 7, "Planetary Aspects: The Formation of Relationship"). Joanna Woolfolk, on the other hand, considers the quincunx a minor aspect (though without providing a rationale for this assessment), grouping it with the semisquare, sesquisquare, and semisextile (Woolfolk, Joanna. *The Only Astrology Book You'll Ever Need*, "Explanation of Terms").

11. Although Marc Edmund Jones's book *The Guide to Horoscope Interpretation* (David McKay, 1941) is still in print, I prefer *The Sabian Symbols in Astrology* (Aurora Press, 1993). For an explanation of Jones's work, I turn to the website *sabiansymbols* (sabiansymbols. com/the-sabian-symbols-story): "The Sabian Symbols are a set of 360 phrases of words that correspond with each of the 360 degrees of the wheel of the zodiac, from Aries 1 to Pisces 30. Consisting from as little as 2 words (Virgo 2: 'A Harem') to as many as 21 words (Taurus 5: 'A Youthful Widow, Fresh and Soul-Cleansed From Grief, Kneels at an Open Grave to Receive the Secret of Eternal Life), each one of these Symbols holds both a story and a unique energy field of their own. These images hold meaning for those degrees of the signs. Although the Symbols have their foundations in astrology, absolutely no knowledge of astrology is needed to use them.The Sabian Symbols were given birth in San Diego, California, in 1925 by Marc Edmund Jones, a noted American astrologer and spiritualist and the gifted clairvoyant Elsie Wheeler. Jones was interested to find a set of word images to go with every degree of the zodiac. Elsie Wheeler was an extraordinary clairvoyant confined to a wheelchair for most of her life. Jones chose Elsie Wheeler as his partner in this "experiment" (as Jones called it) as she had a remarkable ability to 'see' messages, images and symbols."

12. Hand, Chpt. 2, "The Symbol Systems of Astrology."

13. Boland, Yasmin. *Astrology*, Chpt. 8, "Degrees, Aspects and Orbs."

14. Hand, Chpt. 7, "The Aspects: Core Meanings."

15. Arroyo, Stephen. *Stephen Arroyo's Chart Interpretation Handbook*, Chpt. 8, "Understanding Planetary Aspects."
16. *Ibid.*
17. *Ibid.*
18. Kent, April Elliott. *The Essential Guide to Practical Astrology*, Chpt. 16, "Planetary Aspects."
19. Herring, Amy. *Essential Astrology*, Chpt. 10, "The Aspects."
20. Boland, Chpt. 8, "Degrees, Aspects and Orbs."
21. Herring, Chpt. 10, "The Aspects."
22. *Ibid.*
23. *Ibid.*
24. Coincidently, none of the online chart generators I consulted have the exact amount and type of planetary aspects; they range anywhere from twenty-two to thirty-four aspects, with sextile and trine aspects leading the list in each one.

11

Finger of God

Rather than playing ring-around-the-rosy with planets, signs, and houses, the contemporary astrologer is more likely to find their way into the natal chart through planetary patterns, aspect patterns, unaspected planets, and retrograde planets.[1]
Glenn Mitchell, *Discover the Aspect Pattern in Your Birth Chart*

I spoke with my former brother-in-law on the phone today. I don't talk to him that often, but we still keep in touch, as he does with my sister. If I had to look for significant moments in my young adult life, I'd have to say they were the two summers I spent with them in Washington, DC. I was a student at the University of Florida and when summer rolled around I took off. For two summers that meant heading north to DC. I'd jump into my van around sundown, crank up Steppenwolf's "Born to Be Wild," and off I'd go, arriving at my sister and brother-in-law's house around sunrise. I reminded my brother-in-law about that when we talked today and we both had a good laugh. We talked about other things as well: how he quit his day job to become a stand-up comic, how we searched all night for one of his friends who had smoked a little too much weed and had gone missing, and how my brother-in-law had been arrested for flying a kite on the National Mall.

Castor: Your brother-in-law was arrested for flying a kite?

Author: Yep, the "Great Kite Bust," as the *Washington Post* called it, took place in 1970 on a beautiful, flower-popping spring day. The prohibition dated back to an 1892 ordinance that made it illegal to fly a kite over "any street, avenue, alley, open space, public enclosure, or square withing the limits of the cities of Washington and Georgetown."[2] Along with a number of other "longhairs," my brother-in-law got it into his head to challenge the law. It was, after all, the generation that challenged authority on all fronts, and this law needed to be challenged. As my brother-in-law said, "If you want to change the law bad enough, make them enforce it."[3] And he and his buddies did just that: they planned a kite-in on the National Mall. The upshot: he and three others were arrested. But that didn't stop them. They made plans to have another kite-in the following weekend. Friends were called, posters hung, flyers handed out, and when Saturday rolled around instead of a handful of kite flyers, there was a horde of them. But the US Park Police were prepared: they arrived in force in paddy wagons, patrol cars, motorcycles, even on a few oversized horses. Again, my brother-in-law was arrested, this time with ten of his friends. But the wheels of progress that had started to turn the previous weekend turned rather quickly now, especially after the press got ahold of the story. One editorial laid it out quite clearly: "All this could be fine comic relief worthy of the kite trouble Charlie Brown has been enduring for years. But the park police and their superiors are

solid serious, carrying on like classic letter-of-the-law men.
The effect is that they are making fools of themselves in the
public eye, chasing after spring-struck kite fliers while the
town crawls with narcotic pushers, holdup men and other
criminals."[4] Within a month the law was changed and the
festivities began, with a kite-flying celebration (at which park
police handed out over 3,500 kites).

Castor: But what does this have to do with astrology?

Author: Everything. Have you ever heard of a T-square, a
Grand Trine, or a Yod?

Castor: I've heard of Yoda from *Star Wars*.

Author: A Yod is just one of a dozen "aspect patterns"
that involve several planets in a chart. According to Glenn
Mitchell, multi-planet aspect patterns occur when three or
more planets create patterns that result from multiple aspects
between planets."[5] The example Mitchell gives is the Kite,
which is an equilateral triangle composed of three trines (i.e.,
a Grand Trine) with a planet bisecting the midpoint of one of
its trines, creating two sextiles and an opposition.

Castor: I thought a kite was a long stick with a shorter stick
tied to it.

Author: I'm sure it is in your world, but in the world
of astrology, it's a geometric shape—like your kite—that
populates the birth chart.

Castor: Wait. You said an equilateral triangle composed
of three trines, but that doesn't make any sense. How can an
equilateral triangle have three trines of 120° each? That would
create a triangle of 360°. In math, I learned that a triangle has
180°.

Author: Yes, but we're not talking about the angles that planets make to each other. We're talking about the angles they make in relationship to the Earth at the center of the birth chart. In the first case, you're correct: the three angles of a triangle add up to 180°. But when the angles are in relationship to the Earth, we're talking about the 360° of the circle of which the Earth is its center. From this perspective, three trines equal 360°. Before we get into the nitty-gritty of each aspect pattern, let's back up and think about them more holistically. First of all, according to Michael Meyer, an interpreter of the work of Dane Rudhyar, the linking together by aspects of three or more planets forms "a special quality, purpose, and emphasis." In other words, the planets in an aspect pattern are bound together by a relationship of meaning.[6] One of the reasons for this is that the aspects that make up an aspect pattern tend to be of the same "family" of aspects, i.e., either harmonious or challenging. According to Robert Hand, an aspect pattern represents a specific type of "harmonic syndrome," a sympathetic vibration or "coming together" of several related aspects.[7] The example Hand uses to illustrate this point is a plucked guitar string that vibrates not only in the fundamental tone, but also in its respective overtones. In other words, because an aspect pattern usually consists of several aspects of the same family, the aspects tend to be in phase with one another, "so that the peaks of the waves formed by the aspects and overtones occur at the same points around the ecliptic."[8] Knowing this, we can see how some aspect patterns are harmonious while others are more difficult or challenging.

Pollux: I think you just put Castor to sleep.

Author: It appears so.

Castor: I'm not sleeping, just resting my head.

Author: Perhaps talking about a few aspect patterns might wake you up. The problem is which ones do we talk about? For instance, there are classical patterns (Kite, Yod, Grand Trine, Mystic Rectangle, Grand Cross), as well as more contemporary patterns (Bathtub, Envelope, Wreath, Trapeze, UFO, Cradle). In other words, astrologers have quite a few aspect patterns in their toolbox. But which ones are important?

Castor: How about a Grand Cross on a Trapeze in a Bathtub?

Author An interesting image. For this discussion, I think we'll call...

Castor: Loren.

Loren: Good morning, what's on your mind?

Author: The boys and I want to know more about aspect patterns, especially which ones you use when you draw up a chart for a client.

Loren: I have a mixed bag of techniques, a little of this and a little of that. But, in general, I tend to use a handful of patterns, some harmonious, some challenging, and some a mixture of the two. Let's start with one of the most frequently appearing patterns: the T-square.

Castor: We used one of those in drafting class.

Pollux: Not that T-square, dummy.

Castor: I'm not a...

Loren: You're not, but the T-square you used to draw a right angle to another line is shaped like the T-square in astrology. A T-square, also known as a T-cross, occurs when two planets are in opposition to each other with both making a square aspect to a third planet. As its name implies, the pattern resembles the letter "T" with the top of the letter representing the opposition and the leg or support extending downwards at a 90° angle representing the squaring planet.[9] Built on an opposition and two squares, the T-square can be a difficult pattern in a birth chart, signifying tension, obstruction, and conflict. On the other hand, according to Joanna Woolfolk, it can be an energizing influence that motivates an individual to fight and to resolve problems.[10]

Author: I like what Amy Herring says about the T-square. First of all, she recognizes that an opposition represents two parts of a person that are somehow in a stand-off or a push-pull pattern. She calls it the "seesaw effect," where energy can only go to one side or the other. But with a T-square, the stuck or frustrated energy of the opposition gets released or channeled out by the squaring planet, "like lightning striking the highest tree because it was the easiest target."[11]

Pollux: Do you have a T-square in your chart?

Author: Remember when we talked about my unaspected chart pattern...

Castor: *Bowl.*

Author: That's right. My chart pattern is a bowl with a rim opposition between...

Castor: Neptune and Jupiter.

Author: So you really are listening, Castor.

Castor: It's kind of interesting.

Author: So the question is, Do Neptune and Jupiter have a squaring planet?

Castor: How would I know?

Pollux: Uranus in the second house.

Castor: Smarty pants.

Castor: Okay, so Uranus makes a T-square to a Neptune/Jupiter opposition, but what does it mean?

Author: Let's have Loren answer that question.

Loren: According to Robert Jansky, the T-square lends integrative strength and organization to the Bowl pattern, which is only heightened when the rim planets (Neptune and Jupiter) and the planet at the apex of the T-square (Uranus) are in the same "modality" (in your case they are all in cardinal signs).[12]

Castor: Yes, but what does it mean?

Loren: Eleventh-house Jupiter in Aries indicates that when an individual takes charge of his or her creative endeavors, the endeavors may bring good luck. However, the opposition to fifth-house Neptune in Libra indicates that there may be an over-dependence on what others think. This vacillating between the need to create and the need to conform to the expectations of others is the seesawing effect mentioned above. But a T-square offers you a way out, unfortunately it is with another challenging aspect: the square. In your case, the square made by second-house Uranus in Cancer indicates that if you change your point of view and come to see these opportunities in a different way, you'll begin to see their value: the value of self-expression within the limits of what's socially acceptable.

Author: Loren, I'd like to respond to that if you don't mind. Early in my career, I struggled to write children's books. First of all, I learned the craft of children's picture books, like most authors, by studying the work of other authors. I distinctly remember the day that I decided to get serious about my writing. I was teaching second grade in a small public school in Montana and reading a lot of picture books. I had two stacks of books on my desk: in one stack, books that I drooled over as each book was spectacular both for its writing and illustrations; in the other stack, books that I thought were totally uninspiring. I remember thinking that my writing was at least somewhere in between: not spectacular, but not that bad either. That's when I got serious about writing. Since I was learning the craft by imitation (by studying the work of others), I tended to "stay within the lines," hoping to attract an editor to "my work." As I accumulated rejection letters from a number of editors, I noticed a theme in their response to my writing: they often suggested that I "loosen up" and "take more chances" in my writing.

Loren: It appears that early in your career you were caught in a web of your own design: your Neptune/Jupiter opposition.

Castor: So what happened?

Author: Over time I took more ownership of my writing. I know this because, whereas my earliest writing notebooks were filled with excerpts from the writing of others, by my third or fourth notebook all of that had dropped out and I was only recording—and studying—my own writing.

Castor: And you attribute that to Uranus squaring Neptune and Jupiter.

Author: Loren, what do you think?

Loren: Yes, but not exclusively, because you also have
a Wedge that involves your Neptune/Jupiter opposition.
Whereas a T-square involves an opposition and two squares,
a Wedge involves an opposition and a trine and a sextile,
which makes it a more benign or harmonious aspect pattern.
In your case, Pluto is sextile Neptune and trine Jupiter, which
indicates that once you apply yourself, "things" (thoughts,
relationships, work, etc.) really start to flow.

Author: Which means that once I started to "own" my
writing, it started to take off.

Loren: I think so. But you have another Wedge that has
to do with your Neptune/Jupiter opposition, one that is
even more powerful for you. In this case, the focal planet
is Mercury, which trines Neptune and sextiles Jupiter. The
indication here is that once you take a personal point of view,
i.e., own your creative process, your writing will begin to flow
easily and abundantly, and rightly so since Mercury is the god
of communication.

Pollux: Simply fascinating.

Author: Agreed. Loren, what's next?

Loren: The most natural aspect pattern to consider is the
Grand Cross, which is an extension of the T-square. If you
were to "complete" a T-square, what would you do?

Pollux: Draw an opposition to the squaring planet?

Loren: Precisely. Instead of an opposition and two
squares, you'd have two oppositions and four squares. But
perhaps it makes more sense to describe it the way Glenn
Mitchell does: "The Grand Cross pattern is a configuration of

very intense aspects. Two pairs of oppositions are connected by four interlocking squares."[13] Since oppositions are more dynamic or intense than squares, most astrologers focus on the oppositions rather than the squares. Either way you look at it, it's a difficult configuration, often indicating an obsessive, maladjusted personality. However, according to Joanna Woolfolk, it also signifies dynamic energy, intensity, and force, and often appears in the charts of self-made men and women.[14]

Pollux: Does he have a Grand Cross?

Loren: It doesn't look like it.

Castor: So he's not self-made.

Loren: He's independent, but not "self-made" in the way I think you mean. The next aspect pattern to consider is a relative of the Grand Cross: the Mystic Rectangle. If you squeezed a Grand Cross just a tad, instead of a square you'd get a rectangle with two crossing oppositions and two trines and two sextiles.

Castor: That's confusing.

Loren: Again, let me turn to Glenn Mitchell: "The ideal Mystic Rectangle is composed of two opposition aspects, each connected by two trine aspects along the length of the rectangle and two sextile aspects along the width."[15] As you would expect, the Mystic Rectangle is somewhat less challenging than the Grand Cross, given the trines and sextiles which function as "release points" for the tension of the two oppositions. If you count your Midheaven as a "planet" (along with your Ascendant, it is an important point, one of the four major chart angles), you have a Mystic

Rectangle involving a Pluto/Midheaven opposition and a Jupiter/Neptune opposition connected by two trines (Jupiter/ Pluto and Neptune/Midheaven) and two sextiles (Neptune/ Pluto and Jupiter/Midheaven).

Castor: It's not confusing; it's incomprehensible.

Loren: It's really not that hard to understand. The most important thing to remember about a Mystic Rectangle is that it always contains the same polarity of elemental energies (planets will be in either positive signs or negative signs). Additionally, the signs involved will all be compatible (either air/fire or earth/water). Generally speaking, this configuration means that the Mystic Rectangle will be harmonious rather than challenging as it tends not to generate a lot of resistance. In your case, the four planets in your Mystic Rectangle are in positive signs, with the energy split between two fire signs (Aries and Leo) on the eastern half of your chart and two air signs (Libra and Aquarius) on the western half of your chart. With two planets in fire signs on the eastern half of your chart (along with five other planets, all but one in fire and air signs), your self-starting, assertive nature is heightened. However, you have to be careful not to place too much attention on these planets (Jupiter and Pluto) as that might throw the energies in the Mystic Rectangle out of balance. This is particularly true in your case since Jupiter and Pluto are already elevated in your chart. Learning how to balance the energies between the two types of elemental signs, and between the two strong oppositions, will be important to you, and can be done by using the energy of the more harmonious trines and sextiles.

Castor: Why is it called a "Mystic Rectangle?"

Loren: Mitchell offers this answer: "The Mystic Rectangle received its name from Dane Rudhyar. He argued that the pattern represents 'practical mysticism' from its two awareness-revealing, illuminating oppositions. The two trines add creativity to the mix, and the two sextiles intelligent and innovative use of energies."[16]

Castor: Illuminating, creative, intelligent—that sure sounds like someone I know.

Pollux: Yeah, the author, not you.

Castor: *Hey,...*

Author: Moving on, boys. Loren, what's next?

Loren: I think we should discuss the Grand Trine, otherwise known as "The Angle of Joy."

Castor: Angel of Joy?

Pollux: *Angle* of Joy, numbskull.

Loren: It's an equilateral triangle composed of three trines, and, as we learned, a trine is an easy or harmonious aspect, and a major one at that. Next to the T-square, a Grand Trine is one of the most frequently appearing aspect patterns in a birth chart. Given its equilateral structure, each of the planets that make up the vertices of the triangle are always in the same element. The emphasis on a particular element—fire, earth, air, or water—can indicate either an imbalance in the chart or an enormous burst of creative energy. Usually it's the latter, which gives way to the aspect pattern's epithet "The Angle of Joy," as it typically indicates that an individual will be blessed with good luck.[17] This description affirms what Mitchell says about this harmonious aspect pattern: "A Grand Trine is a complete third harmonic pattern. It represents perfect equilibrium and balance that can reveal great talent, ease, or harmony." However, Mitchell goes on to say, "a Grand Trine is often a static, passive structure that doesn't promote the growth that results from confronting the problems of hard aspects."[18]

Castor: It's the stuck-in-a-rut syndrome.

Loren: An interesting way of saying it, but, yes, the energy in a Grand Trine often goes round and round and round: a good thing as it doesn't cause conflict; a bad thing in that it doesn't promote personal growth. Here's a bit longer explanation of this syndrome from astrologer Amy Herring: "Like the trines of which it's composed, the Grand Trine harnesses the energy of each planet into a repeating, harmonious loop, which astrologer Noel Tyl refers to as a 'closed circuit of self-sufficiency.' The planets in a Grand Trine function so well together that they can bring a lot of benefit in the areas of the life in which they are active (via the signs and houses), but like the trines, they are also a grooved track on which the planets are used to expressing themselves. One may be skilled at thinking or acting inside that 'box' but be averse to straying outside of those lines."[19]

Castor: Is he stuck inside a box?

Loren: I think you mean, Does the author have any Grand Trines? Yes, he does. Three of them. Well, not exactly.

Castor: What do you mean?

Loren: He has one *major* Grand Trine and two *minor* Grand Trines. Here's the difference: whereas a major Grand Trine is made up of three planets that trine each other, a minor Grand Trine is made up of one planet that sextiles two planets that are in a trine aspect. Think "families." Trines and sextiles are part of the three-series or triadic aspects that are generally considered easy or harmonious. The vertices of your major Grand Trine are Neptune, Mercury conjunct Mars, and your Midheaven. These form one of those closed circuits of self-sufficiency mentioned earlier, with each planet or point energized by the others. This may explain some of your early writing success in that you have no planets near your Midheaven (only Jupiter is in the upper hemisphere, the realm of social relationships, work, and career opportunities), so Neptune trine Mercury conjunct Mars is pushing the energy from these two trines toward your Midheaven, energizing the "empty" area around the Midheaven. Success is yours as long as Mercury conjunct Mars in particular (the god of communication emboldened by the god of war) is driving their energy toward the Midheaven. Once that energy subsides, as it often does with age, especially since you have no planets near the Midheaven to energize your career aspirations, your "success" (whatever that means to you) will also subside with age, though your aspiration to succeed may not.

Pollux: What about the minor Grand Trines?

Loren: The first minor Grand Trine in your chart is the trine between fifth-house Neptune and first-house Sun, with both of them sextiling fourth-house Pluto. The second minor Grand Trine is the trine between fourth-house Pluto and eleventh-house Jupiter, both sextiling first-house Mercury.

Castor: Is that good?

Loren: The first minor Grand Trine, involving Pluto, Neptune, and the Sun, points to the capacity to be blinded by your own knowledge. What is true? What is illusion? These are questions that might perplex or even consume you. Although you have the capacity for deep, intense self-knowing, you should be prepared to face the dark side of your personality. On the other hand, with your second minor Grand Trine, involving Jupiter, Pluto, and Mercury, the first two support whatever Mercury turns its attention to. In particular, with first-house Mercury in Gemini, you have the ability to throw yourself into a project with great persistence and industry. However, the problem is that you have a hard time walking away from it when you get stuck. In short, where Pluto has a tendency to fixate on something, Jupiter may exaggerate that fixation to the point where you just cannot walk away from it in order to gain perspective.

Author: If I may jump in here. Two things. First of all, what you said about my major Grand Trine is very true. Early in my writing career I had a lot of energy and ambition, which is not unusual, and for close to twenty years I had a lot of success, both in publishing my work and in traveling around the country talking to teachers and students about my writing. After the market collapsed in 2007-2008, everything just fell off the table.

Pollux: But you were not alone in this, right?

Author: That's right. Most of my writing friends were in the same situation. But unlike many of them, I just couldn't seem to gain traction and get moving again. At first I attributed it to advancing age, but the more I thought about it, it wasn't that I had no interest in writing—I did—it's that I had lost interest in the publishing game. Being at the mercy of editors, publicists, bookstore owners, etc., just wasn't interesting to me anymore. I just wanted to write: publish, yes, but on my own terms.

Loren: Very interesting. And what was the other thing you thought about regarding the minor Grand Trines?

Author: It's about not being able to let go of a project when I get stuck. I see this over and over again. I'll be working away, literally tearing my hair out trying to solve a problem (restructuring a chapter, looking for a much-needed quotation, chasing down some tiny bit of information, etc.), and all of a sudden I realize that I've gone down a rabbit hole, at least that's what my wife calls it. I bury myself in whatever it is I'm trying to solve, sometimes for inordinate periods of time. I just can't come up for air and look around until I've finished.

Loren: And you do this in your writing in particular.

Author: Yes, I don't think there's another part of my life in which I do that.

Loren: That's your double Gemini with Mercury and Mars in the first house. Fueled by Mars's energy, Mercury wants to know, to grasp, and then to share. But, above all, Mercury wants to know—to know everything. Then there's Pluto and Jupiter in a minor Grand Trine with Mercury, with the former two keeping Mercury's nose to the grind. What it means to me is that you're probably very productive. More than likely, your productivity has come at a cost.

Author: In two ways. First of all, I have many ideas I want to explore, but I just can't get to them because my laser-like focus on a project just won't let me move on until I've finished it. So, yes, I'm productive, mainly because I finish everything I start—well, almost everything. But here's where I've paid a price: there's a physical cost for my intractability, my laser-like focus. Sitting at a computer everyday, hour after hour, has really taken a toll on my nervous system.

Loren: Nervous system? Imagine that. A Gemini, a double Gemini at that, having issues with his nervous system. I'll bet along with tight shoulders, you have aches and pains in your arms, hands, and fingers.

Author: How did you know that?

Loren: Because Gemini *rules* the nervous system, which includes the shoulders, arms, hands, and fingers (and you can throw in the lungs for good measure). Geminis also exhibit a lot of nervous energy, which can also lead to physical tension. You might want to consider physical exercise like swimming, walking, tai chi, or yoga to lessen the tension in your body.[20]

Author: Something else my wife is always telling me.

Loren: Let's move on to another aspect pattern: the Grand Sextile, a relative of the Grand Trine. Actually, it's two Grand Trines superimposed inversely on top of each other, creating a six-pointed star, which is why this pattern is also called the "Star of David."

Castor: But why is it called a Grand Sextile? Shouldn't it be called a Super-duper Grand Trine?

Loren: With six equally spaced planets around the perimeter of the birth chart, how many degrees separates each one?

Castor: Sounds like math again.

Pollux: Sixty.

Loren: That's right, each planet is separated by 60°, and you learned earlier that a 60° aspect is...

Castor: A sextile.

Loren: Hence the name, Grand Sextile.

Castor: Does he have one?

Ashely: No, because Grand Sextiles don't appear that frequently.

Castor: Why not?

Loren: Imagine trying to get six out of ten planets to space themselves equidistantly around the perimeter of your birth chart at 60° intervals. Rather difficult I'd say. But if you had one (and you don't), it would be a considerably harmonious pattern, with the energy from each planet caught in a continuous closed circuit of six equally spaced vertices. This indicates a very balanced individual, with two or more planets in each of the four hemispheres (upper and lower, eastern and western) and energy flowing in an unobstructed circular manner. Now, while you don't have a Grand Sextile, you do have a close relative to one: a Castle.[21]

Castor: That reminds me of the battlefield in France.

Loren: A Castle is quite easy to explain: it's simply a Grand Sextile missing one planet. Instead of six sextiles created by six equally spaced planets, a Castle is four sextiles created by five equally spaced planets and one trine (stretched across the area where the missing sixth planet should be). Your Castle starts with a Midheaven/Neptune trine and, moving counterclockwise around your chart, involves Jupiter, Mercury, Pluto, and Neptune, each one a sextile apart. All you'd need to have a Grand Sextile is a planet in seventh-house Sagittarius. But you don't, and that makes that portion of the chart a sensitive area, implicating seventh-house activities, primarily dealing with relationships (close friends, spouse, business partner, etc.). In other words, it's an area to pay attention to since it's a break within an otherwise harmonious aspect pattern. Attend to the break, the "release point," and your Castle will function more like a Grand Sextile. The seventh house is further "energized" by the 1st and 7th house axis of boundaries between self and others, with first-house Gemini populated with three planets and seventh-house Sagittarius devoid of any. Castor, what are you thinking about? You look perplexed.

Castor: I'm just dumbstruck by all of this. The fact that you can make sense out of someone's life by "reading" the planets, signs, and houses in someone's birth chart is, well,... *fascinating*.

Pollux: Ditto.

Loren: Good, then let's move on, to another relative of the Grand Sextile: the Cradle.[22]

Castor: It's got to be an easy pattern.

Loren: Why do you say that?

Castor: It's about a baby's cradle. How could that be hard or difficult?

Loren: I see you've never had a baby. But you're right, Castor, a Cradle is more easy-going than it is difficult. The reason: although it has one opposition, it has three sextiles and two trines, which softens the opposition considerably. In other words, the sextiles and trines "cradle" the opposition.

Castor: What does it look like?

Loren: As I said earlier, it is a relative of the Grand Sextile. In the case of a Cradle, instead of removing one planet (which gives you a Castle), remove two consecutive planets. Now you have a Cradle. By removing two planets (which equals three sextiles), you create an opposition that sextiles to two other planets. In other words, it's half of a Grand Sextile.

Castor: Why didn't you say that in the first place?

Loren: That isn't all. Draw a line from each of the opposing planets to the two sextiling planets and internally you've created two trines. So here's a question for you: Do you think the author has more than one Cradle in his chart?

Castor: That's a leading question, so the answer must be yes.

Loren: You saw right through me, didn't you. But why does he have more than one Cradle?

Castor: He has a lot of kids?

Loren: No. It's because, as we learned earlier, the author's chart has more trines than any other aspect, which means that there's a pretty good chance that he has more than one Cradle. In fact, his chart has three Cradles. a Jupiter/Neptune opposition with three sextiles created by Pluto and Mercury; a Pluto/Midheaven opposition with three sextiles created by Mercury and Jupiter; and a Venus/Midheaven opposition with three sextiles created by Mercury and Jupiter.

Castor: Is a Cradle as easy as it sounds?

Loren: It depends upon which planets, signs, and houses are involved. Although a Cradle has an opposition, it also has two trines and three sextiles. So is it "easy" or "hard," or a combination of the two? Another factor to consider is that all of its planets will be in either fire/air or earth/water signs. In your case, all three Cradles are made from a mixture of planets in fire and air signs. This suggests dynamism; it suggests energy that moves of its own accord around the external and internal structure of the Cradle. Since the Cradle is half of a hexagon, it lacks the full circularity of a full hexagon (i.e., a Grand Sextile), which means that the opposition planets set the dominant mode (cardinal, fixed, or mutable) while the sextiling planets often act in a supporting role.[23]

Pollux: I've noticed something: most of the author's aspect patterns fall into either fire or air signs, or a combination of the two.

Loren: The reason is simple: of the twelve "planets" in the author's chart, six appear in air signs and three in fire signs (with two in water signs and one in an earth sign), so you would expect his multi-planet aspect patterns to fall into these elemental signs.[24] Now, of the three Cradles in his chart, the one created from a Jupiter/Neptune opposition that sextiles Pluto and Mercury is the stronger of the three. The Jupiter/Neptune opposition anchored in cardinal signs (Aries and Libra) lends an active quality or drive to the author's personality, along with a streak of independent attitude, even extroversion. Nonetheless, there are challenges: he must learn how to balance the strong cardinal energy with mutable Mercury and fixed Pluto in order to take advantage of the positive, forward-moving energy. Any questions?

Castor: Is it time for lunch?

Author: Soon, Castor, I think we have a couple of more aspect patterns to consider. Loren, what's next?

Loren: Let's look at the Kite, which is a Grand Trine with a fourth planet bisecting the midpoint of one of the three trines creating an opposition. Another way to think about this aspect pattern is to think of a major Grand Trine (the lower half of the kite structure) topped by a minor Grand Trine (the upper half of the kite structure), with the kite's "crossbar" serving as the base for both the major and minor Grand Trines. When you boil it down to its composite aspects, it's an opposition with three trines and two sextiles.[25]

Castor: I don't think I'll ever fly a kite again.

Loren: It's really not that hard. The thing to remember is that a Kite consists of three trines, two sextiles, and an opposition, which means that the harmonious energy trapped in the trines and sextiles has a release valve: the planet that opposes one of the Grand Trine's vertices. But no need to worry: you don't have a Kite, at least not in your chart. But you do have a Yod.

Castor: A Yod?

Loren: Otherwise known as the "Finger of God," a Yod is similar to a Grand Trine, only instead of three trines, a Yod has two quincunxes of 150° each and a sextile. It's as if someone sat on a Grand Trine and squashed it, transforming the equilateral triangle of the Grand Trine into an isosceles triangle of the newly formed Yod, which acts like a Grand Trine in that it captures and circulates the planetary energies among its three vertices, but because a quincunx is a hard or difficult aspect, having a disjointed or stop-and-go energy, a Yod demands more conscious attention to keep the energy flowing. From a geometric perspective, it's easy to see that the Yod is less harmonious than the other patterns discussed, given the narrow, almost arrow-like pointer created by the sextile that connects the two base planets. Hence, its epithet, "Finger of God," which points right to the area of most need.[26]

Castor: But he doesn't have one of those, right?

Loren: Wrong, he has a Yod created by a Pluto/Neptune sextile, both of which are quincunx, or "inconjunct," the North Lunar Node.

Castor: Ooh, I don't like that.

Loren: What I see is a Pluto/Neptune sextile pushing their energy up towards the North Lunar Node, which sits close to the cusp of the eleventh house. If you remember, your chart's upper hemisphere is almost devoid of planets: only Jupiter populates the eleventh house, which is the house of expanding social relationships, often involving social or humanitarian endeavors. But you have no driver—no planets—except Jupiter to help you sustain that impetus. This is where the Yod comes in: your "Finger of God" supports your heartfelt need to live in a harmonious, peaceful world. You desire this deeply, however the preponderance of planets in your lower hemisphere keep you tethered to your private, interior world, which means that your good-intentioned humanitarian aspirations are funneled less into social action and more into the intangibles of your dream world. If you were to act on these aspirations, it would be more through your writing than through direct action.

Author: Incredible. I often dream of joining social causes, especially in these most challenging times, but I never do. In short, I'd rather write about them than actually participate in them.

Pollux: This might explain your latest book that addresses current social themes.[27]

Author: I had a very interesting experience recently related to this. I was riding my bicycle home and passed a corner in my neighborhood where there have been a steady stream of Black Lives Matter protests. I've never stopped. I wave, nod my head, show my support, but I've never stopped. Yesterday, I stopped because I happened to have a copy of my latest book that addresses the recent racial tensions exploding around the country, especially after the deaths of Breonna Taylor in Louisville and George Floyd in Minneapolis. I stopped and gave the BLM organizer a copy of my book, and as I did I blurted, "I don't protest actively, in public; I protest through my writing." As I think about what I said, it's true: I see my activity as a writer as a form of protest, by throwing a book into the pond of ideas I hope to influence the thoughts of others.

Loren: I'd say that's a great place to end this discussion.

Castor: Agreed.

Notes

1. Mitchell, Glenn. *Discover the Aspect Pattern in Your Birth Chart*, Chpt. 10, "How to Recognize Aspect Patterns."

2. Kelly, John. "Until 1970, it was illegal to fly a kite in Washington. Hippies got the law changed." *Washington Post*, April 4, 2020, [URL] www.washingtonpost.com/local/until-1970-it-was-illegal-to-fly-a-kite-in-washington-hippies-got-the-law-changed/2020/04/04/b339f68a-750d-11ea-a9bd-9f8b593300d0_story.html.

3. *Ibid.* For an analysis of the cultural revolution of the 1960s. I suggest Richard Tarnas's book, *Cosmos and Psyche*, especially the first chapter of Part IV titled "From the French Revolution to the 1960s."

4. *Ibid.*

5. Mitchell, Chpt. 10, "How to Recognize Aspect Patterns."

6. Meyer, Michael R. *A Handbook for the Humanistic Astrologer*, Chpt. 4, "Planetary Formations."

7. Hand, Robert. *Horoscope Symbols*, Chpt. 7, "Aspect Patterns: Core Meanings."

8. *Ibid.*

9. Mitchell, Chpt. 10, "How to Recognize Aspect Patterns."

10. Woolfolk, Joanna Martine. *The Only Astrology Book You'll Ever Need*, Glossary.

11. Herring, Amy. *Essential Astrology*, Chpt. 10, "The Aspects."

12. Mitchell, Chpt. 10, "How to Recognize Aspect Patterns."

13. *Ibid.*

14. Woolfolk, Glossary.

15. Mitchell, Chpt. 10, "How to Recognize Aspect Patterns."

16. *Ibid.*

17. Woolfolk, Glossary.

18. Mitchell, Chpt. 15, "The Grand Trine and the Kite."

19. Herring, Chpt. 10, "The Aspects."

20. Woolfolk, Chpt. 4, "Astrology and Health." In general, Mercury rules the brain and nervous system: in Gemini, it rules the nervous system, lungs, and arms; in Virgo, it rules the nervous system and intestines.

21. "Birth Chart: A Guide to Your Astrology," *astro-charts*, [URL] astro-charts.com.

22. *Ibid.*

23. *Ibid.*

24. When counting the "planets" in my original chart, it appears that the computer-analyst-qua-astrologer counts the Sun and Moon (the luminaries), Mercury, Venus, Mars, Jupiter, and Saturn (the

classical planets), Uranus, Neptune, and Pluto (the modern planets), and the Ascendant and Midheaven (the two major chart angles). Although the North Lunar Node is represented in the chart in tenth-house Pisces, it does not appear in the aspect grid below the circular birth chart and, as such, does not show up in the count of elemental signs.

25. Marks, Tracy. *The Art of Chart Interpretation*, Chpt. 1, "The Chart as a Whole: Aspect Configurations."

26. *Ibid.*

27. Nikola-Lisa, W. *This We Pray | Sea of People*. Chicago: Gyroscope Books, 2020.

12

In All Line of Order

Gods of old, and demons, too, they were once—they
still are—the sources of an inspiring light, the wanderers
of night, the far horizon of the landscape of home.[1]
Dava Sobel, *The Planets*

It's been quite a while since I've looked at Joanna Cole
and Bruce Degen's *The Magic School Bus* series. It was very
popular when my daughters were young. They were drawn
to Ms. Frizzle, the somewhat eccentric, but kind, funny, and
resourceful elementary-school teacher, who took her class on
various excursions—to the bottom of the ocean, inside the
human body, through a waterworks system—using a shape-
shifting yellow school bus. One of my favorite titles is the
fourth book in the series, *The Magic School Bus Lost in the Solar
System*.[2] With Arnold's cousin Janet joining the class for a
trip to the planetarium, Ms. Frizzle, finding the planetarium
closed for the day, pushes a button on the bus's dashboard and
turns the bus into a spaceship, whereby Ms. Frizzle and her
class zoom off to explore the solar system by themselves. After
visiting the Moon, the Sun, and the other inner planets, the
bus winds up in the asteroid belt, somewhere between Mars
and Jupiter.

Castor: Where an errant asteroid knocks out a taillight.

Author: Ah, there you are.

Castor: Yep, and we've read most of the books in *The Magic School Bus* series—at night under the covers with a flashlight.

Author: What happens next?

Castor: Ms. Frizzle goes out to fix the taillight, but her tether breaks when the spaceship unexpectedly takes off, leaving her stranded in the asteroid belt.

Pollux: Meanwhile, Arnold's cousin saves the day when she finds Ms. Frizzle's lesson plan book and navigates the spaceship—after exploring the planets in the outer solar system—back to the asteroid belt where they rescue Ms. Frizzle.

Castor: Only none of the kids' parents believe them once they return to Earth. They think they've made the whole thing up. But I believe them.

Pollux: Me, too.

Author: That's all well and good, but it's not why I've been thinking about *The Magic School Bus* series. It's on my mind because I'm not sure what to do next. Should we take a tour of the astrological solar system? It seems a likely next step. Or is there a better way to discuss my natal chart.

Castor: Sounds like we should ring up Loren.

Author: Good idea... Loren, it's us again.

Loren: What's on your mind?

Castor: We're confused. We don't know what to do next.

Loren: It sounds like your question is, How should you dive into the birth chart in order to mine the information in it?

Author: I think that's a fair assessment. I was thinking of a tour of the birth chart, starting in the first house and proceeding counterclockwise around my chart noting house, sign, and planet placements until we arrived at the twelfth house.

Castor: Like the Magic School Bus kids do when they explore the solar system.

Loren: Let's think about this for a moment. Although it's important to know where your planets are in relationship to the signs and houses of your birth chart, this knowledge just scratches the surface of the amount of information that the various factors in a chart represent. I think a linguistic analogy might be useful here: in order to tell a story, an author uses letters to make words, words to make sentences, and sentences to make paragraphs. These are the building blocks an author uses to tell his or her story. When we apply this analogy to astrology, knowing where your planets are in relationship to your signs and houses is like telling a story with only a few phrases made from a handful of letters and words. To get the totality of the story you need more: you need to form sentences from those phrases that combine into paragraphs that coalesce into a full-fledged story.

Castor: It's kind of like a jigsaw puzzle. All of the pieces are in front of you, you just don't know what picture they make yet.

Loren: Excellent analogy, Castor.

Pollux: So what do we do?

Loren: Well, as we're still trying to lay out the overall landscape of a natal chart, I think we should tackle another very important area: the various factors or "points" in a natal chart.

Castor: What do you mean by points?

Loren: For an answer to that question, let me turn to the wisdom of Robert Hand. In *Horoscope Symbols*, Hand divides all items in a birth chart—planets, points, nodes, etc.—into three categories: node-type points, body-type points, and planetary picture-type points.[3]

Castor: I think my head is starting to spin again.

Loren: It's not that difficult. Let me explain. According to Hand, node-type points include the four major chart angles, the twelve house cusps, the East Point, Vertex, and the 0° Aries Point, as well as the lunar and planetary nodes. What these have in common is that all of them are formed by the intersection of two significant planes.

Pollux: Didn't we talk about this earlier when we discussed great and not-so-great circles?

Loren: Yes, we just didn't discuss all of the great circles inscribed within the celestial sphere. We did, however, determine that the plane of every great circle passes through the Earth at the center of the celestial sphere. Take the planets, for instance. Although they revolve around the Sun, from an astrological perspective, i.e., a geocentric perspective, they appear to orbit the Earth, crossing the ecliptic twice in one revolution. We call the place a planet's orbit crosses the ecliptic a "node," which is more a theoretical location than a physical point. In short, it's the place that two great circles intersect. The Moon's orbit around the Earth provides an easy way to understand this phenomena. Astronomers have known for centuries that the Moon's orbit around the Earth is inclined to the Earth's orbit around the Sun about 5.2°, which means that the Moon's orbit crosses the Earth's orbit twice in the course of one revolution, with the crossing points or nodes exactly 180° apart. These are the North and South Lunar Nodes.

Castor: So they're not actually things in the sky; you know, planets and such—just imaginary points.

Loren: Yes, but they do exist in an abstract kind of way, so we count them. But as you'll notice on your chart, only the North Lunar Node is indicated. Why do you think that is?

Castor: The astrologer forgot the other node?

Loren: Not forgot, just thought it unnecessary. Here's why. According to Robert Hand, since the intersection of two planes is always a straight line (called the "nodal axis"), with the nodes exactly 180° apart along the ecliptic, any angular relationship to one end of the nodal axis is similar in its relationship to the other end. For this reason, according to Hand, astrologers only need to consider angular relationships to one end of the nodal pair. By convention, this is usually the North Lunar Node.[4]

Pollux: Which is why the author's chart doesn't list the South Lunar Node.

Loren: But it's there nonetheless. We'll return to the lunar nodes, however for now let's consider body-type points and planetary picture-type points. Body-type points are celestial bodies, either real or hypothesized, that include the ten planets (Sun, Moon, Mercury, Venus, Mars, Jupiter, Saturn, Uranus, Neptune, and Pluto), a handful of large asteroids (Ceres, Vesta, Pallas, and Hygiea), several dozen planetoids (like the recently discovered Chiron), the fixed stars, and a number of hypothetical planets proposed by various astrologers. Planetary picture-type points, the third of Hand's categories, are the least tangible objects: these are mathematical points, the result of various algorithms used by different astrologers, which include Arabian parts (also known as "lots"), midpoints, solstice or antiscia points, among others.[5]

Castor: So that's it? That covers everything?

Loren: Yes, all factors plotted on a natal chart fall within one of these three categories. Of the three, I'm most interested in body-type points as they form the basis for any interpretation of a birth chart. And, as we learned, body-type points include a variety of celestial bodies, all of which are often lumped together under the generic heading "planets." To begin this discussion, we start with the question, What does the word "planet" mean?

Pollux: The term "planet" comes from the root of the Greek word *planetes*, which means "wanderer." I suppose they were given that name since, against the background of fixed stars, they appear "to wander" across the sky.[6] I learned that when we were studying ancient Greece.

Loren: But which "wanderers" are you talking about?

Pollux: "My very educated mother just served us nine pizzas."

Castor: Why are you talking about pizzas?

Pollux: That's the mnemonic I learned to help me remember the order of the planets: Mercury, Venus, Earth, Mars, Jupiter, Saturn, Uranus, Neptune, and Pluto.

Castor: I think I was absent that day.

Loren: That's okay, Castor, because the mnemonic Pollux memorized was handed down to him by his science teacher versed in Western astronomy, not by an astrologer. The planets that most astrologers recognize are: the Sun, the Moon, Mercury Venus, Mars, Jupiter, Saturn, Uranus, Neptune, and Pluto. These are the ten planets of the birth chart.

Castor: Wait a minute. The Sun and Moon aren't planets.

Loren: In the world of astrology, they are. The "classical" planets were seven in number: Sun, Moon, Mercury, Venus, Mars, Jupiter, and Saturn. These were the celestial bodies—the "wanderers"—that our ancestors tracked across the sky against the background of fixed stars before the invention of the telescope. With that spectacular invention, Uranus, Neptune, and Pluto were added to the list, and since Pluto's discovery in 1930 there have been many more celestial bodies discovered: asteroids, comets, planetoids, minor or "dwarf" planets (of which Pluto is now a member), not to mention a slew of exoplanets.[7]

Castor: *Exoplanets?*

Pollux: It's a planet that orbits a star other than our Sun.

Loren: To date, astronomers have discovered hundreds of them.

Castor: You mean, we're not alone in the universe?

Loren: There's always that possibility. Back to planets. Tucked away in the footnote section of *Cosmos and Psyche*, Richard Tarnas describes the classical planets as "all the visible celestial bodies that, unlike the fixed stars, moved through the sky in ways that differed from the simple single motion and eternal regularity of the diurnal westward movement of the entire heavens."[8] The author goes on to say that although a distinction was often made between the Sun and the Moon and the first five visible planets, the astrological tradition generally included the two luminaries or "lights" as part of the planetary lineup. Tarnas acknowledges that even in Shakespeare's day this was known, given the words that the English bard put into the mouth of Ulysses in Act I, Scene III of *Troilus and Cressida*:

> The heavens themselves, the planets and this centre
> Observe degree, priority and place,
> Insisture, course, proportion, season, form,
> Office and custom, in all line of order,
> And therefore is the glorious planet Sol
> In noble eminence enthroned and sphered...[9]

Castor: No wonder I barely passed my literature classes.

Loren: You and me both, Castor, but for all of Shakespeare's wit and wisdom, let us turn to astrologers to help us understand the planets and, in particular, how astrologers subdivide them into meaningful groups. To do that, let's visit the work of several contemporary astrologers and see how they divide up the pie.

Castor: Now you're talking.

Pollux: Not that kind of pie, Castor.

Loren: In *Astrology: A Guide to Understanding Your Birth Chart*, Yasmin Boland divides the planets into *inner* planets (Sun, Moon, Mercury, Venus, and Mars) and *outer* planets (Jupiter, Saturn, Uranus, Neptune, and Pluto). That seems plausible given the difference between the inner "solid" planets and the giant outer "gas" planets (all but Pluto, that is).[10] In *The Astrology Bible*, Judy Hall uses the same categories only with a different lineup in each category: inner planets (Sun, Moon, Mercury, Venus, Mars, Jupiter, and Saturn) and outer planets (Uranus, Neptune, and Pluto).[11] Finally, in *The Essential Guide to Practical Astrology*, April Elliott Kent divides the pantheon of heavenly bodies into *personal* planets (Sun, Moon, Mercury, and Venus), *social* planets (Mars, Jupiter, and Saturn), and *generational* planets (Uranus, Neptune, and Pluto).[12]

Pollux: How do you group the planets?

Loren: Here's my preference: the light-giving *luminaries* (Sun and Moon), the zippy *personal* planets (Mercury, Venus, and Mars), the chatty *social* planets (Jupiter and Saturn), and the slow-beating *generational* planets (Uranus, Neptune, and Pluto).

Castor: Why do you divide them this way?

Loren: Let me present the list again, this time adding the duration of each planet's orbit as they appear to revolve around the Earth: let's skip the luminaries as they present a unique case and start with the *personal* planets, Mercury (88 days), Venus (225 days), and Mars (687 days); then consider the *social* planets, Jupiter (12 years) and Saturn (29 years); and finally end with the *generational* planets, Uranus (84 years), Neptune (165 years), and Pluto (248 years).[13] I think you can see the logic of these groupings from each planet's orbital period around the Sun.

Before we move on, however, I'd like to return to Robert Hand, who analyzes planetary pairings. I find what Hand says about a Sun/Earth pairing quite insightful. According to Hand, from an objective viewpoint, the Sun is the center of the solar system because "it is the dynamic focus of the solar system, providing almost all the radiant energy and holding the system together in its powerful gravitational field."[14] The Earth, on the other hand, is the solar system's subjective center because the ability to experience the solar system is centered here, i.e., in human consciousness. "All the energy put out by the Sun and reflected in various ways by the planets is experienced by us on Earth. Experience by its very nature requires awareness, and the Earth is our center of awareness."[15] That being said, when considering how to subdivide the planets into smaller, meaningful groups, it is quite natural for astrologers to start with a separate category for the Sun and the Moon given their size and irrepressible nature.

Castor: What about the personal planets?

Loren: The personal planets are "personal" because of the way they zip around the zodiac, anywhere between 88 and 367 days. Think of it this way: if the average lifespan of a person is 84 years (I'll tell you why I chose this number later), then the personal planets will "visit" you—your signs and houses— up to four times a year, depending upon which planet we're talking about. As such, they are "personal" because they have the most impact on the development of your unfolding ego-identity, revealing the behavior and characteristics that make you unique (which, of course, is why they are called personal planets). More than any other celestial bodies, they tell you who you are and how you relate to the world around you. Think of it this way: while the personal planets are the sleek speedboats zipping by the shoreline, sending wave after wave crashing upon the beach, the social planets are the touring cruise ships passing every 12 to 29 years, and the generational planets the ore-laden barges chugging along at an interminable 85 to 248 years.

Pollux: So it's not their distance from the Sun, but their relative orbital period that helps to distinguish them.

Loren: Yes, but distance does have something to do with it. The difference in orbital period between Mars (1.88 years) and Jupiter (12 years) is largely a function of the distance Mars and Jupiter are from the Sun. Since we're considering Mars and Jupiter, here's someting else to consider: the "asteroid belt," a torus-shaped region (think: inner tube) between rock-solid Mars and gaseous Jupiter.

Castor: That's where Ms. Frizzle was stuck.

Loren: This is an area that is occupied by a great many small, solid, and irregularly shaped bodies called asteroids or "minor" planets. Although there are other asteroid populations in the solar system, this region is the most dense. Currently, NASA tracks about 10,000 asteroids, way too many for an astrologer to keep tabs on (though software is available to do just that). Since half of the mass of the asteroid belt is contained in the four largest asteroids (Ceres, Vesta, Pallas, and Hygiea), contemporary astrologers often add these to their calculations, leaving the rest to the micro-interest of "asteroid astrologers." But there's another reason as well.

Castor: Because they're almost big enough to be planets?

Loren: It has less to do with their physical attributes and more to do with their symbolism. According to astrologer and

Reiki master Kesaine Walker, the asteroids bring something to the planetary lineup that most of the other planets don't.[16]

Castor: They're square?

Loren: No, they're not square; they're feminine in nature. In fact, aside from Venus and the Moon, they're the only bodies considered to have feminine characteristics.[17]

Castor: They're goddesses!

Loren: Yes, they're goddesses. According to Elizabeth Gulino, author of "Asteroids Are The Goddesses Of Astrology: Here's What They Mean For You," most of the major asteroids in the asteroid belt are named after female figures from either Greek or Roman mythology. Take the four alluded to above: *Juno*, named after Hera, the Greek goddess of love and marriage, was a Roman goddess who watched over all aspects of women's lives; *Ceres*, the counterpart of the Greek goddess Demeter, was the Roman goddess of agriculture, fertility, and motherly relationships; *Pallas*, named after the Greek goddess Athena, was the warrior goddess, the protectress of Athens and other Greek cities, who fought in the name of justice; and *Hygiea*, the daughter of Asclepius, the Greek god of medicine, was who you turned to when your health was in question.[18]

Castor: Impressive.

Loren: Yes, and the feminine energy they brought to astrology was no accident: it arose during the Women's Movement of the 1970s. However, contemporary astrologers don't always concern themselves with asteroids, so let's move on to the social planets, of which there are two: Jupiter and Saturn.

Castor: Are they called "social" planets because they talk a lot?

Loren: It's not so much about talking as it is about their orientation. In contrast to the personal planets that focus on the evolving individual, the social planets relate to the world of people. In general, Jupiter and Saturn describe one's attitudes toward the collectives or groups of people to which an individual belongs. In other words, they often say more about one's social standing and environment than they do about one's inner or personal development. Given their respective orbits—12 and 29 years respectively—they recur throughout an individual's life in an episodic manner.

Pollux: What do you mean "episodic?"

Loren: To answer that, I'll have to talk about why I used 84 years as the average lifespan of an individual earlier. Many occult or esoteric astrologers use that number based less on accurate demographic data than on the need for a reasonable (i.e., mathematically nimble) end date.

Castor: But why 84? Why not 80, or 86, or 92? My grandmother lived until she was 97.

Loren: Yes, but we're not talking about your grandmother. We're talking about the average lifespan of most people, as well as a number that is divisible by seven.

Castor: Why seven?

Loren: According to Rudolph Steiner, an individual's life can be seen as an unfolding series of seven-year periods, i.e., from 0-7, marked by the advent of permanent teeth, 7-14, marked by the onset of puberty, 14-21, marked by an individual's emergence into adulthood, and so on. Although originally set out as 10 seven-year cycles, Steiner's developmental stages have been extended by several of his interpreters to include two additional stages, bringing the full lifespan development to 12 seven-year stages or 84 years.[19]

Pollux: Twelve stages, seven years? That's the same as twelve zodiacal signs and seven classical planets.

Loren: Amazing, isn't it? Another one of Jung's "meaningful coincidences." But it's not just a coincidence; it's the mysterious alignment between the macrocosm and the microcosm. Let's divide the twelve stages of a human life in half. Transpersonal psychologist Ken Wilber, author of *The Atman Project: A Transpersonal View of Development*, does just that, calling the two halves of the human life cycle the "outward arc" and the "inward arc."[20] During the outward arc phase, from birth to age 42, we push outwards or away from our family and close social setting in order to establish ourselves in society. During the inward arc phase, from ages 42 to 84, we take the measure of our life, ultimately pulling back into ourselves to prepare for our final years.

Castor: But how does this relate to Jupiter and Saturn?

Loren: If we take 84 years as the average life span of an individual, with an orbital period of 12 years, Jupiter will return seven times during an individual's lifetime. Saturn, on the other hand, is a little messier: with an orbital period of 29.47 years, it will return just shy of three times during an individual's lifetime. Some astrologers, especially occult astrologers during the late nineteenth century, round Saturn's orbit down to an even 28 years so it will return exactly three times during an average lifetime of 84 years. Twenty-eight is interesting in more ways than one: not only is it closer to the lunar cycle, but also it is divisible by seven, which means it fits nicely into many numerical associations, including Steiner's seven-year developmental cycles. But enough of Jupiter and Saturn, at least for now. Let's move on to the outer planets—Uranus, Neptune, and Pluto. Oh, except I forgot: we need to talk about Chiron.

Castor: *Chiron?*

Loren: In 1977, astronomer Charles Kowal discovered the dried-up husk of an old comet orbiting the Sun between Saturn and Uranus. It was the first identified member of a new class of celestial objects now known as "centaurs" (small "planetoids" orbiting between the asteroid belt and the Kuiper belt, a disk-shaped area filled with small or dwarf "planets" and the remnants of spent comets that orbit the Sun beyond Neptune). Like other planets and asteroids, Chiron is named after a figure in Greek mythology, in this case a centaur who was a teacher and healer, and who, ironically, couldn't heal himself. In a birth chart, Chiron is the "wounded healer," pointing to where an individual has healing powers as the result of their own deep spiritual wounds. Once faced and overcome, those wounds—now powers—can help others overcome something they struggle with in their life as well.[21] Chiron is one of the new generation of astrological points that contemporary astrologers include in their chart analysis. This brings us to the last group of planets to consider. Often called the generational planets, Uranus, Neptune and Pluto form a unique group of planets at the outer edge of the solar system, far enough away at least that we had to wait for the invention of the telescope to discover them. But why do we call them "generational" planets?

Pollux: I assume, given their orbital periods, that they only show up once in a lifetime.

Loren: Precisely, and what that means is that they are not unique to you, at least in the way that the personal planets are. For instance, if you were born in the 1960s, an age known as the "counterculture" generation, the sign and house placement of Uranus, Neptune, and Pluto, will be fairly close to everyone else's born during that decade: they move that slowly (remember, they're the ore-laden barges of the solar system: two-and-a-half centuries alone for Pluto to make its revolution around the Sun). Because of this, the three planetary bodies speak more to the needs and wants of a generation of people than they do to the needs of an individual.

Pollux: If that's the case, why bother with them when analyzing a birth chart?

Loren: Most astrologers don't bother with them. However, they can help clarify areas that are unclear or murky. They're also important to consider, as we've seen, when they are involved in major aspects and aspect patterns.

Castor: They're included in the author's birth chart.

Loren: Yes, and, as such, they add depth to the interpretation of his chart dynamics. In the author's case, they're bunched together, from second-house Uranus to fifth-house Neptune (with fourth-house Pluto in between).

Pollux: Why do astrologers use a natal chart in the first place?

Loren: Simply, it's easier to grasp the dynamic nature of planet, sign, and house relationships presented in a distilled graphic form than it is in a lengthy written form. To do this, as you learned earlier, astrologers have turned words into "glyphs" or symbols.

Pollux: Do astrologers use the same symbols?

Loren: Generally speaking, yes, at least in Western astrology. Of course, it's not *what* they use, but *how* they use it that distinguishes an astrologer. To see these different approaches, we don't have to go very far. In 2004, Rafael Nasser published a book on astrology titled *Under One Sky*.[22] It is a very unique exploration of this fascinating, albeit perplexing, topic. Nasser, with the help of publisher Jodie Forrest, assembled twelve astrologers from different philosophical backgrounds, giving each one the task of analyzing the natal chart of the same person. Each astrologer, working independently, was asked to do a "blind" reading of the subject, who went by the pseudonym "Joyce," based solely on her birth data. Nasser's book really gives you a sense of the myriad of approaches that astrologers use to interpret a natal chart and the particular techniques they employ to that end, approaches that range from Demetra George's "asteroid-centered" approach, to Ken Bowser's "Western sidereal" approach, to Stephen Forrest's "evolutionary astrology" approach, to Wendy Ashley's "mythological" approach.[23]

Castor: Remember that headache I get occasionally...

Author: It's coming back.

Castor: Afraid so.

Loren: And this is just four of the twelve approaches represented in Nasser's book. As you can see, there are a number of ways to...

Castor: Turn the kaleidoscope.

Loren: Yes, I guess you could say that. Different astrologers not only understand the principles of astrology differently, but they also apply those principles in a different manner. Perhaps a better way to say this is that astrologers emphasize different aspects of astrology given their unique philosophical perspective, but also (and I underscore this) to what ends they apply their analysis. In other words, an astrologer interested in event-prediction will probably emphasize different astrological elements than an astrologer interested in their client's personal well-being. In any case, Nasser's book is a "must-have" for any practicing astrologer no matter what their orientation as it covers a wide range of astrological understanding and application.

Castor: I'll consider it.

Notes

1. Sobel, Dava. *The Planets*, Introduction.
2. Cole, Joanna and Bruce Degen. *The Magic School Bus Lost in the Solar System*. New York: Scholastic Press, 1992.
3. Hand, Robert. *Horoscope Symbols*, Chpt. 5, "Other Points in the Chart."
4. *Ibid.*

5. *Ibid.*

6. Herring, Amy. *Essential Astrology*, Chpt. 10, "The Aspects."

7. Orion, Rae. *Astrology For Dummies*, Chpt. 14, "A Guide to Understanding Your Birthchart."

8. Tarnas, Richard. *Cosmos and Psyche*, Notes, Part III: "Through the Archetypal Telescope, Entry #9."

9. Shakespeare, William. *Troilus and Cressida* (1.3.86-91) in *The Complete Works of Wiliam Shakespeare*, MIT Digital Archive, [URL] shakespeare.mit.edu/troilus_cressida/index.html.

10. Boland, Yasmin. *Astrology*, Chpt. 4, "Getting to Know the Planets."

11. Hall, Judy. *The Astrology Bible*, Chpt. 4, "The Planets."

12. Kent, April Elliott. *The Essential Guide to Practical Astrology*, Part IV, "Gods and Monsters: Planets."

13. "Planetary Fact Sheet," *Goddard Space Flight Center*, [URL] nssdc. gsfc.nasa.gov/planetary/factsheet/.

14. Hand, Chpt. 2, "The Symbol Systems of Astrology."

15. *Ibid.*

16. Walker, Kesaine. Kesaine, [URL] kesaine.com/about.

17. For a thorough exploration of the mythology of goddesses and their introduction into contemporary astrology see Demetra George and Douglas Bloch's *Asteroid Goddesses: The Mythology, Psychology, and Astrology of the Re-Emerging Feminine* (Newburyport, MA: Nicolas-Hays, 2003).

18. Gulino, Elizabeth. "Asteroids Are The Goddesses Of Astrology. Here's What They Mean For You," *refinery29*, [URL] www. refinery29.com/en-us/2020/06/9888932/asteroid-day-2020-astrology-meaning/. It was not a woman, however, who discovered Ceres, the first of the large asteroids to be discovered: it was Guiseppe Piazzi, a Sicilian priest and head of the Palermo Observatory, who accidently discovered Ceres between the orbits of Mars and Jupiter in 1801 while correcting errors for a new edition of a star catalog. He named the celestial body "Ceres Ferdinandea," after the Roman and Sicilian goddess of grain, whose

mythological site happened to be nearby, and King Ferdinand IV of Naples and Sicily. For a fuller description, see the entry under "Asteroids" written by Demetra George in William E. Burns's *Astrology Through History*.

19. Monte, Tom. "The 7-year Cycles of Life," [URL] tommonte.com/the-7-year-cycles-of-life/.
20. Wilber, Ken. *The Atman Project*, Chpt. 1, Prologue.
21. Hall, Chpt. 4, "The Planets."
22. Nasser, Rafael. *Under One Sky*. Borego Springs, CA: Seven Paws Press, 2004. Taking a different tact in *Horoscopes Here and Now* (London: Astro-Analytics Publications, 1975), Robert Jansky presents the chart analysis of one hundred twentieth-century celebrities. In my mind, the two volumes—Nasser's and Jansky's—are a perfect complement to each other.
23. *Ibid*. Preface.

13

Healers and Seers

The image of a bearded magus hunched over a candle
lit tome as he painstakingly calculates the position
of the planets has been replaced by the image of a
modern astrologer a mouse click away from powerful
charting tools that would bedazzle the old wizard.[1]
Rafael Nasser, *Under One Sky*

Castor: How do you work?

Pollux: *Castor.*

Loren: That's okay, Pollux. Castor's curiosity is often the
source of his bluntness.

Castor: [smiling]

Loren: First of all, in terms of my philosophical
perspective, I tend to identify with humanistic or
transpersonal astrologers who use astrology in their
therapeutic work. Although I'm not a trained therapist, I view
the astrologer/client relationship through that lens. In other
words, my concern is the client and his or her well-being. I see
my job as helping the client gain insight into their personality
using the multi-faceted tools of astrology. For this approach
we have three people to thank: Alan Leo, Carl Jung, and Dane
Rudhyar. These late nineteenth and early twentieth-century

thinkers helped steer the focus of astrology away from event prediction toward the more contemporary use of astrology as an adjunct to the therapeutic setting. Of course, popular astrology, based on Sun Sign astrology, will always be with us, but the real focus and use of contemporary astrology is in the therapeutic arts. You could say that these three individuals ushered in the Second European Renaissance.

Castor: Second Renaissance?

Loren: After the "Dark Ages," which wasn't as dark as historians made it out to be, Europeans began to rediscover the classical Greco-Roman world. The interest in Hellenic and Roman culture began in southern Europe during the twelfth century, peaking around the middle of the sixteenth century. In high school, where we first learned about the European Renaissance, we memorized the names of Boccaccio, Petrarch, Bruneschelli, Leonardo da Vinci, and Michelangelo, among others. But there was another European Renaissance, during the late nineteenth century. After the Scientific Revolution, which began in the mid-sixteenth century, the doors of understanding opened to modern science and a "mechanistic" view (although some would argue a "nihilistic" view) of the universe. Under the weight of a mechanistic view, the esoteric sciences, of which astrology was but one, fell off the table. They were ridiculed, laughed out of town.

Castor: Why?

Loren: Because people believed "scientific rationalism" was the answer to all of society's problems. But logic and reason, the two pillars of the Scientific Revolution, and the Industrial Revolution which followed on the heels of it, were not enough to satisfy the totality of an individual's yearning. In other words, people hungered for more: a spiritual life that transcended the rigidity of scientific materialism. Into this hunger stepped Alan Leo, Carl Jung, and Dane Rudhyar, three important figures in the world of astrology who breathed new life into astrology at the turn of the twentieth century with their interest in the "occult sciences."

Born William Frederick Allan, British publisher, author, and astrologer Alan Leo (1860-1917) is often regarded as the "Father of Modern Astrology." An early follower of H. P. Blavatsky, the Russian spiritualist who founded the Theosophical Society in 1875, Leo co-founded *The Astrologer's Magazine* (later renamed *Modern Astrology*) in 1889. The magazine did so well that Leo founded the Modern Astrology Publishing Company to publish and distribute other materials based on the British public's growing interest in astrology. By 1910, Leo had published a number of pamphlets and books of his own that were quite successful, including *Astrology for All* (1899), *How to Judge a Nativity* (1904), and *The Key to Your Own Nativity* (1910). Several years later, Leo established the London Astrological Lodge of the Theosophical Society. Through his writings and tireless speaking engagements, Leo helped shift the focus of astrological work from event prediction to personal analysis.

Somewhat skeptical of the esotericism of Blavatsky's theosophical movement, Swiss psychoanalyst Carl Gustave Jung (1875-1961) had an abiding interest in astrology, seeing it as essential to an understanding of the personal mythos of many of his clients' life story. Although a student of the occult sciences, especially Hermeticism, Gnosticism, and Neoplatonism, Jung was careful not to shroud his interest in astrology in esoteric jargon. Preferring the newly emerging terminology of psychology, to which he and his one-time mentor Sigmund Freud are credited, Jung understood the horoscope not only as a psychological map of character, but also as a meaningful narrative, one mythic in scope. This is consistent with Jung's idea, expressed early in his profession, that the signs of the zodiac—indeed, all celestial phenomena imbued with symbolic value—are nothing more than projections of the unconscious.[2]

Person-centered astrology, also known as transpersonal astrology, would not get off the ground until French-born American author, modernist composer, and humanist Dane Rudhyar (1895-1985) began applying the concepts of both Leo and Jung to his growing interest in astrology.[3] Born Daniel Chennevière in Paris, Rudhyar (whose pseudonym is a cognate of several Sanskrit words for "god") was a sickly child, who turned to music and philosophy to compensate for his lack of physical vigor. At the age of 21, with a degree in music from the Paris Conservatoire in his back pocket, Rudhyar sailed to New York City to showcase his orchestral arrangements and original compositions with the New York Metropolitan Opera. As a result of his stay in America, Rudhyar became exposed to Oriental philosophy and Western occultism, the latter of which led him to a serious study of Blavatsky's Theosophy. He was introduced to astrology by the American astrologer Marc Edmund Jones, who became Rudhyar's mentor. After becoming a naturalized citizen of the

United States in 1926, Rudhyar split his time between the East and West Coasts. More than Leo and Jung, Rudhyar's work became the foundation upon which subsequent generations of humanistic or person-centered astrologers would stand.

Castor: Wasn't it Einstein who said, I stand upon the shoulders of giants.

Pollux: I think it was Isaac Newton.

Loren: In reality, everyone stands upon the shoulders of those who came before them: I stand upon the shoulders of Leo, Jung, and Rudyhar. They provide a solid platform, i.e., philosophical orientation, in which to operate as an astrologer.

Castor: Which leads us to, Just how do you work?

Loren: To answer that question, let's start with a quote from *Stephen Arroyo's Chart Interpretation Handbook*: "One needs to focus on what is important for the person in order not to get lost in endless possibilities. If one tries to do a 'complete reading' for a person, there is no end to it; it is really an absolute impossibility. How could any of us ever sum up such a complex, infinite, and ever-changing mystery as a human being?"[4] In other words, in order to avoid the trap of "endless possibilities," an astrologer needs a roadmap, a set of concrete guidelines to help him or her through the maze of chart indicators. Here's my roadmap, based on years of experience and the wisdom of others.[5]

I read the chart as a whole, looking for the unaspected global chart pattern. Is it a bowl, a bundle, a seesaw, a locomotive, a splash, or a fan? This is the most helpful starting point for me. Then, I take a close look at the Primal Triad: the

Rising sign, the Sun sign, and the Moon sign, with a particular emphasis on the Sun/Moon relationship. While considering the Rising sign and Ascendant, I ascertain the overall chart ruler and calculate the chart's dispositors, determining if there are several or a final or sole dispositor.

This usually leads me to some other questions about planets: How many planets are near or on the cusp of the major chart angles? Which is the most elevated planet? Which planet is the most heavily aspected? Is there a leading planet? How many planets are in their own signs? Their own house? What is the rising planet? Is there a stellium? A planet in singleton?

I also look at the preponderance of planets by polarity, quality, element, and house. How many planets are in positive and negative signs? How many planets are in cardinal, fixed, and mutable signs? How many planets are in fire, earth, air, and water signs? How many planets are in angular, succedent, and cadent houses?

Finally, using the five major Ptolemaic aspects, I consider planetary relationships, both bi-planetary aspects (conjunction, sextile, trine, etc.) and multi-planet aspect patterns (T-square, Yod, Grand Trine, etc.). I also look at the most frequently appearing aspect, the most aspected planet, any unaspected planets, and aspects or aspect patterns involving the inner or personal planets. Usually, this is more than enough information to prepare me for a client consultation.

Castor: Is this the format you use when you consult with a client?

Loren: Oh, no. This is the background "noise," if you will. Or, more positively, it's the knowledge base that I acquire before I meet with a client. What I do in a consultation, whether it be face-to-face or digital, is listen.

Castor: *Listen?*

Pollux: Something Castor is still trying to master.

Loren: Like many contemporary astrologers, I come from a psychological orientation, in particular a person-centered perspective. In this setting, I see it as my role to come armed to the hilt with information about the client based on a reading of his or her chart, but it is up to the client to draw it out of me.

Castor: I don't get it.

Loren: It's simple. A client is only ready to "hear" you once they've opened themselves up to questioning. In other words, you can talk to a client all day long about what you've found in his or her natal chart, but if the client is not receptive to what you have to say, nothing will get through. So I try to create as welcoming an environment as I can and gently prod the client to ask questions. Think of a client as a flower bud in early spring. It is only with time, patience, and effort—conscious attention—that you can coax it to bloom, to reach its maximum potential. That's what I do.

Pollux: It's like you're an astrological gardner.

Loren: An astrological gardner? I like that.

Castor: So when do we get to ask questions?

Loren: I thought you'd never ask.

Castor: When will I get a new bicycle?

Pollux: Not *that* kind of question, Castor. Something about us, about growing up, something you've always wondered about. Like, why do you talk so much?

Castor: I don't talk...

Author: Hold on, boys. Actually, I'm going to ask the questions. After all, it is my chart.

Castor: *Rats!*

Author: Loren, I know there are a gazillion questions I could ask you—about my childhood, love life, finances, career, family, etc.—but as we learned earlier, there just isn't time to answer them all since it would take longer to do a full chart analysis of a life than it would to live it. So let me ask you one question and see where it takes us. When I had my chart read in the mid-1980s by the computer-analyst-qua-astrologer, he told me that I had all of the Writers Destiny Marks except one...

Castor: Contact with publishers.

Pollux: *Castor.*

Castor: Well, it's true.

Author: Yes, it's true. But what are Writers Destiny Marks? And what did he mean that I lacked contact with publishers? Since I've averaged a book a year for the last thirty years, I really want to know what he was thinking about or, better yet, what he was "seeing" in my natal chart.

Loren: Actually, I've never heard of Writers Destiny Marks. It could be that it's your astrologer's own term, coined from what I would call "indicators" of writing talent or potential. That being the case, I'd say you have two questions: the one having to do with writing; the other with publishing. As you know, these are not one and the same. There are many writers who don't publish their work, for a variety of reasons. Let's begin with indicators in your chart that suggest a proclivity for writing. According to the authors of the online blog post, "Writing Talent in Astrology," a career in writing usually involves Gemini, Mercury, and the third house.[6]

Pollux: That's Ptolemy's natural zodiac: Mercury in Gemini in the third house.

Loren: Yes, that's the most comfortable arrangement in which these three factors find ease of expression given their unique qualities: Mercury (communication) in Gemini (logic, memory, and thinking) in the third house (the house of communication, early childhood education, and siblings).

Castor: Siblings? That's odd.

Loren: Remember, each house of the natal chart covers a variety of human experience.

Castor: But the author doesn't have Mercury and Gemini in the third house.

Loren: Not too many people do. It's a rare occurrence for your natal chart to line up exactly with Ptolemy's natural zodiac. Nonetheless, knowing where Gemini and Mercury are and what is in the third house is very important. Let's start, not with Gemini, or Mercury, or the third house; let's start with the first house, which is...?

Pollux: The house of identity and personality development.

Castor: It's also the house of your Rising sign, the sign that determines the "face" you put on when you greet the world.

Loren: So a first-house Gemini means that you have a quicksilver mind: you're alert, observant, a real information-processor. But that's your face, your persona; your real or deeper self is hidden behind it in the house of your Sun sign.

Castor: Which in the author's case is still first-house Gemini.

Loren: Which means that the author has no place to hide.

Castor: *No place to hide...* What do you mean?

Loren: Remember, there are always advantages and disadvantages to anything. When it comes to the positive side of being a double Gemini, the two—Rising and Sun sign—conspire to give you great energy. In other words, they amplify the positive qualities of the Gemini personality. On the other hand, since the Rising sign is your mask or persona, and the Sun sign is your deep or true Self, when the two appear in the first house—the house of identity—it's hard to find a place to hide.

Castor: Why would you want to hide?

Loren: We usually hide when faced with an unfamiliar situation: we hide behind our mask (Rising sign) which enables us to face the unknown without risking our deeper self (Sun sign). But when the two are together, there's nowhere to hide.

Author: If I might jump in here, I think I can give you an example. When I was in my twenties, I went to a week-long meditation retreat. A couple of days into it, the retreat organizers decided to hold a concert the last night of the retreat and they asked retreat-goers to audition to be in the show's lineup. I showed up with my guitar, sang a few songs, and was invited to join the group. Not only that, but they wanted me to be the opening act. Wow, what an honor. There was only one dress rehearsal, which was a couple of hours before the concert. I was first and I was a wreck. I couldn't contain my nervousness, no matter what I did. After the rehearsal one of the organizers approached me and said that they had rearranged the lineup and thought it best that I go on toward the end of the show. That was a real blow to my ego. Somehow I got through the show, I don't remember how, and I only tried the "public concert" approach one other time, with the same results unfortunately. I just couldn't control my fear of being front-and-center.

Castor: Stage fright.

Author: Yes, Castor, I had a very bad case of stage fright that I couldn't shake.

Loren: In other words, you couldn't hide behind your Rising sign since it is the same as your Sun sign.

Castor: Did you give up playing guitar in public?

Author: No, I just pivoted and started playing in restaurants and coffeehouses. In this situation, I'm not front-and-center. I'm off to the side and no one's looking at me directly, expecting me to perform. In this situation, I easily lose myself in the music.

Loren: Which brings up several other qualities of Gemini. According to Jodie Forrest, Geminis come into the world "wearing the mask of the Perceiver, the Communicator, the Observer, and the Storyteller."[7] Let's apply that to your coffeehouse performances. In these settings you're all of the above: you communicate or tell stories with your guitar while observing the audience in order to perceive or gauge their response.

Pollux: It's like you've reversed roles: instead of the audience staring at you, now you stare at the audience.

Author: I guess you could say that.

Loren: And you could also say that this is a very good example of the positive, mutable, air quality of a Gemini. Let's circle back to the "Writing Talent in Astrology" post and look at a fuller description of the role of Gemini when it comes to indicating writing talent: "Gemini is the sign of writing. Gemini is the most communicative zodiac sign with the strongest talent for verbal self-expression. People with a strong Gemini have a way with words, they are versatile, smart, observe every detail, and they have what it takes to be a writer."[8] In other words, a favorably placed Gemini is usually a strong indicator of writing talent, and Gemini in the first house is considerably well-placed. But it's not everything.

Castor: Why not?

Loren: Because there are other factors to consider, starting with the zippy, personal planet Mercury. Here's how astrologer Arlan Wise describes Mercury: "He is known by many names: Hermes, Thoth, the Lord of Holy Words, in Norse he is Loki, the Native Americans call him Coyote. He is Raven to the Inuit, and Lugas (god of trade who gives things back and forth) to the Celts. The Hellenistic astrologers called him 'the twinkling one.' Vedic mythology sees him as 'the prince.' He is Jung's *puer aeternus*, the perpetual youth."[9]

Pollux: Castor.

Castor: No more than you.

Loren: Let me once again consult the blog post "Writing Talent in Astrology" and see what the authors have to say about the importance of Mercury: "In astrology, Mercury rules everything related to thinking and communication. This planet governs reading and writing, books, journals, newspapers, everything that enables us to share our thoughts with each other. When talking about writing talent in astrology, Mercury is the most important planet to consider in the natal chart. Writers are often Mercury dominants."[10] And your writing friend is, if nothing else, Mercury dominant. Not only does he have Mercury in the first house, the house of Gemini, Mercury is conjunct his Ascendant, with Mars and the Sun close behind. All of this adds up to an all-important first-house stellium.

Castor: *Stellium?*

Pollux: I assume it has to do something with stars since *stella* is Latin for stars.

Loren: Yes, but in this case, we're talking about the "wandering" stars.

Castor: The planets.

Loren: According to Dane Rudhyar, a stellium "is a multiple conjunction; a complex accentuation which involves more than two planets located in a small area." Rudhyar goes on to distinguish between a stellium by house and sign. In the first, four or five planets are within the same house; in the second, four or five planets are within the same sign. In both cases, the focus should be on the house or sign more so than on the planets, which might actually dull or blur each other. In other words, according to Rudhyar, "What stands out is the quality represented by house or sign rather than the activity symbolized by the several planets."[11]

Castor: Wait, you said there has to be four or five planets in a house or sign to make a stellium. The author only has three: Mercury, Mars, and the Sun.

Loren: If you count the Ascendant, which is just off the first-house cusp, then he'd have four "planets" in the sign of Gemini and in his first house, which makes both sign and house important. If you remember, Geminis are all about...

Castor: Logic, memory, and thinking.

Loren: Yes, but it's not that simple. There are many aspects to a Gemini personality. Here's what one of my chart consultants says about Geminis: "Extremely active by nature, you like to get around, meet people and do varied things. Very restless, you just can't seem to stay put. To keep your mind stimulated, you need to be involved in several projects at once, and may be known as a Jack-of-all-trades. You like to read, write letters and talk—constantly. Seemingly ageless, you will always appear much younger than you really are. Adaptable and inquisitive, lively and versatile, you are always open to new ideas and experiences."[12] Since the author is a double Gemini with a first-house stellium no less, with a strongly placed Mercury, he has all of these qualities and then some.

Castor: And then some?

Loren: Yes, and then some, which means that we have to look more closely at Mercury, which we learned earlier is not only the author's chart ruler, but also the author's sole dispositor: in other words, all things—planets, signs, and houses—lead to Mercury.[13] It is, along with Jupiter, a high-focus planet, a planet that exerts maximum influence. When

it combines with either the Sun and/or Mars, especially in the
first house, Mercury's presence indicates the ability to express
thoughts and ideas easily. According to astrologer John Hayes,
this combination all but guarantees that words and ideas will
be conveyed with authority and decisiveness, and that mental
processes will be sharp, incisive, and come with an abundance
of energy.[14]

Author: This may be so, but I didn't realize this until
well into adulthood. I was, as you stated earlier, a Jack-of-all-
trades...

Castor: And master of none.

Pollux: *Castor.*

Castor: But that's the saying, "Jack-of-all-trades and master
of none."

Author: It's okay. Castor's right. I was a master of nothing,
until I figured out that I was destined to be a writer. You see,
when I was a young adult I suffered from the Jack-of-all-trades
syndrome considerably. I just couldn't figure out who I was
or what I wanted to do. I knew it would be related to music or
art, either visual or performance, maybe even both, but I just
couldn't figure it out, so I tried everything: I tried puppetry,
painting, acting, storytelling, music, even dance.

Loren: Thanks to your favorably placed Venus and
Neptune.

Author: The funny thing about it is throughout this
period, a period that lasted a good ten years or more, I was
always writing, but I never identified myself as a writer.
Finally, after these excursions into various art forms fell away,
I realized that the one thing I did consistently was write.

That's when I dove headfirst into that world, becoming much more serious and disciplined about writing.

Loren: It doesn't surprise me. You just can't overlook the importance of Mercury in your chart. Not only is Mercury your chart ruler and sole dispositor, but it is also an "angular planet" (a planet close to the cusp of any of the four major angles), and an angular planet conjunct your Ascendant. It's also your chart's "leading planet" (the first planet over the horizon after the Ascendant, which is different from Jupiter which "leads" your bowl-shaped chart pattern). All of this adds up to one thing: *words, words, words*. According to noted astrologer Tracy Marks, Mercury is your strongest planet and Gemini your strongest sign. Their combined presence also makes your first house your strongest house. And if that's not enough, Mercury is also implicated in more aspects than any other planet in your chart. And we haven't even talked about the effect of Mars and the Sun in your first house.

Castor: *Ugh*, this is endless.

Loren: No, just the impact of a first-house stellium in Gemini, which I think you can sum up like this: you're a writer, or someone who loves words, given the presence of Mercury (from whence you get a passion for words) in first-house Gemini (in a mind that is quick and alert), fueled both by the Sun (who gives you an abundance of energy and confidence) and Mars (who adds drive and assertiveness to the mix). In fact, if you didn't write, I'd be concerned.

Castor: Could we please end here. My head is spinning.

Loren: Yes, let's take a break, and while we do, I'm going to dig up a research study that I think you'll find interesting.

Notes

1. Nasser, Rafael. *Under One Sky*, Preface.

2. Greene, Liz. *Jung's Studies in Astrology*, Chpt. 1, "Jung's Understanding of Astrology." It was Jung who first connected the ancient art of astrology to the emerging practice of psychotherapy. To Jung, astrology was nothing less than the summation of all psychological knowledge gleaned by our ancestors. In other words, astrology was always "psychological" in orientation, even though it was put toward other ends.

3. According to Laura Andrikopoulos, the term "transpersonal astrology" was first used by Dane Rudhyar in 1930. It referred to a form of astrology that went beyond Jungian psychological description and analysis. It recognized astrology as a "spiritual path that opened the individual up to spiritual forces that could transform consciousness." Many contemporary transpersonal astrologers trace their roots back to the transpersonal psychology of Robert Assagioli who, along with Abraham Maslow, was instrumental in shaping humanistic psychology. Assagioli's work has been the inspiration for Bruno and Louise Huber, founders of the "Huber Method" that emphasizes the use of astrology for psychological and spiritual growth, London-based astrologers Howard Sasportas and Liz Greene of the Centre for Psychological Astrology, and Richard Tarnas's "archetypal astrology." See Laura Andrikopoulos's entry on "Transpersonal Astrology" in William E. Burns's *Astrology Through History*.

4. Arroyo, Stephen. *Stephen Arroyo's Chart Interpretation Handbook*, Chpt. 9, "Guidelines to Chart Synthesis."

5. Loren's approach to chart synthesis and interpretation is an amalgamation of ideas gleaned from Stephen Arroyo's *Chart Interpretation Handbook* (Chpt. 9, "Guidelines to Chart Synthesis"), Tracy Marks' *The Art of Chart Interpretation* (Part I: "Techniques of Chart Synthesis and Interpretation"), and Judy Hall's *The Astrology Bible* (Chpt. 8, "Piecing It All Together").

6.   "Writing Talent in Astrology: Indicators of Writers and Poets in the Birth Chart," *Advanced Astrology* (August 23, 2020), [URL] advanced-astrology.com/writing-talent-in-astrology.

7.   Forrest, Jodie. *The Ascendant: Your Rising Sign*, Chpt. 11, "The Ascendant and Evolutionary Astrology."

8.   "Writing Talent in Astrology," *Ibid.*

9.   Wise, Arlan. "Mercury: The Writer's Friend," *Constellation News* (Sept. 20, 2019), [URL] www.astro.com/astrology/ivccn_ article190920_e.htm.

10. *Ibid.*

11. Rudhyar, Dane. *The Astrology of Personality*, Chpt. 11, "Form and the Pattern of Planetary Aspects."

12. *Astrolabe*, [URL] alabe.com/chartservice/natal.html.

13. Mercury is not only my chart ruler and final or sole dispositor; it is also astrologer Arlan Wise's as well: "Mercury is my final dispositor, as is so with many writers and authors and people who work with words. He rules five planets and two angles in my chart and I've gotten to know him well over the years. He sits with me when I write and he loves it when I teach writing workshops for astrologers..." Wise, Arlan. "Mercury: The Writer's Friend," *Constellation News* (Sept. 20, 2019), [URL] www.astro.com/ astrology/ivccn_article190920_e.htm.

14. Hayes, John. "Indicators of Writing Ability in the Horoscope," [URL] www.johnhayes.biz/Articles/writingAbility.htm.

14

Universal Scheme of Things

If there is any principle that we should keep in mind as we develop the art of chart synthesis, it is this: Start with the characteristics that are most extreme, most powerful, most outstanding, and let the rest of the chart interpretation take shape around them.[1]

Michael R. Meyer, *A Handbook for the Humanistic Astrologer*

It's taken a while, but I finally found it: a research study by the UK-based research group Capricorn Research Astrology (CRA). The question members of the group tried to answer was, Is Mercury the writer's planet?[2] To answer this question, they analyzed the natal charts of over two thousand individuals who described themselves as professional writers. The first thing the group looked at was the most common combination of planet and zodiacal sign. Their research indicated that Venus in Taurus led the list, followed by Mercury in Capricorn, with the Sun in Aries a close third. They also found that most successful writers, like many famous people, have the Sun in their first-house Rising sign. When it comes to conjunctions to the Ascendant, Mercury and Jupiter led the list at 137%, with Venus third at 131%.

Author: That's interesting, because I have both the Sun and Mercury in my first house with Mercury conjunct my Ascendant.

Loren: That's a pretty strong one-two punch, if you ask me. However, what really piqued my interest was CRA's analysis of three subgroups in the study: novelists, poets, and journalists.

Castor: What, no children's book writers?

Loren: I think we'll find that most children's book authors fall into the poets' group, especially those, like our author, who write for younger children. Before we get to that group, let's take a look at novelists and journalists. When it comes to the former, novelists seem to have a very strong Venus placement (remember: Venus in Taurus heads the list). In fact, novelists are the most Venusian of the three groups with the top scoring aspect being Venus conjunct Uranus at 143% followed by Venus conjunct Ascendant at 136%. They also have a very strong Mars/Jupiter opposition (143%). Finally, the most common Sun sign is Pisces (120%), with no dominant house position for any sign or planet.

Journalists, on the other hand, have a different configuration with several strong aspects involving Mercury, Jupiter, and the Ascendant. Here are the top six aspects that indicate a strong preference for the craft of journalism: a Mercury/Ascendant conjunction (166%), a Sun/Jupiter conjunction (157%), a Neptune/Ascendant opposition (153%), a Neptune/Sun conjunction (141%), a Jupiter/Ascendant conjunction (136%), and a Mars/Jupiter opposition (136%).

Pollux: Out of the six, the author only has a Mercury/ Ascendant conjunction.

Loren: Yes, but it's the highest scoring aspect when it comes to journalists. Venus also appears in the list of major aspects, but not near the top: Venus conjunct Ascendant appears at a non-statistically significant 105%. When it comes to signs, whereas Leo is the most common Sun sign (121%), Venus in Sagittarius (139%) heads the list of planets appearing in a particular sign. Finally, like novelists, journalists don't seem to have a dominant house position for any sign or planet.

Castor: And that brings us to poets.

Loren: Poets seem to favor Mercury, Mars, and Venus. When it comes to the latter, Venus in Cancer is statistically significant at 131%, with an even higher score of 159% for a Venus/Jupiter conjunction. But it's really Mercury's position and aspect relationships that determine a predilection for poetry. We find Mercury in the first house statistically significant at 155% and the Sun behind it at 143%. What's really interesting is that Mercury's score in the twelfth house (143%) is also quite high, creating a strong focus around the Ascendant for both Mercury and the Sun.

Pollux: Which is where these two planets are in the author's first house.

Loren: So he's not only a writer, but a writer with a poetic bent.

Castor: What about Gemini? Is that high for poets?

Loren: Actually, the most common Sun sign is Capricorn (117%), though it's not statistically significant. What is

statistically significant, and almost staggering, is a Mercury/
Jupiter conjunction that weighs in at 170%, followed by a
Mercury/Mars opposition (162%). In addition to the Mercury/
Mars opposition, there's also a Sun/Mars opposition (159%)
and a Neptune/Mars conjunction (142%), making Mars,
second to Mercury, more impactful for poets than for novelists
or journalists.

After all is said and done, when it comes to a talent for
speaking and writing, whether you're a novelist, a journalist,
or a poet, it's all about Mercury, Mars, and the Sun in the first
house. They're a potent combination, but we can't stop at the
first house, no matter how populated with planets it is. We
must also consider the third and fifth houses.

Castor: What's so important about them?

Loren: I think you know about the third house already.

Pollux: It's the house of communication and the natural
home of Gemini and Mercury.

Loren: But Mercury is somewhere else...

Castor: In first-house Gemini.

Loren: Yes, but the author's third house is not empty. You'll
find sparkling Venus there, which is a very good placement.
According to the article "If You Want to Be a Writer, What Sign
Should You Be," planets in the third house indicate the type
of writing an individual might favor. Here's a synopsis of what
the authors of this study found: Mercury (a journalist), Mars
(a political or sports writer), Jupiter (a writer of religious or
philosophical tracts), Saturn (a writer of law books or how-to
manuals), Uranus (a technical writer), Pluto (a writer interested
in erotica or other taboo subjects), and Venus (a poet).[3]

Castor: But that doesn't match up to the results of the CRA study.

Loren: Not exactly, though we did see that journalists have a strong Mercury presence, and poets, although linked to Mercury and Mars, have a Venusian emphasis. With Venus, the goddess of art and beauty, in the author's third house, there's a strong urge to write in a pleasing, lyrical manner.[4] What I found, aside from the chart consultants I tapped and the articles I read, is that you can't get away from the heavy emphasis on Mercury in the author's chart, and since Mercury is linked to the third house of communication as its natural ruling planet, Venus becomes an important planet to consider, especially since in third-house Leo it is disposited by the author's first-house Sun (which, in turn, is disposited by Mercury).

In the Koch house system, the author's third house actually spans two signs: Cancer ruled by the Moon and Leo ruled by the Sun. So we must also look to the Moon in fifth-house Libra as another important energetic zone. Since there is an emphasis on both Venus in third-house Leo and the Moon in fifth-house Libra, it is no wonder that the author writes in a lyrical, poetic manner. Now, he may not write poetry in the traditional sense; but more than likely his writing has a lyrical, even musical, quality to it no matter the genre.

Author: I totally relate to this. As I tell my wife, I live in a world of sound and words. The sounds are musical sounds: if I'm not listening to music, I'm usually creating it. Of course, this translates to my writing. I wrote an article about this years ago.[5] The central premise was that words have both meaning and sound. When I write I often pay more attention to the sound of words than I do to their meaning. It's not that meaning isn't important, it's just that my writing has to "flow" in an aesthetically pleasing and lyrical manner.

Loren: And let's not forget Neptune, also in the fifth house. Whereas the Moon represents your intuitive, emotional self, Neptune represents your dreamy, imaginative self.

Author: When I first started writing picture books for children, I studied the work of authors who wrote in a dreamy, lyrical manner, what editors (many of whom despised this type of writing) call mood or "tone" poems. One of my favorite books was *Owl Moon* by the well-known and highly esteemed children's book author Jane Yolen.[6] The award-winning book was so dreamy, so lyrical, so imaginative: I loved it, and read it over and over and over. My first book, *Night Is Coming*, is really an homage to *Owl Moon* and to all of the other tone poems I was reading and analyzing. (Ironically, I found out later that Jane Yolen had as much trouble publishing *Owl Moon* that I did publishing *Night Is Coming*.)[7]

Loren: More than likely that dreamy, lyrical style comes from third-house Venus (your "inner poet") and fifth-house Neptune (your imaginative, intuitive self). Although Mercury, Mars, and the Sun in first-house Gemini give you the urge— and talent—to write, it's third-house Venus and fifth-house Neptune that give your writing that artistic flair; there is grace, charm, and beauty in your writing thanks to these favorably placed planets. As one of my chart consultants says, "You are verbally expressive, diplomatic, and aim to be tactful. You easily win others over with your words, whether it's because of a likable facility with language, a beautiful voice, or a judicious use of words."[8]

This might be a good time to talk about some of your planetary aspects that involve Mercury and Venus, the most important being Mercury sextile Venus (that is, at a two-sign or 60° angle to each other), which gives you more than a pleasing writing voice, but also an excellent speaking voice: "Like a poet, you have a way with words, lulling people into a trance when they hear you speak or read your writing. You understand the mechanics of having a creative and pragmatic mindset. There's a grace to your self-expression that easily captivates those around you."[9]

Author: I've always enjoyed reading work aloud, and not just mine, other authors as well.

Loren: For a fuller explanation of the gifts that a Mercury-sextile-Venus aspect brings you, let me turn to another chart consultant: "You can appreciate the finer, more aesthetic things of life because you have a well-developed sense of form, proportion, design and beauty. With such skills you could perhaps be successful as an artist, sculptor, fashion designer, craftsmen, interior decorator, creative writer, or jewelry designer. This aspect usually gives talent in the arts, whether it be writing, poetry, speaking or musical ability. You may possess a lovely singing voice. You have the ability to bring harmony to situations through your expert use of the spoken word."[10]

Castor: Wait a minute, this doesn't say that he'll be a writer. He could be any number of things: artist, sculptor, fashion designer, craftsmen, interior decorator, creative writer, or jewelry designer.

Loren: Yes, but you're only looking at Mercury sextile Venus. You have to combine that aspect with all of the other indicators in his chart, which, as we've seen, point to a Mercury dominant chart, and that means *words, words, words*.

Castor: Okay, okay, I think I get it: he writes dreamy, imaginative stories for children (Neptune conjunct the Moon in fifth-house Libra) in a song-like, lyrical manner (Venus in third-house Leo), all of which is driven by a quick mind, a strong sense of self, and a mastery of language (Mercury, Mars, and the Sun in first-house Gemini), which he can't wait to share using his sweet, melodious voice (first-house Mercury sextile third-house Venus).

Loren: I'd say you passed your astrology class with flying colors.

Castor: [smiling].

Pollux: But what about fifth-house Saturn in Virgo?

Loren: Oh, yes, we must not ignore that, especially since Virgo is ruled by Mercury (remember, all roads lead to Mercury). Let's start with Virgo. When we dip our toe into Virgo we find a sign that is critical, discriminating, precise, fastidious, modest, and discreet. In other words, Virgo wants to take stock, to analyze—and judge—before committing, and it does so once everything is precise, predictable, and well-ordered. Saturn is a great complement to Virgo since Saturn is all about structure, control, and restriction.

Author: *Structure. Control. Restriction.* I totally relate to this. If I don't maintain a steady, predictable work routine,

I tend to get antsy. In other words, I don't need external deadlines to motivate me to work.

Loren: Which can be good and bad. The upside is that you get things done; the downside is that you don't step away from your work enough to gain perspective, to see the big picture or direction of your writing. That's where your fifth-house Saturn in Virgo comes in. The combination tells me that you seek order and structure, i.e., predictable routines, in order to control your work environment and maintain your highly goal-directed activities.[11] With Saturn in Virgo in the fifth house, the house of creative endeavors (and Mercury in Gemini in the first house), it is no wonder that you have chosen writing as your profession *and* have had success in it. But your success has been incremental: Saturn gives gifts over time and with much effort.[12]

Author: You're right about that: everything has come with effort. I feel like I have to pull each and every piece of writing, especially longer pieces for the adult market, out of me in a protracted and laborious manner.

Loren: That is also the effect of Sun square Saturn, a difficult aspect (90°), but one that adds resilience to your character: you have an underlying grit and determination that allows you to achieve your goals, albeit in a slow and steady manner. Much like a tree, you put emphasis on "building a strong trunk" from which all things flow.[13] Here's what one of my chart consultants says about your work ethic and self-critical attitude: "As the Sun rules our conscious mind, it does enough censoring on its own. It is the 'adult' within us. Saturn, on the other hand, is more like the 'parent' within us.

We need parents to guide us when we are children, and to some degree as adults, but for the most part, we don't need to be censored indefinitely—something that seems to be the case with Saturn-Sun hard aspects, except that the censoring and parenting is coming from within."[14]

Author: What should I do?

Loren: Step back from your writing routine once in awhile and relax. Go for a walk, spend an afternoon in your garden, take a bike ride. You actually have a very interesting dynamic between your Mercurial self and your Sun-in-Virgo, nose-to-the-grindstone self. The former wants things fast, the faster the better so you can move on to other things, other ideas, other writing projects. But you fight that tendency, or at least Saturn in fifth-house Virgo does. It wants to drill down and get it right, at any cost, so you might belabor a piece of writing, often stuck on the smallest detail. But be careful, don't let work and its routine drive you crazy, don't let "order" become the be-all and end-all of your life. Seek balance in your life: remember the first- and seventh-house axis of boundaries between self and others. Whereas your first house is a box of dynamite (Mercury, Mars, the Sun, and your Ascendant), your seventh house is a wasteland, devoid of any planets. In other words, to activate the latter—the seventh house of others—will take effort on your part in order to balance it with the strong first-house emphasis on yourself.[15]

There's something else you should consider, another aspect in your chart: Saturn sesquisquare (135°) your Midheaven. What this aspect indicates is that you are a perfectionist by nature, especially when it comes to mapping out strategy for achieving your life goals. You are often more interested in the successful step-by-step completion of each specific task related to your writing than in getting there as soon as possible. At times, this can cause you problems because you get sidetracked by trying to make sure that minor details are properly taken care of at the expense of forward motion.[16] Couple this with what we learned earlier about the Jupiter/Pluto trine in one of your minor Grand Trines, and you can easily see how you arrive at a fixation—often exaggerated—on some small, often inconsequential, detail in your writing.

Castor: It's down the rabbit hole!

Pollux: *Castor.*

Loren: Your saving grace, however, is that you have great persistence, endurance, patience and staying power.[17] Now, back to your question about writing and publishing. I think we can say hands down that you have an abundance of natal chart indicators—Writers Destiny Marks, if you will—that point to a career as a writer. As to the question of publishing, well, that's a horse of a different color. Let's go back to the author's global chart pattern...

Castor: *Bowl.*

Loren: Yes, a bowl defined by a Jupiter/Neptune opposition, with most of the author's planets in the lower or northern hemisphere. Individuals with this type of hemispheric bowl usually want to keep their writing to themselves. Generally, these are people who value their privacy and are remiss to share their inner world with others. But our author has several forces in his chart that push his writing into the world: along with being a double Gemini and having a first-house stellium (both of which indicate a strong sense of self and purpose), the author has a series of aspect patterns that act as a slingshot hurling energy into his upper hemisphere, the hemisphere of business partnerships, social liaisons, career aspirations, and group memberships. What this means is that poor, lonely eleventh-house Jupiter isn't as lonely as it appears. Not only are their various "nodes" in the author's upper hemisphere (i.e., North Lunar Node, Chiron, Part of Fortune, Midheaven, etc.), but the energy from the lower half of his chart is constantly being funneled into the upper half by several aspect patterns that use a fifth-house Neptune and eleventh-house Jupiter opposition as a slingshot hurling energy toward the author's Midheaven. And just what is the Midheaven or Medium Coeli? According to Michael Meyer, it is "the point of social integration and political power, revealing the individual's orientation to social experiences."[18] In other words, it describes the individual's position in the outer world and the power he or she has over others.

Castor: "Power over others." Ooh, I like that.

Loren: Yes, but power that is more persuasive than authoritative, especially in a Mercury-dominant chart. Now, as to the Midheaven, according to Tracy Marks, the Midheaven indicates the nature of the profession in which an individual is most likely to experience fulfillment, enabling them to achieve success and status. It is: "How we relate to society at large, how we seek to be recognized or to 'belong,' and how we orient ourselves toward concrete goals and bring about our success or failure in the public sphere are all described by the sign of our Midheaven and the location of its ruler by sign, house and aspect."[19]

Pollux: It sounds like it's not just the Midheaven, but also the sign in which it finds itself and the location of the sign's ruling planet.

Castor: It's the same old, same old. Nothing is straightforward. Everything is related, layer upon layer.

Loren: And that is the key to understanding astrology. You can't look at one or two, or even three, factors in a chart. It's a full kaleidoscope of imagery and meaning.

Pollux: So what's the author's Midheaven sign?

Loren: The Midheaven, which sits on the cusp of the tenth house, is firmly situated in the sign of Aquarius.

Castor: *It is the dawning of...*

Pollux: Cool it, Castor, we've already heard that.

Loren: According to April Elliott Kent, Aquarius in the tenth house signifies "a freedom-loving iconoclast," someone who is called to work that allows them to reach large numbers of people with an expansive, positive message.[20] Someone, often an entrepreneur or someone who is self-employed, who values freedom and originality above all other qualities in his or her work. In short, you are unconventional and unique and seek employment that is forward-looking and progressive, and that provides tangible benefits to society.[21]

Author: If I might comment on that. Although I have spent much of the last thirty years writing, I was a teacher first.

Loren: A very suitable profession not only for a Mercury-dominant individual, but also for someone with Aquarius in the tenth house.

Author: In fact, I've always seen myself as a teacher first and a writer second.

Loren: That's your lower hemisphere filled with planets pulling you back into yourself.

Author: First, I taught children…

Loren: Thanks to your favorably placed third-house Venus and fifth-house Neptune/Moon conjunction.

Author: Then, after receiving my doctorate, I taught teachers in a graduate education program. It was a very progressive, student-centered program based loosely on Harold Bloom's "Great Books" model.

Loren: Unconventional and unique?

Author: Yes, not your regular, everyday academic program.

Loren: So let's add to the mix tenth-house Aquarius's ruling planet. But first, before we identify this planet, a few general thoughts about rulership. According to Stephen Arroyo, "The ruling planet of the Midheaven sign is important not only due to its general symbolic meaning, but also due to the fact that its house position so often shows where your real vocation comes into clearest focus. That house represents a field of experience which feels like your true calling at a very deep level."[22]

Castor: If the Midheaven is in Aquarius, then the ruling planet is Uranus in the second house.

Loren: Yes, *except…*

Castor: You always say that.

Loren: Except, according to Arroyo, if your Midheaven is in a sign that has both a traditional ruler and a modern ruler, the house position of the traditional ruler is usually more important than that of the modern ruler.[23]

Pollux: Which means that instead of second-house Uranus, we have to look at fifth-house Saturn, Aquarius's traditional ruler.

Loren: And that means two things will be important to the author: children and creativity.

Author: I don't think you could sum up my life and career more succinctly.

Pollux: But what about this publishing thing?

Loren: We're getting there. The next question we have to ask is, Are there any planets near the Midheaven?

Castor: Nope.

Loren: Which doesn't mean that you won't have a satisfying or successful career. Far from it, it means that the issues related to career and social status are not as important for you as they are for others.[24] Here's another way to think about it: "Planets at the Midheaven or in the tenth house represent strength in the public or outer world—the world of ambition and status. Planets in the tenth house indicate the conscious motivation behind a person's actions."[25] I want to underscore "conscious motivation" because the author wants success, even fame, but he is not consciously motivated to achieve this. In other words, his success is derived from disciplined work that in-and-of-itself is rewarding (whether it brings external rewards or not); everything else, as they say, is icing on the cake.

Castor: *Cake?*

Pollux: There's no cake, Castor. It's just a saying.

Castor: Doesn't hurt to ask.

Author: I think I know what Loren means though, and perhaps it explains the idea that I have all of the Writers Destiny Marks except contact with publishers. I've always been motivated to write, but I've not always been motivated to find a publisher for my work. It is hard work, and often unrewarding. But I did do it...

Loren: You can thank fifth-house Saturn in Virgo for your "never-give-up" work ethic.

Author: But even working hard, trying to get my writing out into the world, there have always been bumps in the road.

Loren: You might look to fourth-house Pluto in Leo for that, after all Pluto—the Great Disrupter—is a high-focus planet in your chart, given its placement and involvement in several bi-planetary aspects and multi-planet aspect patterns.

Author: Often, I would sell a manuscript to an editor only to find out later that she had left her position for another job, or that the company had been sold to a large conglomerate. In both cases, the door slammed shut without the possibility of further sales. On two occasions I had manuscripts canceled because of a downturn in the economy. Once, I sold a manuscript to a senior editor, but when the illustrations came in, they were horrid, I mean utterly miserable. Unfortunately, the editor was retiring and no one at the publishing house wanted to take up the project, so the house canceled the project. And then there was the time I sold a manuscript to a small company: first, the acquiring editor left for another job; then her replacement left for another job; then, if that wasn't enough, the illustrator came down with a disabling disease and couldn't finish the work. Guess what? Project canceled.

Loren: Disruption after disruption after disruption. Oh, that Pluto.

Castor: I'd say it's time to give up and look for a new profession.

Loren: But not our author. He did what his chart indicates. He looked toward the sign in his Midheaven—Aquarius in the tenth house—and forged on to greater heights, or, should I say, to an independent writing and publishing life.

Castor: Self-publishing?

Loren: Yes, the world of independent, do-it-yourself digital publishing is a perfect match for this author as it provides maximum freedom both in terms of controlling the publishing process, but, more importantly, in providing maximum freedom in his writing.

Author: But I didn't plan it that way.

Loren: No, that's your overly-cautious, conservative streak, for which you can thank fifth-house Saturn in Virgo.

Author: It really just kind of happened. After the market crash in 2008, I was talking to a few editors and they all said the same thing: Come back in a year or two. Not only are we not buying manuscripts right now, but we're slowing down production on everything. Well, I wasn't ready to slow down.

Loren: Here, you can thank your Mercury-dominant chart with a first-house solar stellium, which gives you an abundance of mental energy, drive, and self-confidence.

Author: After talking with several other editors, I decided to try my hand at independent publishing, more as a way of keeping my head in the game. I saw it as a place-marker, a temporary foray in the world of independent digital publishing. I'd jump back into the "real" world of publishing once the economy turned around. So I looked for a manuscript in my files that probably wouldn't sell under normal circumstances. I pulled out a travelogue that I'd been keeping, a tongue-in-cheek look at my travels to schools as a children's book author.[26] I dusted it off, added a few more vignettes, tapped a graphic artist friend of mine to do the layout, and published it myself. It was an enjoyable experience, but I still saw it as a place-marker, a temporary reprieve given current economic conditions.

Loren: Again, the effect of conservative fifth-house Saturn in Virgo.

Author: More time elapsed, still no sales to a traditional publisher, so I decided to self-publish again. I did the same thing: I looked for a manuscript in my files that probably wouldn't sell. This time I pulled out a very dreamy piece of lyrical writing titled "Gaya Lives in a Blue House."[27] A children's picture book, yes, but for a very small niche. I was sure I would have a hard time selling it, so I published it myself. Again, I tapped my graphic artist friend to do the layout, as well as my wife to do the illustrations. It was a much more involved process, which I managed from beginning to end.

Loren: Not only do you seek to control your work schedule; you seek to control your entire creative output.

That's the push-pull tension between eleventh-house Jupiter (expansion) and fifth-house Saturn (restriction).

Author: As a picture-book author, I'm usually involved only at the front end of the editorial process—if that. Once the piece is handed off to the illustrator, I'm shown the door. I learned that early in my career. I received the "folded-and-gathered" galley sheets from an editor with a post-it note attached to it. The note read, "Here's your book, how do you like it?" Well, I wrote the editor a three-page letter telling her exactly what I thought. She wrote back to remind me that the question was rhetorical, i.e., it was too late to suggest changes. But as an independent author/publisher, this is not the case: I take a hands-on approach during the entire process. Not only that, but I found out after my third self-published book that I actually enjoy all of the stages of publishing a book. Now, I don't just write a book: I write, design, publish, promote, and sell my own work.

Loren: And in doing so, you have—whether consciously or not—addressed what your computer-analyst-qua-astrologer told you almost forty years ago: that you have all of the Writers Destiny Marks except one...

Castor: Contact with publishers.

Loren: Except now, that is not a condemnation; it is an affirmation of your spirit, of what you long for—complete, unfettered self-expression. And there are several facets in your chart to thank for that, but most of all Jupiter, your most elevated planet.

Castor: What do you mean, "most elevated planet?"

Loren: A chart's most elevated planet is the planet that is closest to an individual's Midheaven, and since Jupiter is the only planet in the author's upper hemisphere, it is, by default...

Castor: The author's most elevated planet.

Loren: When you think of this giant gas planet, remember Jupiter expands whatever it touches. According to Glenn Mitchell, when Jupiter is the most elevated planet, "the individual can feel compelled to exude confidence about matters relating to career." This is because an elevated Jupiter, more than any other indicator, is one of the leading astrological indicators for popularity and success.[28]

Castor: *Wow*.

Pollux: Double wow.

Loren: But we're not through. According to the authors of "Writing Talent in Astrology," not only does Jupiter, the most beneficial planet in astrology, expand everything it touches, but it also brings luck and good fortune. Furthermore, when Jupiter is in a harmonious aspect with Mercury (as it is in the author's chart with Jupiter sextile Mercury), it enhances or elevates writing success. Why? Because when it comes to writing, Jupiter *rules* publishing. And, to push this even further, the author's eleventh-house Jupiter is in Aries, a full-on, take-no-prisoners sign, which indicates that if the author takes charge of his own creative endeavors, those endeavors will bring him luck.[29]

Author: And they have: ten self-published books in the last ten years, with several of them winning recognition by a handful of national literary award organizations.

Loren: What more can you ask for? Not recognition or success, but living up to your potential, potential that lies dormant in the seed-pattern of your natal chart at the time of your birth. Look at it. It's all there. Perhaps the most fitting way to end this discussion is to cite humanistic astrologer Dane Rudhyar again: "The fundamental concept on which astrology is based is that everything that is 'born' (i.e., that begins to operate as an individual factor in a specific environment) at a particular time and point of space is organized according to a particular seed-pattern or archetype symbolized by its birth chart. This seed-pattern defines what that organism (or organized field of activity) SHOULD be if it fulfills its function in the universal scheme of things..."[30]

Author: I guess, in the universal scheme of things, I was born to be a writer.

Loren: But "born to be a writer" does not automatically make you one. You have to take ahold of your fate, your destiny—that special combination of gifts and challenges—and make it manifest in the world. It's the only way you can fulfill your birthright, expressed in your natal chart, that points from the moment of birth to your unique place in the universal scheme of things.

Pollux: Universal scheme of things...

Castor: *Gosh.*

Notes

1. Meyer, Michael R. *A Handbook for the Humanistic Astrologer*, Part 3, The Technique and Procedure of Astrological Interpretation, Chpt. 1, "The Process of Astrological Interpretation."

2. "Mercury - The Writer's Planet ?" *Capricorn Astrology Research* (no date), [URL] astrologyresearch.co.uk/mercury-the-writers-planet.

3. "If You Want to Be a Writer, What Sign Should You Be?" *Ohio Astrology* (February 12, 2012), [URL] ohioastrology.com/2012/02/12/if-you-want-to-be-a-writer-what-sign-should-you-be/.

4. "Writing Talent in Astrology: Indicators of Writers and Poets in the Birth Chart," *Advanced Astrology* (August 23, 2020), [URL] advanced-astrology.com/writing-talent-in-astrology.

5. Nikola-Lisa, W. "Sound and Sense in Children's Picture Books," *Language Arts*, 74 (3), pp. 168-171.

6. Yolen, Jane. *Owl Moon*. New York: Philomel, 1987.

7. Nikola-Lisa, W. *Night Is Coming*. New York: Dutton Children's Books, 1991.

8. *Astrology Cafe*, [URL] www.astrologycafe.com.

9. *Astro-Charts*, [URL] astro-charts.com.

10. *Just Things Astrology*, [URL] justastrologythings.com/pages/chart/.

11. *Just Things Astrology*, [URL] justastrologythings.com/pages/chart/.

12. Pickett, *Ibid*.

13. *Astro-Charts*, [URL] astro-charts.com.

14. *Cafe Astrology*, [URL] cafeastrology.com.

15. *Astro-Charts,* [URL] astro-charts.com.

16. *Astrolabe*, [URL] alabe.com/chartservice/natal.html.

17. *Just Things Astrology*, [URL] justastrologythings.com/pages/chart/.

18. Meyer, Part 2, Astrological Principles, Chpt. 2, "The Axes of Individual Selfhood and the Circle of Houses."

19. Marks, Tracy. *The Art of Chart Interpretation*, Chpt. 1, "The Chart as a Whole."

20. Kent, April Elliott. *The Essential Guide to Practical Astrology*, Chpt. 9, "Celestial Navigation: Angular Houses."

21. Orion, Rae. *Astrology for Dummies*, Chpt. 11, "What You See vs. What You Get: The Rising Sign (And More)."

22. Arroyo, Stephen. *Stephen Arroyo's Chart Interpretation Handbook*, Chpt. 6, "The Ascendant (or Rising Sign) & the Midheaven."

23. *Ibid.*

24. *Astrolabe*, [URL] alabe.com/chartservice/natal.html.

25. Woolfolk, Joanna Martine. *The Only Astrology Book You'll Ever Need*, Chpt. 9, "How to Interpret Your Horoscope."

26. Nikola-Lisa, W. *Hey, Aren't You the Janitor? And Other Tales from the Life of a Children's Book Author*. Chicago: Gyroscope Books, 2011.

27. ———. *Gaya Lives in a Blue House*. Illustrated by Barbara Cooper. Chicago: Gyroscope Books, 2012.

28. Mitchell, Glenn. *Discover the Aspect Pattern in Your Birth Chart*, Chpt. 19, "Most Elevated Planet."

29. Pickett, *Ibid.*

30. Rudhyar, Dane. *Person Centered Astrology*, Chpt. 9, "Astrology as Karma Yoga."

Reader's Guide

I've held off including charts, graphs, and other visual aids in this project since it has always been my intention to write a personal narrative than produce a technical manual. However, if astrology is anything, it is a visual experience. Whether you look up at the night sky or look down at a natal chart, it is all about visualizing: seeing houses, signs, and planets in relationship to each other. To help you see these relationships, astrologers often use a natal chart made from a set of concentric circles or "wheels," where each wheel contains either the houses of the ecliptic, the signs of the zodiac, or the idiosyncratically orbiting planets. In this guide I'm going to focus on how these wheels work, which is essential knowledge for anyone interested in the serious study of chart interpretation.

Let's start with the basic architecture of the natal chart. It is, as mentioned above, a set of concentric circles or wheels, each one—when filled—containing information about the location of houses, signs, and planets at the moment of an individual's birth. It is circular because the circle is an apt metaphor for the zodiac, a band or pathway approximately 18° wide that contains the twelve signs of the zodiac, the apparent pathway of the Sun around the Earth known as the ecliptic, and the planetary orbits.

In Figure 1 below note that the Earth, and by extension, the *natus*, the one born, is at the center of the chart. In astrology, everything is "seen" from the vantage point of the Earth, considered by astrologers the subjective center of the universe. The set of concentric circles around the Earth represent the house, sign, and planet wheels, each one with a separate function and unique movement.

Notice that the natal chart highlights four important points or angles: the Ascendant (ASC), the Midheaven *Medium Coeli* (MC), the Descendant (DSC), and the Lower Heaven or *Imum Coeli* (IC). These are created by the intersection of two fundamental lines—the "Line of the Horizon" (ASC/DSC) and the "Line of the Meridian" (MC/IC)—that divide the natal chart into four quadrants, with each endpoint associated with a seasonal marker: ASC (spring equinox), IC (summer solstice), DSC (fall equinox), and MC (winter solstice).

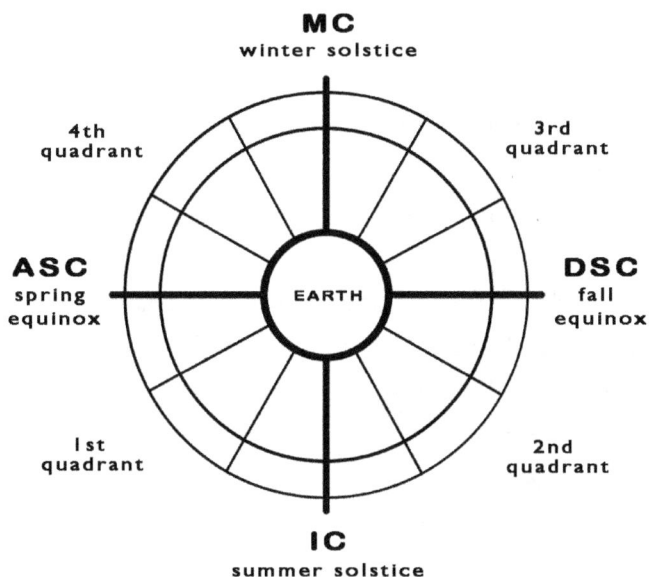

MC
winter solstice

4th quadrant

3rd quadrant

ASC
spring equinox

EARTH

DSC
fall equinox

1st quadrant

2nd quadrant

IC
summer solstice

Figure I
the four seasonal markers

The fully articulated natal chart, however, is divided into twelve segments (Figure 2), each one representing 30° along the ecliptic, with each segment or wedge representing both a natal house and a sign of the zodiac. For this sample chart, I've chosen an "equal house" approach in which the houses and signs are divided equally into 30° segments. Although there are other house division approaches that yield houses of unequal size, for our purposes I've chosen the equal house approach for its simplicity.

In Figure 2, I've numbered the houses of the natal chart 1 through 12. Although the numbers appear in the outer ring, they don't have to: that's just a personal preference rather than a default setting. They could just as easily be placed in the middle or inner ring. The important point to remember is that there are twelve of them, with each house representing a different sphere or area of life, i.e., 1st house (House of Self), 2nd house (House of Possessions), 3rd house (House of Communication), 4th house (House of Home and Family), 5th house (House of Creativity), and so forth.

Whereas the signs and planets of the natal chart "move" depending upon the time, date, and location of birth, the houses don't. They are fixed locations along the ecliptic. For this reason, using the analogy of a clock, the cusp or beginning of the 1st house will always be on or near the nine o'clock position (i.e., the Ascendant), the cusp of the 2nd house will always be on or near the eight o'clock position, the cusp of the 3rd house on or near the seven o'clock position, and so forth. This is especially true for this chart because it is based on an equal house approach where each house takes up exactly 30° along the ecliptic.

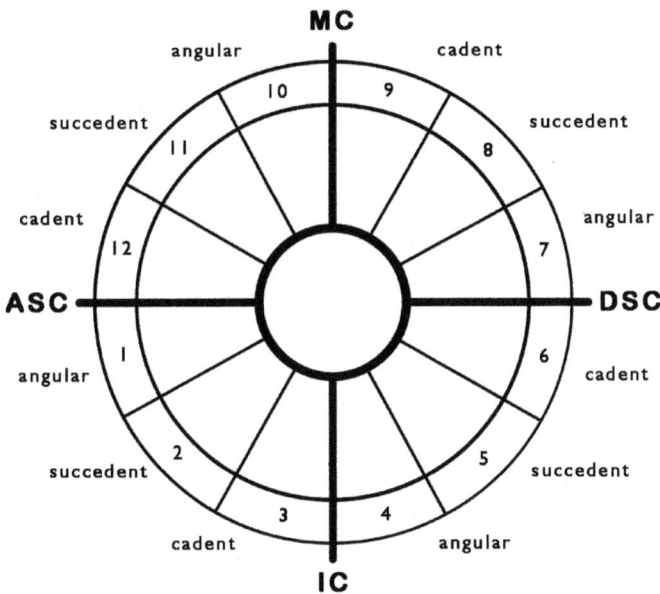

Figure 2
natal houses with their respective qualities

Here are a couple of other things to notice. First of all, the houses follow a counterclockwise direction. The natal chart tracks two types of movement: the annual revolution of the Earth around the Sun and the diurnal or daily rotation of the Earth on its axis. Whereas the first movement is signified by the counterclockwise direction of the houses as they follow the signs around the ecliptic, the second movement is represented by the apparent clockwise progression of the signs and planets as the Earth rotates counterclockwise on its axis.

Notice also that each house in Figure 2 is associated with a particular type of quality or energy—*angular, succedent,* or *cadent*—that appear in each quadrant in the same order as we move counterclockwise around the chart. Despite what sign and and/

or planets appear in a particular house, the energy of that house will always be the same, either angular, succedent, or cadent, thus influencing or "coloring" the sign and planets in that house, with angular houses points of initiation representing action, succedent houses points of purpose representing stability, and cadent houses points of transition representing change and adaptation. With this knowledge, let's turn our attention to the dynamic qualities of the chart, beginning with the twelve signs of the zodiac.

Anyone who studies astrology is familiar with the signs of the zodiac, after all that's what we're interested in—our Sun sign, which is the sign that the Sun was progressing through at the moment of our birth. Since there are twelve signs of the zodiac and twelve months of the year, the Sun takes approximately one month to travel through a sign. This may or may not be true for the natal houses; it all depends upon which house division system an astrologer uses. Just as the natal houses start in the 9 o'clock position on the left-hand side of the chart, so do the signs of the zodiac (Figure 3), with Aries in the first house on the day of the spring equinox and the other eleven signs arranged, like the natal houses, counterclockwise around the chart. This is the Ptolemaic "natural" or "tropical" zodiac (Claudius Ptolemy was a 2nd-century astrologer and mathematician whose work laid the foundation for Western astrology). It is the default zodiac—the starting point for Western astrologers—based on the four seasons of the year (hence the name "tropical," a reference to the four "turning points"—*tropos*—marking the beginning of each new season). Although the exact dates depend upon the year in question, the signs of the zodiac generally adhere to the following calendar, beginning with 1st-house Aries at the time of the spring equinox:

1st-house *Aries* (March 21 - April 19)

2nd-house *Taurus* (April 20 - May 20)

3rd-house *Gemini* (May 21 - June 21)

4th-house *Cancer* (June 22 - July 22)

5th-house *Leo* (July 23 - August 22)

6th-house *Virgo* (August 23 - September 22

7th-house *Libra* (September 23 - October 23)

8th-house *Scorpio* (October 24 - November 21)

9th-house *Sagittarius* (November 22 - December 21)

10th-house *Capricorn* (December 22 - January 19)

11th-house *Aquarius* (January 20 - February 18)

12th-house *Pisces* (February 19 - March 20)

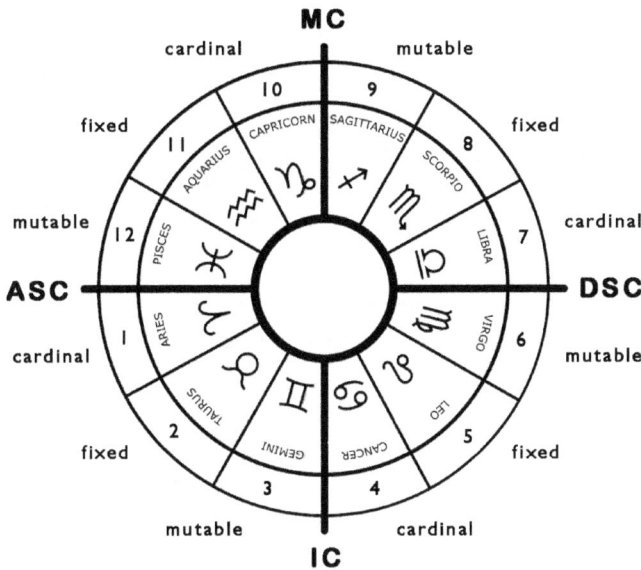

Figure 3
signs of the zodiac with their respective qualities

Like the houses, each sign is influenced by a particular energy or quality. In the case of signs, the qualities are *cardinal, fixed,* and *mutable,* and, like house qualities, they follow a three-part repeating sequence, i.e., Aries (*cardinal*), Taurus (*fixed*), Gemini (*mutable*), Cancer (*cardinal*), Leo (*fixed*), Virgo (*mutable*), and so forth. Additionally, the sign energies act like their house counterparts: cardinal energy initiates, fixed energy maintains, and mutable energy adapts. However, here's where they differ: whereas the angular, succedent, and cadent qualities are attached to a particular house and don't move around the natal chart, just as the houses don't move, the cardinal, fixed, and mutable energies are attached to particular signs and move around the chart as the signs move. What this means is that you could have a fixed Aquarius in an angular 1st house, or a mutable Virgo in a cadent 12th house, or a cardinal Libra in a succedent 8th house. When the two sets of qualities line up—angular/cardinal, succedent/fixed, and cadent/mutable—the combined energies exert the most influence on the sign and planets in that house.

In Figure 4 below, I've added the hours of the day, beginning at sunrise (6:00 a.m.) on the day of the spring equinox. Since the Earth spins counterclockwise on its axis, it gives the appearance of the signs—and the planets—rising in the East and setting in the West. With the Earth taking approximately 24 hours to complete a full rotation on its axis, it also appears that each sign takes approximately two hours to clear the horizon. In our equal house approach, the two-hour blocks begin on the cusp of each new house, i.e., 1st house cusp (Sunrise/6 a.m.), 12th house cusp (8 a.m.), 11th house cusp (10 a.m.), 10th house cusp (Noon/12 p.m.), and so forth around the natal chart. A knowledge of the time associated with each house cusp is important to understand how an astrologer "recalibrates" the sign wheel based on the moment of birth, which is necessary in order to identify an individual's Rising sign. I've done this in Figure 4, which is the hypothetical natal chart of an individual born in North America between December 22 and January 19 in the sign of Capricorn at 11:30 p.m.

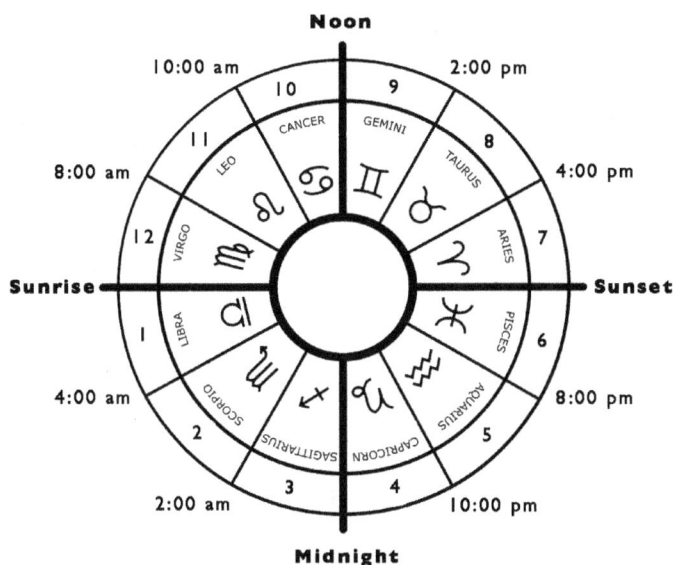

Figure 4
4th-house Capricorn yielding 1st-house Libra rising sign

Notice that Capricorn is no longer in the default 10th house (see Figure 3), but now falls within the 4th house. The reason for this is that the sign wheel is rotated counterclockwise until Capricorn, our hypothetical individual's Sun sign, is in the house of the time of birth which, at 11:30 p.m., falls within the 4th house.

This shows us how the house and sign wheels differ: whereas the house wheel remains fixed in place, the sign wheel rotates as a unit, always keeping the original sequence of signs intact. The rotation of the sign wheel enables an astrologer to determine an individual's Rising sign. He or she does this by rotating the sign wheel clockwise until the Sun sign (10th-house Capricorn) aligns with the birth time (4th-house Cancer), revealing a new sign—the Rising sign—in the 1st house, which in this case is Libra.

For people born between 4:00 a.m. and 6:00 a.m., the Rising sign and Sun sign are the same. This is because when you rotate the sign wheel so that the Sun sign aligns with the birth time, the two—the Rising sign and the Sun sign—occupy the 1st house. If you were born in the middle of June, between 4:00 a.m. and 6:00 a.m., as I was, both your Sun sign and your Rising sign would be in the 1st house, and you would be known as a double Gemini or a Gemini rising. However, most people aren't born at sunrise; they're born at various times of day or night, which yields a Sun sign and a Rising sign in different houses and, by extension, different signs.

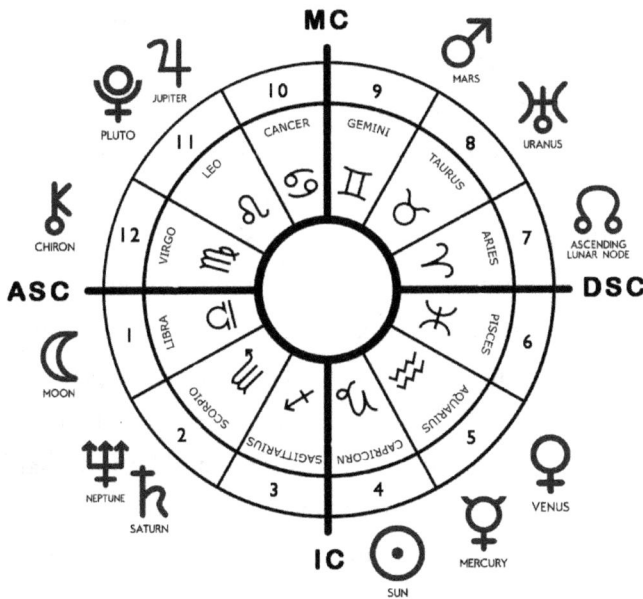

Figure 5
4th-house Capricorn Sun Sign with planet placements

Let's return to our hypothetical case, a person born in North America between December 22 and January 19 at 11:30 p.m. As we saw in Figure 4, they would have a 4th-house Sun sign in Capricorn and a 1st-house Rising sign in Libra. Now all we have to do is add the planets in their positions around the zodiac at the time of birth, which to an astrologer begins with the newborn's first breath of air. You'll notice in Figure 5 that I've added twelve "planets" (a catch-all phrase that can include the major and minor planets, a variety of asteroids, important planetary nodes, even mathematical points). Generally, astrologers in the West work with ten planets: the *personal* planets (Mercury, Venus, and Mars), the *social* planets (Jupiter and Saturn), and the *generational* planets

(Uranus, Neptune, and Pluto). But twelve signs, twelve houses, and *ten* planets is mathematically awkward, so astrologers add two more "planets" in order to bring the total to twelve (here I've added the North Lunar Node and the asteroid Chiron).

Unlike the signs that move on a fixed wheel as one entity, or the houses that don't move at all, the planets move idiosyncratically, each one with its own unique orbital speed around the Sun, anywhere from Mercury's 88 days to Pluto's 248 years (which means there could be two or three planets in a house or none at all). It is the planets, the most dynamic part of the natal chart, combined with the signs and houses, that lay the groundwork for chart interpretation. With a fully articulated natal chart, an astrologer has all of the tools that he or she needs to begin the process of chart analysis and interpretation. But as I said at the outset of this addendum, this guide is focused on how a natal chart works and not on what each discrete part means, which makes this a good place to stop.

Bibliography

Arroyo, Stephen. *Arroyo's Chart Interpretation Handbook: Guidelines for Understanding the Essentials of the Birth Chart*. Sebastopol, CA: CRCS Publications, 1989.

————. *Astrology, Psychology, and the Four Elements: An Energy Approach to Astrology and Its Use in the Counseling Arts*. Sebastopol, CA: CRCS, 1975.

Barton, Tamsyn. *Ancient Astrology*. London & New York: Routledge, 1994.

Bates, Graham. "The Astronomy of Houses," *Urania Trust* [Dec. 2014 & March 2015], https://www.uraniatrust.org/astrology/astronomy-of-houses.

Beck, Roger. *A Brief History of Ancient Astrology*. Malden: Blackwell, 2007.

Bloch, Douglas and Demetra George. *Astrology for Yourself: A Workbook for Personal Transformation*. Lake Worth, FL: Ibis Press, 2006.

Bobrick, Benson. *The Fated Sky: Astrology in History*. New York: Simon & Schuster, 2005.

Boland, Yasmin. *Astrology: A Guide to Understanding Your Birth Chart*. Carlsbad, CA: Hay House Inc., 2016.

Boxer, Alexander. *A Scheme of Heaven: The History of Astrology and the Search for Our Destiny in Data*. New York: W. W. Norton & Company, 2020.

Burns, William E. (ed). *Astrology Through History: Interpreting the Stars from Ancient Mesopotamia to the Present*. Santa Barbara, CA: ABC-CLIO, LLC, 2018.

Campion, Nicholas. *Astrology and Cosmology in the World's Religions*. New York: New York University Press, 2012.

Clement, Stephanie Jean. *Aspect Patterns: What They Reveal & How They Are Triggered*. Woodbury, MN: Llewellyn Worldwide, 2007.

Couprie, Dirk L. *Heaven and Earth in Ancient Greek Cosmology: From Thales to Heraclides Ponticus*. New York: Springer, 2011.

Edington, Louise. *The Complete Guide to Astrology: Understanding Yourself, Your Signs, and Your Birth Chart*. Emeryville, CA: Rockridge Press, 2020.

Forrest, Jodie. *The Ascendant: Your Rising Sign*. Borrego Springs, CA: Seven Paws Press, Inc., 2013.

Forrest, Steven. *The Changing Sky: Learning Predictive Astrology*. Borrego Springs, CA: Seven Paws Press, 2014.

———. *The Inner Sky: How to Make Wise Choices for a More Fulfilling Life*. Borrego Springs, CA: Seven Paws Press, 2012.

———. *The Night Speaks: How Astrology Works*. Borrego Springs, CA: Seven Paws Press, 2016.

Genuth, Sara Schecner (ed). *Comets, Popular Culture and the Birth of Modern Cosmology*. Princeton: Princeton University Press, 1997.

Gerwick-Brodeur, Madeline and Lisa Lenard. *The Complete Idiot's Guide to Astrology*. New York: Alpha Books, 2007.

Greene, Liz. *The Astrological World of Jung's Liber Novus: Daimons, Gods, and the Planetary Journey*. London & New York: Routledge, 2018.

———. *Jung's Studies in Astrology: Prophecy, Magic and the Qualities of Time*. London & New York: Routledge, 2018.

———. *The Luminaries: The Psychology of the Sun and Moon in the Horoscope*. York Beach, ME: Red Wheel/Weiser, 1992.

———. *Relating: An Astrological Guide to Living with Others on a Small Planet*. York Beach, ME: Samuel Weiser, 1978.

Hall, Judy. *The Astrology Bible: The Definitive Guide to the Zodiac*. London: Octopus Publishing Group Ltd, 2009.

Hamaker-Zondag, Karen. *Elements & Crosses as the Basis of the Horoscope*. York Beach, ME: Samuel Weiser, 1984.

———. *The House Connection: How to Read the Houses in an Astrological Chart*. York Beach, ME: Red Wheel/Weiser, 1994.

———. *Planetary Symbolism in the Horoscope*. York Beach, ME: Red Wheel/Weiser, 1992.

———. *Psychological Astrology: A Synthesis of Jungian Psychology and Astrology*. York Beach, ME: Red Wheel/Weiser, 1990.

Hand, Robert. *Essays on Astrology.* ARHAT Media, 1999.

———. *Horoscope Symbols.* Atglen, PA: Schiffer Publishing, 1981.

———. *Whole Sign Houses: The Oldest House System.* ARHAT Media, 1999.

Herring, Amy. *Essential Astrology: Everything You Need to Know to Understand Your Natal Chart.* Woodbury, MN: Llewellyn Publications, 2016.

Holden, James H. *A History of Horoscopic Astrology: From the Babylonian Period to the Modern Age.* Tempe, AZ: American Federation of Astrologers, 2006.

Hopper, Vincent Foster. *Medieval Number Symbolism: Its Sources, Meaning, and Influence on Thought and Expresion.* New York: Columbia University Pres, 1938.

Houlding, Deborah. *The Houses: Temples of the Sky.* Swanage, England: Wessex Astrology, 2006.

Howell, Alice O. *The Heavens Declare: Astrological Ages and the Evolution of Consciousness.* Second Edition. Wheaton, IL: Quest Books, 2006.

———. *Jungian Symbolism in Astrology: Letters from an Astrologer.* Wheaton, IL: Quest Books, 1987.

———. *Jungian Synchronicity in the Astrologial Signs and Ages: Letters from an Astrologer.* Wheaton, IL: Quest Books, 1990.

Jacobsen, Theodor S. *Planetary Systems from the Ancient Greeks to Kepler.* Seattle, WA: University of Washington Press, 1999.

Jaffé, Aniela, "Symbolism in the Visual Arts," in Carl Jung (ed.), *Man and His Symbols* (p. 236). New York: Dell Publishing, 2012.

Jansky, Robert Carl. *Astrology, Nutrition, and Health.* Atglen, PA: Schiffer Publications, 1997.

———. *Horoscopes: Here and Now.* London: Astro-Analytics Publications, 1975.

———. *Interpreting the Aspects.* London: Astro-Analytics Publications, 1978.

———. *Planetary Patterns.* London: Astro-Analytics Publications, 1977.

Jones, Marc Edmund. *Essentials of Astrological Analysis.* Bloomington, IN: Trafford Pubishing, 2006.

———. *Patterns of Consciousness.* Conshohocken, PA: Infinity Publishing, 2010.

————. *The Planetary Nodes and Collective Evolution*. Portland, OR: Raven Dreams Press, 2020.

————. *The Sabian Symbols in Astrology*. Santa Fe, NM: Aurora Press, 1993.

Kempton-Smith, Debbi. *Secrets from a Stargazer's Notebook: Making Astrology Work for You*. New York: Topquark Press, 1999.

Kent, April Elliott. *The Essential Guide to Practical Astrology: Everything from Zodiac Signs to Prediction, Made Easy and Entertaining*. Two Moon Publishing. Kindle Edition, 2015.

Leo, Alan. *Esoteric Astrology: A Study in Human Nature*. London: Modern Astrology Office, 1913.

————. *Symbolism and Astrology: An Introduction to Esoteric Astrology*. New York: Cosimo, 2005.

———— and H. S. Green. *The Horoscope in Detail. Astrological Manuals, No. IV*. London, 1906.

Leo, Bessie. *The Life and Work of Alan Leo, Theosophist, Astrologer, Mason*. London: Modern Astrology Office, 1919.

Lewi, Grant. *Astrology for the Millions*. Woodbury, MN: Llewellyn Publications, 1992.

Lewis, James. *The Astrology Book: The Encyclopedia of Heavenly Influences*. Canton: MI: Visible Ink Press, 2003.

Marks, Tracy. *The Art of Chart Interpretation: A Step-by-Step Method of Analyzing, Synthesizing & Understanding the Birth Chart*. Lake Worth, FL: Ibis Press, 2009.

Maxwell-Stuart, P. G. *Astrology: From Ancient Babylon to the Present Day*. Stroud, UK: Amberley, 2012.

McCaffery, Ellen. *Astrology: Its History and Influence in the Western World*. New York: Charles Scribner's Sons, 1942.

————. *Graphic Astrology: The Ellen McCaffery Home Study Course*. Richmond, VA: Macoy Publishing Co., 1952.

Mitchell, Glenn. *Discover the Aspect Pattern in Your Birth Chart: A Comprehensive Guide*. Woodbury, MN: Llewellyn Worldwide, 2020.

Orion, Rae. *Astrology for Dummies*. Hoboken, NJ: Wiley Publishers, 2007.

Papon, Donald. *The Lure of the Heavens: A History of Astrology*. New York: Samuel Weiser, 1980.

Parker, Julia and Derek Parker. *Parker's Astrology: The Definitive Guide to Using Astrology in Every Aspect of Your Life*. London and New York: DK, 2020.

Phelps, Ruth. *The Universe of Numbers*. San Jose, CA: Amorc, 2015.

Rochberg, Francesca. *Babylonian Horoscopes*. Philadelphia: American Philosophical Society, 1998.

Rossi, Safron and Keiron Le Grice. *Jung on Astrology*. London & New York: Routledge, 2017.

Rudhyar, Dane. *The Astrology of Personality: A Re-formulation of Astrological Concepts and Ideals, in Terms of Contemporary Psychology and Philosophy*. Santa Fe, NM: Aurora Press, 1991.

————. *Person Centered Astrology*. Sante Fe, NM: Aurora Press, 1980.

Sasportas, Howard. *Direction and Destiny in the Birth Chart*. Eastbourne, England: Gardners Books, 2002.

————. *The Inner Planets: Building Blocks of Personal Reality*. York Beach, ME: Red Wheel/Weiser, 1993.

————. *The Twelve Houses: Exploring the Houses of the Horoscope*. London: Flare Publications, 2007.

Schwartz-Salant, Nathan (ed.). *Jung on Alchemy*. Princeton, NJ: Princeton University Press, 1995.

Steiner, Rudolph. *Astronomy and Astrology: Finding a Relationship to the Cosmos*. Forest Row, England: Rudolph Steiner Press, 2012.

Steyson, Julia. *Astrology Uncovered: A Complete Guide to Horoscope and Zodiac Star Signs*. Copyright, Julia Steyson, 2018.

Tarnas, Richard. *Cosmos and Psyche: Intimations of a New World View*. New York: Viking, 2006.

Tester, Jim. *A History of Western Astrology*. New York: Ballantine Books, 1987.

Thompson, Gary D. *Ancient Zodiacs, Star Names, and Constellations: Essays and Critiques: The Influence of Religion and Astronomy on the Development of Astrology*. Copyright, Gary D. Thompson, Melton West, Australia, 2018.

Tierney, Bil. *All Around the Zodiac: Exploring Astrology's Twelve Signs.* Woodbury, MN: Llewellyn Publications 2001.

———. *Dynamics of Aspect Analysis.* Sebastopol, CA: CRCS Publications, 2015.

Tompkins, Sue. *Aspects in Astrology: A Guide to Understanding Planetary Relationships in the Horoscope.* New York: Simon & Schuster/ Destiny Books, 2002.

von Franz, Marie Louise. *Psyche and Matter.* Boston, MA: Shambhala Publ., 1992.

Wehr, Gerhard. *Jung & Steiner: The Birth of a New Psychology.* Translated from the German by Magdalene Jaeckel. Great Barrington, MA: Anthroposophic Press, 2002.

Whitfield, Peter. *Astrology: A History.* New York: Harry N. Abrams, 2001.

Woolfolk, Joanna Martine. *The Only Astrology Book You'll Ever Need.* Lanham, MD: Taylor Trade Publishing, 2008.

Zor, Karni. *Stories of Ancient Astrology: A Fascinating View into the History of Astrology in Different Cultures Around the Globe.* Copyright, Karni Zor, 2018.

Acknowledgments

This is less a series of acknowledgments and more a road map of necessary explanations. First of all, contrary to the usual format, I have placed each chapter's footnotes at the end of its respective chapter. In doing so, I hope that the reader will read not only the source of the footnotes, but also the added commentary that is sprinkled throughout.

Secondly, since I wrote this book during most of the COVID-19 pandemic, I did not have recourse to my usual lending library, i.e., the State of Illinois I-Share Interlibrary Loan System. As such, I was limited to e-books from a variety of sources, which means that the precise location of a quotation was not always available. So I made the executive decision to list author, title, and chapter from which each quotation or excerpt is taken in order to standardize the citation format. Perhaps it might also encourage the reader to read more of the context surrounding the excised quotation, which is not a bad secondary outcome.

When I began writing this project, I did so from a first-person perspective. Whereas I wanted a piece of writing that was thoroughly researched, I also wanted it to be accessible to most readers, i.e., casual in tone. As I progressed, several other "voices" appeared; namely, Castor and Pollux (who act not only as my alter ego, but also, especially in the case of Castor, as a bit of comic relief). Another useful voice to emerge later in the book was "Loren," my consultant on all things astrological. As these voices appeared and gained strength, the writing became somewhat of a cross between a Galilean dialogue and a Seinfeld episode (i.e., an information-driven discussion bolstered by a dose of humor).

As for Loren, she does not exist. She is an amalgamation of two threads: several online sources (in particular, free and proprietary online astrological natal chart generators) and Sarah Pickett, a bona fide astrologer who goes by the pseudonym "Sarandipity, the Chicago Astrologer." You can view her bona fides and/or contact her at www.facebook.com/sarandipitythechicagoastrologer. My exposure to Sarah came in two ways: first of all, early in this project, I took an entry level class on astrology at the Discovery Center in Chicago; secondly, while well into the project, I sat with her as she poured over my natal chart, adding much needed context to the original interpretation of my chart conducted in the mid-1980s.

I followed up Sarah's reading and interpretation of my natal chart with a seminar on "Celestial Happenings," sponsored by the Jung Center in Evanston, IL, conducted online (a casualty of COVID-19 sequestering) by Chicago-based astrologer Brian Allemana of Soul Rise Astrology (soulriseastrology.com). Brian, too, added much needed context to my original chart interpretation, especially in the case of Jupiter and its role in my chart.

A word about the online natal chart generators that I used. Although most of the resources for this project came from books and articles on various aspects of astrology, both historical and contemporary, I'm indebted to several online astrology websites for their natal chart analyses. I found the following natal reports particularly helpful: Astrolabe's Professional Natal Report (www.astrolabe.com), Liz Greene's Natal Chart Report from Astro-Charts (www.astro-charts.com), Just Astrology Things' Planet

Positions and Major Aspects Report (justastrologythings.com), and Astrology Cafe's Natal Report (www.astrologycafe.com).

Also, I'd be remiss if I didn't thank the folks at the Coffee Joint on Irving Park Road in Chicago, especially Gato, Michelle, and "Z" (a.k.a. Makenzie), who humored me as I ranted on for well over a year about the curious world of astrology.

I'd also like to thank Deb Tremper of Six Penny Graphics who once again has taken my ideas and thrown them into the world in a fully realized fashion (something I'll never quite master; not enough Capricorn in me, or something like that). Anyway, thanks Deb, you're a wiz.

Finally, I'd like to thank my family for putting up with my incessant babbling about the history, mechanics, and peculiarities of astrology, especially my wife who, two years ago, couldn't wait for me to stop babbling about major league baseball when I was working on an early history of the New York Yankees, only to find herself submerged by a tsunami of astrological ramblings; but being the good Leo that she is, she powered through it—thanks.

About the Author

W. Nikola-Lisa is professor emeritus of the School of Education at National-Louis University, where he taught in a progressive graduate teacher education program. A long-time resident of Chicago, Mr. Nikola-Lisa is the author of over thirty books. His books for young readers include the award-winning *Bein' With You This Way* and the ever-popular *Shake Dem Halloween Bones*. For the middle-grade reader, he's the author of *How We Are Smart*, a multicultural look at Howard Gardner's theory of multiple intelligences, and the semi-autobiographical novel *Shark Man*. For older readers, he's written *The Men Who Made the Yankees*, an early history of the American League's New York franchise, and *From Lectern to Laboratory*, an exploration of how developments in science and technology in the early to mid-nineteenth century led to changes in the curriculum of America's antebellum colleges. For more information about the author and his work, please visit www.nikolabooks.com.

www.ingramcontent.com/pod-product-compliance
Lightning Source LLC
Chambersburg PA
CBHW060311030426
42336CB00011B/995